THE WORDS WE LIVE BY

YOUR ANNOTATED GUIDE TO THE CONSTITUTION

THE WORDS WE LIVE BY

YOUR ANNOTATED GUIDE TO THE CONSTITUTION

Linda R. Monk

A Stonesong Press Book

New York

HYPERION
77 West 66th Street
New York, NY 10023-6298

Copyright © 2003 Linda R. Monk and The Stonesong Press, Inc.

THE STONESONG PRESS
27 West 24th Street
New York, NY 10010

Judy Pray, Executive Editor
Paul Fargis, President
Alison Fargis, Vice President, Development
Ellen Scordato, Vice President, Editorial

Design and production by Laura Smyth, Smythtype
Photo research by Michele Camardella

ISBN 978-0-7868-6720-2

Library of Congress Cataloging-in-Publication Data

Monk, Linda R.
    The words we live by : your annotated guide to the constitution / Linda R. Monk.
        p. cm.
    "A Stonesong Press book."
    Includes bibliographical references and index.
    ISBN 978-0-7868-6720-2
    1. Constitutional law—United States—Popular works. 2. Constitutional history—United States—
Popular works. I. Title.

KF4550.Z9 M66 2003
342.73'02—dc21   2002038826

A Stonesong Press Book
FIRST EDITION
10 9 8

Information regarding extracts and citations can be found in the endnotes on page 264.
Photo credits can be found on page 288.

Pages 40, 101, 247, and 262: Reprinted by permission.
Pages 70 and 74: Copyright © 2000 by The New York Times Co. Reprinted by permission.
Pages 81, 141, and 160: Copyright © 2001 by The New York Times Co. Reprinted by permission.
Page 32: *Wall Street Journal.* Eastern Edition [Staff Produced Copy Only] by John Fund. Copyright 2001 by
Dow Jones & Co. Inc. Reproduced with permission of Dow Jones & Co. Inc., in the format Trade Book via
Copyright Clearance Center.
Page 52: *Wall Street Journal.* Eastern Edition [Staff Produced Copy Only] by Ted Nugent. Copyright 2001 by
Dow Jones & Co. Inc. Reproduced with permission of Dow Jones & Co. Inc., in the format Trade Book via
Copyright Clearance Center.
Page 75: Reprinted by permission of International Creative Management, Inc. Copyright © 2001 by Arthur Miller.
First appeared in Harper's.
Page 106: *Wall Street Journal.* Eastern Edition [Staff Produced Copy Only] by Robert Bork. Copyright 2001 by
Dow Jones & Co. Inc. Reproduced with permission of Dow Jones & Co. Inc., in the format Trade Book via
Copyright Clearance Center.
Page 211: Reprinted by permission of Linda Chavez and Creators Syndicate, Inc.

For my beloved husband, Stephen,
with whom all things are possible.

Contents

Acknowledgments

I am grateful to the creative team who helped bring this book to fruition. At Stonesong Press, Paul Fargis provided both the original concept and the primary impetus for the book, and Judy Pray's persistence and positive attitude kept the project on track. Mary Ellen O'Neill, our editor at Hyperion, demonstrated her commitment throughout the book's development. The book's principal content reviewer was Dr. John W. Winkle, III, professor of political science at the University of Mississippi, and he has been my mentor in constitutional law for more than twenty-five years. Ralph Eubanks, director of publishing for the Library of Congress and a fellow Ole Miss alum, knew this was the right project for me and encouraged me to take it.

Another team of generous colleagues and friends offered insightful comments on early drafts of the manuscript. These include: Susan Kulp, Jim Mengert, Clare Merrill, Chuck Sass, Elizabeth Scanlon Thomas, and Ralph Watkins. In addition, author Rachel Simon shared her hard-won wisdom of the writing process with me countless times.

During the research for this book I realized how deeply indebted I am to Benjamin Franklin for establishing the public library. I am privileged to be a patron of one of the best in the country, the Fairfax County Public Library in Virginia. A special thank-you goes to the staff and volunteers of the Martha Washington Branch, who dealt with my literally hundreds of requests with professionalism and good cheer.

I am blessed with a circle of beloved friends and family who are always willing to help me incarnate the impossible. I would also like to thank the "council of midwives" who coached me through the birth pangs of this book, especially Sheila Foster and the School for Women Healers. Most of all, my love and gratitude go to my life partner and husband, Stephen G. Cook, for his unwavering support. This book truly would not have been possible without him.

THE CONSTITUTION AS CONVERSATION

Many Americans think of the Constitution as words on paper preserved under glass at the National Archives in Washington, D.C. But the Constitution is also the product of an ongoing conversation among Americans about the meaning of freedom in their daily lives.

America's conversation about liberty included women and men of all classes, races, and religions—enslaved and free. The slaves of Massachusetts petitioned for their "unalienable right to freedom" in 1777 with words echoing the Declaration of Independence. White men without property sought the right to vote. The Cherokee Nation, although deprived of its land, believed that American Indians should be protected under the Constitution. Women argued that they, too, were included in "We the People." In this book, you will hear the voices of America's founders and fanatics, of Supreme Court justices and civil rights workers. Among this cacophony are rock star Ted Nugent, first-grader Ruby Bridges, actor Charlton Heston, gay rights activist Michael Hardwick, ex-con Clarence Earl Gideon, and pro-life protester Norma McCorvey.

As these stories prove, the Constitution is not self-enforcing and depends upon citizens for its support. Judge Learned Hand emphasized this fact during World War II:

> I often wonder whether we do not rest our hopes too much upon constitutions, upon laws, and upon courts. These are false hopes; believe me, these are false hopes. Liberty lies in the hearts of men and women; when it dies there, no constitution, no law, no court can save it.

For the Constitution to have meaning, it must be not only the words we recite, but also the words we live by.

"Every morning we wake up and decide that we want to live in a constitutional republic."

—Garrett Epps, author

PART I:

THE CONSTITUTION OF THE UNITED STATES

"Liberty wasn't guaranteed by the Constitution. It was only given a chance."

—Stephen Chapman, *Chicago Tribune*

The Constitution that the framers signed in 1787 was the beginning of an experiment in liberty. It was also the culmination of more than 150 years of practical experience with self-government in America. But although the American colonies had declared their independence from Britain, by 1787 they had yet to prove they could maintain a stable form of government.

The fifty-five men who gathered in Philadelphia during that hot summer of 1787 had a sense of failure as well as promise. Congress had charged them only with amending–not discarding–the Articles of Confederation, America's first constitution. But James Madison, George Washington, and others came to the Federal Convention (later known as the Constitutional Convention) with the outlines for a new charter. After months of secret deliberations, they agreed on a structure of government that was designed to preserve American liberty.

This new government consisted of three separate branches: the legislature, the executive, and the judiciary. These branches exercised checks on each other's power, because the framers feared the concentration of authority in any one group. Similarly, the framers divided power between the national government and the states. And, most radically of all, the new Constitution would be approved by the people themselves, not the state legislatures. It was the most democratic document the world had ever witnessed.

But even the framers themselves did not think the Constitution was perfect. As Washington pointed out, the Constitution contained a provision for amendments to allow the people to change it as they saw fit. The outcome of the framers' efforts is still not certain. As Justice Oliver Wendell Holmes later said of the Constitution: "It is an experiment, as all life is an experiment."

PREAMBLE

We the People of the United States, in Order to form a more perfect Union, establish Justice, insure domestic Tranquility, provide for the common defence, promote the general Welfare, and secure the Blessings of Liberty to ourselves and our Posterity, do ordain and establish this Constitution for the United States of America.

THE PREAMBLE: WE THE PEOPLE

preamble
a clause at the beginning of a constitution or statute that explains the reasons for its passage

The introductory passage to the Constitution is known as the **Preamble,** although the original text does not give it that title. The Preamble states the general purposes of the Constitution. After winning independence from the British in the Revolutionary War, Americans sought to "secure the Blessings of Liberty" through a permanent form of government. Their first attempt, the Articles of Confederation, was a loose association of the thirteen independent states. Ratified in 1781, the Articles existed only six years before a new Constitution was proposed in 1787.

Writing in the first of the Federalist papers, a series of newspaper articles supporting the ratification of the Constitution, Alexander Hamilton pointed out the unique status of the American people in creating their new government:

This artwork by Mike Wilkins illustrates the Preamble using the license plates of all fifty states.

It has been frequently remarked that it seems to have been reserved to the people of this country, by their conduct and example, to decide the important question, whether societies of men are really capable or not of establishing good government from reflection and choice, or whether they are forever destined to depend for their political institutions on accident and force.

popular sovereignty

principle that the people are the source of all governmental power

We the People...

These first three words of the Constitution are the most important. They clearly state that the people—not the king, not the legislature, not the courts—are the true rulers in American government. This principle is known as **popular sovereignty.**

But who are "We the People"? This question troubled the nation for centuries. As Lucy Stone, one of America's first advocates for women's rights, asked in 1853: "'We the People'? Which 'We the People'? The women were not included." Neither were white males who did not own property, American Indians, or African Americans—slave or free. Justice Thurgood Marshall, the first African American on the Supreme Court, described this limitation:

"The adoption of the Constitution was...the most participatory, majoritarian, and populist event the Earth had ever seen."

—Akhil Reed Amar

> For a sense of the evolving nature of the Constitution, we need look no further than the first three words of the document's preamble: 'We the People.' When the founding fathers used this phrase in 1787, they did not have in mind the majority of America's citizens....
>
> The men who gathered in Philadelphia in 1787 could not...have imagined, nor would they have accepted, that the document they were drafting would one day be construed by a Supreme Court to which had been appointed a woman and the descendant of an African slave.

Through the amendment process, more and more Americans were eventually included in the Constitution's definition of "We the People." After the Civil War, the Thirteenth Amendment ended slavery, the Fourteenth Amendment gave African Americans citizenship, and the Fifteenth Amendment gave black men the vote. In 1920, the Nineteenth

Gentlemen of Their Time *Justice Ruth Bader Ginsburg*

Even though the framers did not realize it, says Justice Ruth Bader Ginsburg, the equal worth of all people is essential to the Constitution.

It manifests no disrespect for the Constitution to note that the framers were gentlemen of their time, and therefore had a distinctly limited vision of those who counted among "We the People." Not until the adoption of the post–Civil War Fourteenth Amendment did the word "equal," in relation to the stature of individuals, even make an appearance in the Constitution. But the equal dignity of all persons is nonetheless a vital part of our constitutional legacy, even if the culture of the framers held them back from fully perceiving that universal ideal. We can best celebrate that legacy by continuing to strive to form "a more perfect Union" for ourselves and the generations to come.

Amendment gave women the right to vote nationwide, and in 1971, the Twenty-sixth Amendment extended suffrage to eighteen-year-olds.

Dead White Guys *Charlton Heston*

In a speech to the Free Congress Foundation in 1997, Charlton Heston, who became president of the National Rifle Association, celebrated the role of white men in the nation's founding.

The Constitution was handed down to guide us by a bunch of those wise old dead white guys who invented this country. Now, some flinch when I say that. Why? It's true…they were white guys. So were most of the guys who died in Lincoln's name opposing slavery in the 1860s. So why should I be ashamed of white guys? Why is "Hispanic pride" or "black pride" a good thing, while "white pride" conjures up shaved heads and white hoods?

…of the United States,…

Like most documents, the Constitution needed a good editor. That person was Gouverneur Morris, who served on the Constitutional Convention's Committee of Style. Morris was the Constitution's chief draftsman, while James Madison was the chief architect. Morris's task was to shape the verbiage of committees into ringing prose. He commented on his work years later: "Having rejected redundant and equivocal terms, I believed it to be as clear as our language would permit."

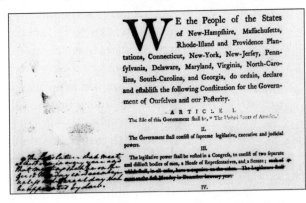

This early draft of the Preamble lists all the original thirteen states, rather than referring to "the United States" as a whole.

In the Constitution's Preamble, Morris's phrasing had substantive as well as stylistic consequences. The original draft of the Preamble referred to all thirteen states. But, in part because no one knew exactly which states would become the nine required to ratify the Constitution, Morris condensed the Preamble into the familiar words of today: "We the People of the United States."

Even after the Constitution's ratification, the United States was still evolving from a loose confederation of states into a cohesive national union. Only the Civil War finally achieved the latter. As historian Shelby Foote noted: "Before the war, it was said, 'The United States are.'…After the war, it was always 'the United States is.'…And that sums up what the war accomplished. It made us an 'is.'"

…in Order to form a more perfect Union,…

The first constitution of the United States, the Articles of Confederation, was a failure—or so many advocates of a stronger central government

"What a triumph for our enemies... to find that we are incapable of governing ourselves."

—George Washington

believed. Under the Articles, the states retained virtually all powers, and the national government was considered merely a "firm league of friendship" among them.

After only five years under the Articles, trade problems among the states prompted a conference at Annapolis, Maryland, in 1786. There, Alexander Hamilton made a motion, adopted by the conference, that a convention be held in Philadelphia in 1787 to amend "such defects as may be discovered to exist" in the Articles. The Continental Congress approved of the plan, resolving that such a convention be held "for the sole and express purpose of revising the Articles of Confederation."

Once in Philadelphia, however, the convention delegates quickly scrapped the Articles altogether and began drafting a new constitution. Representing twelve states–all except Rhode Island–they convened on May 25, 1787. Under the leadership of George Washington, the delegates met behind closed doors for almost four months. Their final product, signed on September 17, was presented to Congress, which then submitted it to the states for ratification. The Constitution was ratified in 1788, and the new government took office in 1789 with George Washington as president. A revolution had been achieved without a single drop of blood. A more perfect union had begun.

...establish Justice, insure domestic Tranquility, provide for the common defence, promote the general Welfare, and secure the Blessings of Liberty to ourselves and our Posterity,...

The Preamble sets forth the Constitution's goals, but the Supreme Court has ruled that it is not an independent source of rights. For instance, one cannot file a lawsuit based on the Preamble, as the Court held in *Jacobson v. Massachusetts* (1905). Henning Jacobson had refused to comply with a Massachusetts law mandating vaccination for smallpox, claiming that the law violated his "liberty" as secured by the Preamble. The Court disagreed, saying: "Although...one of the declared objects of the Constitution was to secure the blessings of liberty..., no power can be exerted to that end by the United States, unless, apart from the Preamble, it be found in some express delegation of power, or in some power to be properly implied therefrom."

...do ordain and establish...

Under the terms of the Preamble, "We the People," not the states, "ordain and establish" the Constitution. During the Constitutional Convention, James Madison said that the difference between a government established by state legislatures and one founded on the people directly was "the true difference between a league or treaty, and a Constitution." But Patrick

Henry, who refused to attend the convention because he "smelt a rat," took exception to the Preamble's language. He argued that the convention had exceeded its power by abandoning the Articles of Confederation. Asked Henry during the Virginia ratifying convention: "Who authorized them to speak the language of, We, the People, instead of We, the States?... The people gave them no power to use their name."

But as specified in Article VII, the Constitution was ratified by the people through state conventions, not by the state legislatures. The Supreme Court pointed to this fact in *McCulloch v. Maryland* (1819). Chief Justice John Marshall wrote for the unanimous Court: "The government proceeds directly from the people; is 'ordained and established' in the name of the people.... Its powers are granted by them and are to be exercised directly on them and for their benefit." However, Justice Clarence Thomas and other members of the Rehnquist Court have disagreed with Marshall's analysis. According to Thomas, the "source of the Constitution's authority is the consent of the people of each individual state, not the consent of the undifferentiated people of the nation as a whole." In this view, the states retain significant power over the national government.

A Firm League of Friendship *Articles of Confederation*

Contrasted to the Constitution's Preamble, the Articles of Confederation make clear that the states are sovereign and the national government has little power.

The Articles of Confederation and Perpetual Union Between the States of New Hampshire, Massachusetts Bay, Rhode Island and Providence Plantations, Connecticut, New York, New Jersey, Pennsylvania, Delaware, Maryland, Virginia, North Carolina, South Carolina, Georgia.

Article I. The stile of this confederacy shall be "The United States of America."

Article 2. Each State retains its sovereignty, freedom, and independence, and every power, jurisdiction, and right, which is not by this confederation expressly delegated to the United States, in Congress assembled.

Article 3. The said States hereby severally enter into a firm league of friendship with each other for their common defence, the security of their liberties and their mutual and general welfare; binding themselves to assist each other against all force offered to, or attacks made upon them, or any of them, on account of religion, sovereignty, trade, or any other pretence whatever.

...this Constitution for the United States of America.
The U.S. Constitution is the oldest written **constitution** of a nation still being used. From the beginning, Americans and others have disagreed about its relative merits. Federalists believed that, by creating a stronger national government, the Constitution would enable the United States to survive among the competing powers of Europe and provide a surer safeguard for liberty at home. Antifederalists feared that the new Constitution would create a new form of tyranny, especially since it lacked

constitution

a society's most fundamental and most important law

a bill of rights. Only by promising that the new Congress would make passage of a bill of rights its top priority did the Federalists secure ratification of the Constitution.

To British prime minister William Gladstone, the U.S. Constitution was "the most wonderful work ever struck off at a given time by the brain and purpose of man." But according to Justice Thurgood Marshall, the U.S. Constitution was "defective from the start, requiring several amendments, a civil war, and momentous social transformation to attain the system of constitutional government, and its respect for the individual freedoms and human rights, we hold as fundamental today." The

Of the fifty-five delegates who attended the Constitutional Convention, thirty-nine actually signed the Constitution. George Washington's "rising sun" chair is pictured behind him.

With All Its Faults *Benjamin Franklin*

Acknowledging that the Constitution had limitations, Benjamin Franklin still believed that it was as close to perfection as human beings could achieve.

I agree to this Constitution, with all its faults, if they are such: because I think a general government necessary for us, and there is no form of government but what may be a blessing to the people if well administered.... I doubt too whether any Convention we can obtain, may be able to make a better Constitution: For when you assemble a number of men to have the advantage of their joint wisdom, you inevitably assemble with those men all their prejudices, their passions, their errors of opinion, their local interests, and their selfish views. From such an assembly can a perfect production be expected? It therefore astonishes me, Sir, to find this system approaching so near to perfection as it does....

Constitution was not perfect, but rather perfectible–through the amendment process.

At the Constitutional Convention, Benjamin Franklin stated that he approved of the Constitution "with all its faults" because he did not think a better one was possible at that time. The oldest delegate to the convention at eighty-one, Franklin was too weak to give speeches and instead offered his opinions through written remarks delivered by a fellow Pennsylvania delegate. Franklin reportedly signed the Constitution with tears in his eyes. But if Franklin was willing to sign a document so full of errors, according to one tart-tongued Boston critic, "no wonder he shed a tear." Perhaps Franklin's last words to the convention gave the best assessment of the prospects of the new republic. As the other delegates were signing the Constitution, Franklin remarked to those nearby that, throughout the convention, he had wondered whether the sun carved on the back of George Washington's chair was rising or setting. "Now," he said, "I have the happiness to know that it is a rising and not a setting sun."

Does Founding Father Know Best?

Some writers have referred to the 1787 Constitutional Convention as the "miracle at Philadelphia." Indeed, George Washington wrote in 1788: "It appears to me…little short of a miracle, that the delegates from so many different states… should unite in forming a system of national government, so little liable to well founded objections." Others have extrapolated from the miracle metaphor to attribute divinely inspired wisdom to the "founding fathers," a phrase first used by Warren G. Harding in 1918 before he was elected president. Some legal scholars have referred to this point of view as "founding father knows best," an allusion to a 1950s television program. But Washington himself cautioned against such a view. He wrote in 1787: "I do not think we are more inspired, have more wisdom, or possess more virtue, than those who will come after us."

ARTICLE I

SECTION. 1. All legislative Powers herein granted shall be vested in a Congress of the United States, which shall consist of a Senate and House of Representatives.

SECTION. 2. The House of Representatives shall be composed of Members chosen every second Year by the People of the several States, and the Electors in each State shall have the Qualifications requisite for Electors of the most numerous Branch of the State Legislature.

No Person shall be a Representative who shall not have attained to the Age of twenty five Years, and been seven Years a Citizen of the United States, and who shall not, when elected, be an Inhabitant of that State in which he shall be chosen.

Representatives and direct Taxes shall be apportioned among the several States which may be included within this Union, according to their respective Numbers, which shall be determined by adding to the whole Number of free Persons, including those bound to Service for a Term of Years, and excluding Indians not taxed, three fifths of all other Persons. The actual Enumeration shall be made within three Years after the first Meeting of the Congress of the United States, and within every subsequent Term of ten Years, in such Manner as they shall by Law direct. The Number of Representatives shall not exceed one for every thirty Thousand, but each State shall have at Least one Representative; and until such enumeration shall be made, the State of New Hampshire shall be entitled to chuse three, Massachusetts eight, Rhode-Island and Providence Plantations one, Connecticut five, New-York six, New Jersey four, Pennsylvania eight, Delaware one, Maryland six, Virginia ten, North Carolina five, South Carolina five, and Georgia three.

When vacancies happen in the Representation from any State, the Executive Authority thereof shall issue Writs of Election to fill such Vacancies.

The House of Representatives shall chuse their Speaker and other Officers; and shall have the sole Power of Impeachment.

SECTION. 3. The Senate of the United States shall be composed of two Senators from each State, *chosen by the Legislature thereof,* for six Years; and each Senator shall have one Vote.

Immediately after they shall be assembled in Consequence of the first Election, they shall be divided as equally as may be into three Classes. The Seats of the Senators of the first Class shall be vacated at the Expiration of the second Year, of the second Class at the Expiration of the fourth Year, and of the third Class at the Expiration of the sixth Year, so that one third may be chosen every second Year; *and if Vacancies happen by Resignation, or otherwise, during the Recess of the Legislature of any State, the Executive thereof may make temporary Appointments until the next Meeting of the Legislature, which shall then fill such Vacancies.*

No Person shall be a Senator who shall not have attained to the Age of thirty Years, and been nine Years a Citizen of the United States, and who shall not, when elected, be an Inhabitant of that State for which he shall be chosen.

The Vice President of the United States shall be President of the Senate, but shall have no Vote, unless they be equally divided.

The Senate shall chuse their other Officers, and also a President pro tempore, in the Absence of the Vice President, or when he shall exercise the Office of President of the United States.

The Senate shall have the sole Power to try all Impeachments. When sitting for that Purpose, they shall be on Oath or Affirmation. When the President of the United States is tried, the Chief Justice shall preside: And no Person shall be convicted without the Concurrence of two thirds of the Members present.

Judgment in Cases of Impeachment shall not extend further than to removal from Office, and disqualification to hold and enjoy any Office of honor, Trust or Profit under the United States: but the Party convicted shall nevertheless be liable and subject to Indictment, Trial, Judgment and Punishment, according to Law.

SECTION. 4. The Times, Places and Manner of holding Elections for Senators and Representatives, shall be prescribed in each State by the Legislature thereof; but the Congress may at any time by Law make or alter such Regulations, except as to the Places of chusing Senators.

The Congress shall assemble at least once in every Year, and such Meeting shall be *on the first Monday in December,* unless they shall by Law appoint a different Day.

SECTION. 5. Each House shall be the Judge of the Elections, Returns and Qualifications of its own Members, and a Majority of each shall constitute a Quorum to do Business; but a smaller Number may adjourn from day to day, and may be authorized to compel the Attendance of absent Members, in such Manner, and under such Penalties as each House may provide.

Each House may determine the Rules of its Proceedings, punish its Members for disorderly Behaviour, and, with the Concurrence of two thirds, expel a Member.

Each House shall keep a Journal of its Proceedings, and from time to time publish the same, excepting such Parts as may in their Judgment require Secrecy; and the Yeas and Nays of the Members of either House on any question shall, at the Desire of one fifth of those Present, be entered on the Journal.

Neither House, during the Session of Congress, shall, without the Consent of the other, adjourn for more than three days, nor to any other Place than that in which the two Houses shall be sitting.

SECTION. 6. The Senators and Representatives shall receive a Compensation for their Services, to be ascertained by Law, and paid out of the Treasury of the United States. They shall in all Cases, except Treason, Felony and Breach of the Peace, be privileged from Arrest during their Attendance at the Session of their respective Houses, and in going to and returning from the same; and for any Speech or Debate in either House, they shall not be questioned in any other Place.

No Senator or Representative shall, during the Time for which he was elected, be appointed to any civil Office under the Authority of the United States, which shall have been created, or the Emoluments whereof shall have been increased during such time; and no Person holding any Office under the United States, shall be a Member of either House during his Continuance in Office.

SECTION. 7. All Bills for raising Revenue shall originate in the House of Representatives; but the Senate may propose or concur with Amendments as on other Bills.

Every Bill which shall have passed the House of Representatives and the Senate, shall, before it becomes a Law, be presented to the President of the United States: If he approve he shall sign it, but if not he shall return it, with his Objections to that House in which it shall have originated, who shall enter the Objections at large on their Journal, and proceed to reconsider it. If after such Reconsideration two thirds of that House shall agree to pass the Bill, it shall be sent, together with the Objections, to the other House, by which it shall likewise be reconsidered, and if approved by two thirds of that House, it shall become a Law. But in all such Cases the Votes of both Houses shall be determined by yeas and Nays, and the Names of the Persons voting for and against the Bill shall be entered on the Journal of each House respectively. If any Bill shall not be returned by the President within ten Days (Sundays excepted) after it shall have been presented to him, the Same shall be a Law, in like Manner as if he had signed it, unless the Congress by their Adjournment prevent its Return, in which Case it shall not be a Law.

Every Order, Resolution, or Vote to which the Concurrence of the Senate and House of Representatives may be necessary (except on a question of Adjournment) shall be presented to the President of the United States; and before the Same shall take Effect, shall be approved by him, or being disapproved by him, shall be repassed by two thirds of the Senate and House of Representatives, according to the Rules and Limitations prescribed in the Case of a Bill.

SECTION. 8. The Congress shall have Power To lay and collect Taxes, Duties, Imposts and Excises, to pay the Debts and provide for the common Defence and general Welfare of the United States; but all Duties, Imposts and Excises shall be uniform throughout the United States;

To borrow Money on the credit of the United States;

To regulate Commerce with foreign Nations, and among the several States, and with the Indian Tribes;

To establish an uniform Rule of Naturalization, and uniform Laws on the subject of Bankruptcies throughout the United States;

To coin Money, regulate the Value thereof, and of foreign Coin, and fix the Standard of Weights and Measures;

To provide for the Punishment of counterfeiting the Securities and current Coin of the United States;

To establish Post Offices and post Roads;

To promote the Progress of Science and useful Arts, by securing for limited Times to Authors and Inventors the exclusive Right to their respective Writings and Discoveries;

To constitute Tribunals inferior to the supreme Court;

To define and punish Piracies and Felonies committed on the high Seas, and Offences against the Law of Nations;

To declare War, grant Letters of Marque and Reprisal, and make Rules concerning Captures on Land and Water;

To raise and support Armies, but no Appropriation of Money to that Use shall be for a longer Term than two Years;

To provide and maintain a Navy;

To make Rules for the Government and Regulation of the land and naval Forces;

To provide for calling forth the Militia to execute the Laws of the Union, suppress Insurrections and repel Invasions;

To provide for organizing, arming, and disciplining, the Militia, and for governing such Part of them as may be employed in the Service of the United States, reserving to the States respectively, the Appointment of the Officers, and the Authority of training the Militia according to the discipline prescribed by Congress;

To exercise exclusive Legislation in all Cases whatsoever, over such District (not exceeding ten Miles square) as may, by Cession of particular States, and the Acceptance of Congress, become the Seat of the Government of the United States, and to exercise like Authority over all Places purchased by the Consent of the Legislature of the State in which the Same shall be, for the Erection of Forts, Magazines, Arsenals, dock-Yards, and other needful Buildings;—And

To make all Laws which shall be necessary and proper for carrying into Execution the foregoing Powers, and all other Powers vested by this Constitution in the Government of the United States, or in any Department or Officer thereof.

SECTION. 9. The Migration or Importation of such Persons as any of the States now existing shall think proper to admit, shall not be prohibited by the Congress prior to the Year one thousand eight hundred and eight, but a Tax or duty may be imposed on such Importation, not exceeding ten dollars for each Person.

The Privilege of the Writ of Habeas Corpus shall not be suspended, unless when in Cases of Rebellion or Invasion the public Safety may require it.

No Bill of Attainder or ex post facto Law shall be passed.

No Capitation, or other direct, Tax shall be laid, *unless in Proportion to the Census or enumeration herein before directed to be taken.*

No Tax or Duty shall be laid on Articles exported from any State.

No Preference shall be given by any Regulation of Commerce or Revenue to the Ports of one State over those of another; nor shall Vessels bound to, or from, one State, be obliged to enter, clear, or pay Duties in another.

No Money shall be drawn from the Treasury, but in Consequence of

Appropriations made by Law; and a regular Statement and Account of the Receipts and Expenditures of all public Money shall be published from time to time.

No Title of Nobility shall be granted by the United States: And no Person holding any Office of Profit or Trust under them, shall, without the Consent of the Congress, accept of any present, Emolument, Office, or Title, of any kind whatever, from any King, Prince, or foreign State.

SECTION. 10. No State shall enter into any Treaty, Alliance, or Confederation; grant Letters of Marque and Reprisal; coin Money; emit Bills of Credit; make any Thing but gold and silver Coin a Tender in Payment of Debts; pass any Bill of Attainder, ex post facto Law, or Law impairing the Obligation of Contracts, or grant any Title of Nobility.

No State shall, without the Consent of the Congress, lay any Imposts or Duties on Imports or Exports, except what may be absolutely necessary for executing its inspection Laws: and the net Produce of all Duties and Imposts, laid by any State on Imports or Exports, shall be for the Use of the Treasury of the United States; and all such Laws shall be subject to the Revision and Controul of the Congress.

No State shall, without the Consent of Congress, lay any Duty of Tonnage, keep Troops, or Ships of War in time of Peace, enter into any Agreement or Compact with another State, or with a foreign Power, or engage in War, unless actually invaded, or in such imminent Danger as will not admit of delay.

ARTICLE I: THE LEGISLATIVE BRANCH

The duty of the legislative branch is to make the laws. Congress is the only branch of the U.S. government that existed prior to the Constitution, although it took a different form. The framers of the Constitution expected that Congress would overshadow the newly created executive and judicial branches, and they spelled out its powers in considerable detail. They also placed explicit limits on the powers of Congress, to balance its weight against the other branches. Thus, Article I is the longest part of the Constitution–longer than Articles II and III combined, which cover both the executive and the judiciary.

Article I contains the laundry list of federal powers–among them to collect taxes, borrow money, regulate commerce, establish post offices, and declare war. It also allows Congress to make all laws "necessary and proper" for carrying out the powers specifically granted, a broad source of authority in the modern regulatory state. Article I holds two compromises that were essential to the formation of the Union: equal representation of the states in the Senate, and the valuation of a slave as three-fifths of a person.

SECTION 1. All legislative Powers...

The Constitution establishes a system of **separation of powers** among the three branches of government. The framers of the Constitution derived their ideas about the separation of powers from the French philosopher Montesquieu, and they divided the U.S. government into the legislative, executive, and judicial branches. Article I gives Congress the power to make the laws; Article II gives the president the power to enforce the laws; and Article III gives the judiciary the power to interpret the laws.

But the framers did not make the boundaries between those branches absolute. Instead, they created a system of **checks and balances,** in which each branch exercised some restraint on the power of the other. For instance, Congress has the power to pass laws, but the president can veto those laws. The president can make treaties, but the Senate must approve them. Judges have life tenure to give them independence, but the president and the Senate together select judges. James Madison described the principle of checks and balances in *Federalist* 51: "Ambition must be made to counter ambition. The interest of the man must be connected with the constitutional rights of the place."

This system of checks and balances is so intricately woven throughout the Constitution that some scholars believe it negates the separation of powers. According to political scientist Richard Neustadt: "The constitutional convention of 1787 is supposed to have created a government of 'separated powers.' It did nothing of the sort. Rather, it created a government of separated institutions *sharing* powers."

...herein granted shall be vested in a Congress of the United States,...

The institution of Congress existed in several forms prior to the Constitution. At the dawn of the American Revolution, the colonies began to act collectively through the First Continental Congress in 1774. The Second Continental Congress convened in 1775, and its Declaration of Independence the next year gave birth to the United States of America. The Continental Congress carried out the functions of national government through 1781, when the newly independent states adopted the Articles of Confederation, the first Constitution of the United States.

Under the Articles, Congress was the entire government—referred to as "the United States, in Congress assembled." There were no separate

---

separation of powers

the constitutional doctrine of dividing governmental power among the legislative, executive, and judicial branches

checks and balances

the constitutional doctrine in which each branch of government shares some of the powers of the other branches in order to limit their actions

If Men Were Angels *James Madison*

Writing in Federalist 51, *James Madison explains the constitutional principles of separation of powers and checks and balances, as well as the vagaries of human nature.*

The great security against a gradual concentration of the several powers in the same department consists in giving to those who administer each department the necessary constitutional means and personal motives to resist encroachments of the others....

Ambition must be made to counteract ambition. The interest of the man must be connected with the constitutional rights of the place. It may be a reflection on human nature that such devices should be necessary to control the abuses of government. But what is government itself but the greatest of all reflections on human nature? If men were angels, no government would be necessary. If angels were to govern men, neither external nor internal controls on

government would be necessary. In framing a government which is to be administered by men over men, the great difficulty lies in this: you must first enable the government to control the governed; and in the next place oblige it to control itself. A dependence on the people is, no doubt, the primary control on the government; but experience has taught mankind the necessity of auxiliary precautions.

executive or judicial branches. The framers of the 1787 Constitution created these two new branches of government because the Confederation Congress could not effectively handle all the business of the United States. While the framers believed that Congress would be the principal arm of government, they did not want to give it the unbridled power of England's Parliament. Therefore, Article I limits Congress to the legislative powers "herein granted." The Constitution does not acknowledge a

The role of government agencies expanded greatly during the New Deal.

prerogative of the legislature to make laws on any subject whatsoever; the laws must be related to a power granted in Article I.

However, Article I also states that all such legislative powers are vested in Congress. This means that Congress cannot delegate its lawmaking function to other branches of government, chiefly the executive. During the New Deal, Congress created a host of administrative agencies, usually as part of the executive branch, to implement a wide array of new laws. These agencies began making their own rules and regulations, known as administrative law. If such agencies go too far in their rule making, they can violate the Constitution's delegation of legislative power to Congress.

> "Reader, suppose you were an idiot. And suppose you were a member of Congress. But I repeat myself."
>
> —attributed to Mark Twain

...which shall consist of a Senate and House of Representatives.
The delegates to the Constitutional Convention in 1787 disagreed vehemently about how the states would be represented in the legislative branch. Under the Articles of Confederation, each state had an equal vote in a unicameral Congress that consisted of one house. Small states wanted to continue this system, and their delegates promoted the New Jersey Plan at the Constitutional Convention. Large states, however, supported the Virginia Plan, which would create a bicameral Congress with membership in both houses to be based on population.

Finally, in a move called the Great Compromise, the framers agreed to a bicameral legislature that had different formulas for representation in each house. Membership in the House of Representatives, or lower house, would be based on a state's population, whereas each state was represented equally in the Senate, or upper house. The House of Representatives would be elected by the people, but state legislatures would choose senators. Besides solving the problem of state representation, a bicameral legislature also slowed down the legislative process. This was a good thing to many of the framers, who worried about excessive government power. When Thomas Jefferson questioned the role of the Senate in the 1790s, George Washington allegedly asked: "Why did you pour that coffee into your saucer?" "To cool it," said Jefferson. "Even so," replied Washington, "we pour legislation into the senatorial saucer to cool it."

When the First Congress met in 1789 in New York City, it got off to a bad start. The Congress was scheduled to convene on March 4, but a quorum of legislators had not arrived by then. The House of Representatives finally achieved a quorum on April 1–which, as some noted at the time, was All Fools' Day. The Senate reached a quorum a few days later, but criticism of Congress has remained a national pastime ever since. Why is Congress so often the subject of ridicule? Some legislators speculate that it is because Congress is the branch of government closest to the people themselves. Familiarity breeds contempt, according to this view. In the words of political historian James MacGregor Burns, "We enjoy bashing Congress because they are us."

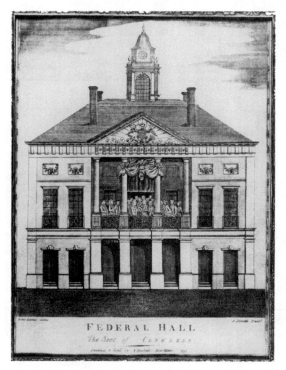

FEDERAL HALL
The Seat of CONGRESS

The first Congress under the Constitution met in 1789 at Federal Hall in New York City. The capital of the United States would move to Philadelphia in 1790, before occupying its permanent home in Washington, D.C., in 1800.

SECTION 2. The House of Representatives shall be composed of Members chosen every second Year by the People of the several States, and the Electors in each State shall have the Qualifications requisite for Electors of the most numerous Branch of the State Legislature.

The framers of the Constitution designed the House of Representatives to be close to the people. Some thought yearlong terms would best serve this goal, while others supported three-year terms. The framers agreed on two years, but some Americans argue that terms for the House should be changed to four years. Under the current system, these critics say, a member of Congress is constantly running for reelection and has no time to focus on long-term goals. That's exactly the point, according to supporters of short terms—frequent elections keep a member of Congress close to the people. Consequently, the House of Representatives is known as "the people's house."

The House of Representatives was the only part of the new U.S. government under the Constitution of 1787 to be chosen by the people themselves. State legislatures selected senators (prior to the Seventeenth Amendment), the electoral college picked the president, and the president and the Senate together appointed judges. Rather than setting a uniform national standard for voting, Article I allows the states to determine what the qualifications for voters shall be. However, later amendments to the Constitution did establish national standards regarding race, gender, age, and property requirements for voting.

In most states at the time of the Constitution's ratification, only free white men who owned property could vote. Unlike other states, New Jersey's 1776 constitution gave the vote to "all inhabitants" who owned property. Thus, women and free persons of color voted in New Jersey until that right was specifically revoked in 1807. During the 1820s, as part of the movement toward Jacksonian democracy, many states removed property requirements for voting. In 1870, the Fifteenth Amendment gave black men the right to vote in federal and state elections, and in 1920 the Nineteenth Amendment protected the same right for women nationwide.

Because of varying state requirements for voting, a woman was elected to Congress before the Nineteenth Amendment was ratified. Western states were among the first to grant women full suffrage, in order to encourage settlement there. In 1916, Montana elected Jeannette Rankin to the U.S. House of Representatives, where she became the first female member of Congress.

"We're half the people; we should be half the Congress."
—Rep. Jeannette Rankin

Jeannette Rankin, the first woman to serve in Congress, was elected to the House of Representatives as a Republican from Montana in 1916 and again in 1940. A dedicated pacifist, Rankin voted against U.S. entry into both World War I and World War II.

The expansion of voting rights continued in 1964 with the Twenty-fourth Amendment's prohibition of poll taxes, which discouraged poor people from voting. And in 1971, the Twenty-sixth Amendment lowered the minimum age for voting from twenty-one to eighteen. More constitutional amendments have dealt with voting than any other issue.

In Whom Is the Right of Suffrage? *Benjamin Franklin*

Arguing against property qualifications for voting, Benjamin Franklin used the humorous story of a man and his jackass to make a powerful point.

Today a man owns a jackass worth fifty dollars and he is entitled to vote; but before the next election the jackass dies. The man in the mean time has become more experienced, his knowledge of the principles of government, and his acquaintance with mankind, are more extensive, and he is therefore better qualified to make a proper selection of rulers—but the jackass is dead and the man cannot vote. Now, gentlemen, pray inform me, in whom is the right of suffrage? In the man or in the jackass?

No Person shall be a Representative who shall not have attained to the Age of twenty five Years, and been seven Years a Citizen of the United States, and who shall not, when elected, be an Inhabitant of that State in which he shall be chosen.

This part of Section 2 is known as the Qualifications Clause. It sets forth the basic requirements to be a member of the House of Representatives. There is a similar clause for the Senate in Section 3. Besides a minimum age of twenty-five, other qualifications for the House of Representatives include seven years of U.S. citizenship and residence within the state from which elected. However, the representative does not have to live in a particular congressional district within the state.

The Constitution puts no specific limit on the number of terms a member of Congress may serve, either in the House or the Senate. In *U.S. Term Limits v. Thornton* (1995), the Supreme Court ruled that individual states cannot restrict the terms for members of Congress. To do so, said the Court, would be to allow states to change the qualifications for office specified in Article I. Such action would require a constitutional amendment, according to the Court. Justice Clarence Thomas dissented, arguing that the Constitution was silent on the issue of term limits for Congress and did not forbid the states to enact them. In *Cook v. Gralike* (2001), the Supreme Court also held unconstitutional a Missouri law requiring ballots to indicate that a congressional candidate opposed term limits (known as "scarlet letter" laws).

Proponents of term limits believe they are necessary to keep Congress from becoming a professional class of politicians who are captive to special interests, rather than citizen legislators who rotate in and out of government. Supporters of congressional term limits emphasize that incumbents are rarely defeated for reelection. They also point to the Twenty-second Amendment, which restricts the number of terms the president can serve.

Opponents say that term limits are built into the Constitution in the form of elections; the people can always refuse to reelect an incumbent. They add that expertise in the legislative branch is important to deal with an increasingly complex world. Opponents of term limits point out that Congress, unlike the president, does not have a large permanent bureaucracy to rely on for independent information, and so must draw on the experience of its own members.

> **"We already have term limits— they are called elections."**
>
> —Rep. Henry Hyde

To Restore Congress *George Will*

In his book Restoration, *journalist George Will argues that term limits will restore public respect for Congress and halt the growth of an overexpansive government.*

My reflex is to recoil from proposals for constitutional change. However, under the accumulating weight of evidence I, like millions of other Americans, have been driven to the conclusion that something must be done to restore Congress to competence and respect, and that term limits can do it....

If government now is so omnipresent (because it strives to be omniprovident) and so arcane that it makes a permanent legislative class indispensable, that is less an argument in favor of such a class than it is an argument against that kind of government. It is an argument for pruning the government's claims to omnicompetence. It is an argument for curtailing government's intrusiveness at least enough so that the supervision of the government can be entrusted to the oversight of intelligent lay people. Or amateurs. Sometimes called citizens.

Representatives and direct Taxes shall be apportioned among the several States which may be included within this Union, according to their respective Numbers, which shall be determined by adding to the whole Number of free Persons, including those bound to Service for a Term of Years, and excluding Indians not taxed, three fifths of all other Persons.... Under the Great Compromise, large states would have more seats than small states in the House of Representatives, but they would also have to pay more taxes. Representation based on population was thus a two-edged sword. Direct taxes—primarily those derived from the value of land—would be apportioned among the states according to population as well. Today, the federal government seldom uses direct taxes to raise revenue, preferring the income tax instead.

Besides how states would be represented in Congress, another critical stumbling block at the Constitutional Convention was whether slaves would be counted in a state's population, both for representation and taxation purposes. The framers faced a dilemma: if slaves were property, they should not be counted at all for representation purposes; if they were persons, they should be counted fully–even as women, children, indentured servants, and others who could not vote were also counted. However, including slaves as persons would only increase the political power of the slaveholding South. After extended debate between delegates supporting and opposing slavery, the framers agreed to the Three-Fifths Compromise, which included a fraction of a state's slaves in its population total. This formula was changed by the Fourteenth Amendment, after slavery was abolished.

Under the Constitution, Native Americans living on tribal land were not taxed and not included in a state's population for representation purposes. The framers regarded the Indian tribes as independent nations, although subsequently the U.S. government encroached on most of their power. As discussed more fully in Section 8 of Article I, Native Americans have a unique constitutional status. They are dual citizens both of their tribe and, since 1924, of the United States. Prior to that date, American Indians who left tribal lands were sometimes recognized as citizens of a state, but often not. Native Americans living on reservations, and therefore not taxed, were not allowed to vote by Arizona and New Mexico until 1948.

The Slaveholding Republic

Three provisions in the 1787 Constitution specifically address slavery, although the word *slave* is never mentioned. Article I, Section 2 includes three-fifths of all slaves in a state's population for representation and taxation. Section 9 of Article I forbids Congress to prohibit the slave trade prior to 1808. And Article IV, Section 2 requires states to return fugitive slaves to their owners. During the Constitutional Convention, the framers disagreed over how to deal with slavery. But most delegates recognized that, without some protection of slavery, southern states would not join the Union. Many of the framers regarded slavery as a matter of state law that the Constitution could not prohibit.

Because of its slavery provisions, abolitionist William Lloyd Garrison referred to the Constitution as "a covenant with death, and an agreement with hell." However, historian Don Fehrenbacher disagrees. In his book *The Slaveholding Republic*, Fehrenbacher states: "The Constitution as it came from the hands of the framers dealt only minimally and peripherally with slavery and was essentially open-ended on the subject." Abraham Lincoln and his Republican party also believed that the Constitution did not require slavery to be protected, but the Supreme Court ruled otherwise. In 1857, the Court held in *Dred Scott v. Sandford* that, under the Constitution, the United States could not forbid slavery in new territories. The debate over whether the Constitution guaranteed slavery culminated in the Civil War, and was finally resolved in 1865 with the ratification of the Thirteenth Amendment.

The actual Enumeration shall be made within three Years after the first Meeting of the Congress of the United States, and within every subsequent Term of ten Years, in such Manner as they shall by Law direct.

The Constitution requires that the entire population of the United States be counted every ten years. This census is then used to determine how many representatives each state should have in Congress. Traditionally, the census was conducted by an actual head count of each individual. Today, many Americans argue that a statistical sampling of the nation would more accurately count racial minorities. Congress now uses information from the census to make decisions about federal funding, in addition to the apportionment of representatives. In a 1996 case, the Supreme Court ruled that sampling was not required by the Constitution to adequately represent minorities. In 1999, the Court held that sampling for apportionment purposes violated the Census Act, but a majority did not rule on whether Article I prohibited sampling.

The first census was held in 1790. At that time, the United States consisted of about 4 million people, 17 percent of whom were slaves. In 2000, the total U.S. population was more than 280 million—making the nation seventy times larger than first envisioned by the framers. Many of the framers believed that a republic could not exist in a very large country. In addition to population, the census also includes demographic data such as race and gender.

The Number of Representatives shall not exceed one for every thirty Thousand, but each State shall have at Least one Representative; and until such enumeration shall be made, the State of New Hampshire shall be entitled to chuse three, Massachusetts eight, Rhode-Island and Providence Plantations one, Connecticut five, New-York six, New Jersey four, Pennsylvania eight, Delaware one, Maryland six, Virginia ten, North Carolina five, South Carolina five, and Georgia three.

The Constitution says that the total number of representatives shall not be greater than one for every 30,000 citizens. During the ratification debates over the Constitution, opponents argued that such a ratio was inadequate to properly represent the country. But even using the original ratio in the Constitution, the House of Representatives would have consisted of about 9,400 members after the 2000 census. Faced with the ever increasing size of the House, Congress voted in 1929 to limit the number of representatives to 435. Based on the 2000 census, the population ratio per representative is about 1 for every 646,000 citizens.

reapportionment

the process by which Congress allocates the number of representatives for each state, based on changes in the census

redistricting

the process by which each state draws the boundaries of its congressional districts, according to the number of representatives allocated by Congress

Once the census has been held, Congress must then allocate the number of representatives per state, a process known as **reapportionment.** This number varies every decade according to changes in a state's population. When a state's representation changes, it must then redraw the boundaries of its congressional districts—which is called **redistricting.** According to the Supreme Court's ruling in *Wesberry v. Sanders* (1964), a state's congressional districts must be equal in population.

However, because each state must have at least one representative, the population of congressional districts can vary widely across the nation. For instance, in the 2000 reapportionment, Wyoming received one representative for its 500,000 residents, while Montana also received only one representative for its 900,000 residents. Montana had sued after the 1990 census to have congressional districts be more equal nationwide, but the Supreme Court ruled that such districts only have to be equal within states.

State legislatures have often drawn oddly shaped congressional districts in order to preserve the political power of the majority party, a practice known as gerrymandering. In a series of cases in the 1990s, the Supreme Court held that such redistricting, when drawn primarily along racial lines, can violate the Fourteenth Amendment's guarantee of equal protection—even when designed to address past discrimination in voting.

Governor Elbridge Gerry of Massachusetts drew a salamander-shaped election district in 1812 to help his political supporters. His critics added wings, claws, and a head to a map of the district, dubbing it the "Gerry-mander."

Etch-a-Sketch Gerrymanders *John Fund*

A columnist for the Wall Street Journal, *John Fund believes that gerrymandering predetermines the outcome of elections, so that voting becomes meaningless.*

[The 2000] census has set in motion the redrawing of political districts. In many states, the process will result in sundered communities, Etch-a-Sketch gerrymanders, court suits, and charges of discrimination....

Block by block computer maps of the nation allow the party in power to create maps with tortuous nooks and crannies. Too often, the result is a plan that allows elected officials to choose their voters, rather than the other way around.

[In 1981], the late Rep. Phil Burton created an infamous gerrymander that he called "my contribution to abstract art." One district was an incredible 385-sided figure.... States could adopt standards that prevent the worst gerrymandering abuses by demanding contiguity and compactness....

Unless districts are fairly drawn to preserve competition and the idea of a political community, many elections, basically predetermined, will be rendered meaningless. When voters learn the truth, it becomes yet another reason for them to stop voting—as they are doing in growing numbers.

When vacancies happen in the Representation from any State, the Executive Authority thereof shall issue Writs of Election to fill such Vacancies.

The governor of a state can call a special election to fill a vacant House seat, such as when a member dies in office. However, because House terms last only two years, some governors have declined to incur the cost of a special election if less than a year remains in the term.

The House of Representatives shall chuse their Speaker and other Officers;...

The Speaker of the House of Representatives is the highest officer in the legislative branch. Originally, the Speaker was just a moderator, maintaining order and parliamentary procedure during congressional debate. But over time the Speaker became a very powerful leader in Congress, using political influence to determine the success of legislation.

The power of the office reached its apex under Speaker Joseph G. "Uncle Joe" Cannon (R-Ill.), but in 1910 the House voted to limit his power to select the membership and leadership of congressional committees. Today, party leaders in the House make committee assignments, and the committee members choose their own chairs; however, the speaker still plays a crucial role in designing legislative strategy. The Speaker is elected by a majority vote in the House, but practically the

Speaker Joe Cannon presided over the House of Representatives from 1903 to 1913.

An Attempt to Herd Cats *Speaker Newt Gingrich*

In 1995, Rep. Newt Gingrich (R-Ga.) became speaker of the House, the first Republican in that office in forty years. Dissent within his own party caused Speaker Gingrich to leave office four years later, as recounted in his book Lessons Learned the Hard Way.

The Speaker is the third-ranking constitutional officer. That in itself might seem weighty

enough. In addition, the day-to-day job requires him not only to preside over, but to attempt to lead, 435 strong-willed, competitive, and independent-minded people. (Some wag has likened this to an attempt to herd cats.) After all, if these people had not in the first place been heavily endowed with all three of these characteristics—will, competitiveness, and independence of mind—they

would never have been able to get through the process of winning a primary, followed by a general election, followed by the requirement that they represent 600,000 of their fellow Americans in the nation's capital. So if they sometimes made difficulties for one another, and for me, that was one of the great strengths of the system.

Speaker is chosen at a caucus of the ruling political party. Under the Presidential Succession Act of 1947, the Speaker is next in line after the vice president to become president.

All Politics Is Local *Speaker Thomas P. "Tip" O'Neill*

From 1977 to 1987, Rep. Tip O'Neill (D-Mass.) served as Speaker of the House. He became well known for his trademark slogan: "All politics is local."

I lost the first race I ever ran, for the Cambridge City Council, by 160 votes because I took my own neighborhood for granted. My father took me aside after the election and told me, "All politics is local. Don't forget it."...

A politician learns that if a constituent calls about a problem, even if it's a streetlight

out, you don't tell them to call City Hall. You call City Hall. Members of the House learn this quicker than anyone else because they only have a two-year term. They learn that if you don't pay attention to the voters, you soon will find yourself right back there with them.

Rep. Tip O'Neill served in the House for thirty-four years.

impeachment

the process by which a civil officer of the United States is charged with wrongdoing

...and shall have the sole Power of Impeachment.

This provision of Article I is the first of several in the Constitution that deal with **impeachment,** the process by which a civil officer of the United States is accused of wrongdoing. Section 2 of Article I gives the House of Representatives the sole power to impeach, or make an accusation against

President Andrew Johnson receives a summons from Congress in 1868 during his impeachment.

an official. Section 3 of Article I designates the Senate as the trier of guilt or innocence, establishes the procedures to be used for such a trial, and specifies punishment. Article II, Section 2 prevents the president from issuing pardons in cases of impeachment, and Section 4 sets forth who may be impeached and upon what grounds.

Only twice in U.S. history has the House impeached a president–Andrew Johnson in 1868 and Bill Clinton in 1998. Both were acquitted. The House Judiciary Committee voted to impeach

President Richard Nixon in July 1974, but he resigned before the full House voted on the charges. Details of specific impeachments are discussed in the Article II chapter.

My Faith in the Constitution Is Whole *Rep. Barbara Jordan*

When the House Judiciary Committee began hearings on the impeachment of President Richard Nixon in July 1974, Rep. Barbara Jordan (D-Tex.) noted that as an African American and a woman, she was not included in the original definition of "We the People." Yet as a member of the House her duty was to defend the Constitution.

Earlier today, we heard the beginning of the preamble to the Constitution of the United States, "We the People." It is a very eloquent beginning. But, when that document was completed on the 17th of September in 1787, I was not included in that "We the People." I felt somehow for many years that George Washington and Alexander Hamilton just left me out by mistake. But, through the process of amendment, interpretation, and court decision, I have finally been included in "We the People."

Today, I am an inquisitor. I believe hyperbole would not be fictional and would not overstate the solemnness that I feel right now. My faith in the Constitution is whole, it is complete, it is total. I am not going to sit here and be an idle spectator to the diminution, the subversion, the destruction of the Constitution.

SECTION. 3. The Senate of the United States shall be composed of two Senators from each State, *chosen by the Legislature thereof,* for six Years; and each Senator shall have one Vote.

Each state is equally represented in the Senate, which according to Article V cannot be changed even by constitutional amendment. This equal representation means that a senator in California has about 34 million constituents while a senator in Wyoming has about 500,000. Originally, senators were chosen by state legislatures, but the Seventeenth Amendment, ratified in 1913, provided for direct election of senators.

During the Constitutional Convention, the framers decided to give senators longer terms than representatives–which, according to James Madison, would give senators more expertise in public policy. The Senate tends to have a more collegial air than the House of Representatives due to its smaller size and the longer terms of its members. The Senate often refers to itself as "the world's greatest deliberative body." Before direct election of senators, critics during the Progressive Era called the Senate a "millionaire's club," charging that rich people bribed state legislatures for Senate seats.

Immediately after they shall be assembled in Consequence of the first Election, they shall be divided as equally as may be into three Classes. The Seats of the Senators of the first Class shall be vacated at the Expiration of the second Year, of the second Class at the Expiration of

the fourth Year, and of the third Class at the Expiration of the sixth Year, so that one third may be chosen every second Year;...

The Constitution rotates the terms of office for senators so that the entire Senate is not up for reelection at the same time. Therefore, no more than one-third of the Senate is being elected every two years. This practice preserves the continuity of the Senate as a political body, whereas the House of Representatives is elected anew on a biennial basis.

...and if Vacancies happen by Resignation, or otherwise, during the Recess of the Legislature of any State, the Executive thereof may make temporary Appointments until the next Meeting of the Legislature, which shall then fill such Vacancies.

This provision in the Constitution was also changed by the Seventeenth Amendment. Now, when a vacancy in the Senate occurs, the governor may appoint a replacement who serves until a special election is called or until the next general election, as specified by the state legislature. In 2000, Governor Mel Carnahan of Missouri, a candidate for the U.S. Senate, died in an airplane crash only three weeks before the general election. Carnahan's name remained on the ballot, and he became the first dead man ever elected to the Senate. The new governor of Missouri appointed Carnahan's widow, Jean, to the seat.

In 1870, Sen. Hiram Revels of Mississippi became the first African American to serve in Congress, filling the Senate seat previously held by Jefferson Davis, president of the Confederacy.

No Person shall be a Senator who shall not have attained to the Age of thirty Years, and been nine Years a Citizen of the United States, and who shall not, when elected, be an Inhabitant of that State for which he shall be chosen.

The minimum age and length of citizenship is higher for senators than for representatives, which some scholars say indicates that the framers intended for the Senate to be a more experienced and august body than the House of Representatives. The age and citizenship requirements must be reached before a senator is sworn in, but not necessarily at the time of election. However, a candidate must be a resident of the state when elected.

The Vice President of the United States shall be President of the Senate, but shall have no Vote, unless they be equally divided.

The vice president is the only U.S. official who is a member of two branches of government: the executive and the legislative. The vice president is next in line for the presidency but otherwise has no specific executive branch duties. However, the Constitution does designate the vice president as the Senate's presiding officer and tiebreaker. The vice president's power to cast a vote in a divided Senate is one of the checks and balances that the executive branch has over the legislative branch, and it has been used several times in U.S. history to help the president win passage of controversial laws.

John Adams: A Government of Laws, Not Men

The first vice president of the United States was John Adams (1735–1826), who came in second to George Washington in the electoral vote for president. As vice president, Adams began by using up much of the first Senate's time unsuccessfully pursuing a grand title for the president.

Instead, Adams earned the nickname "His Rotundity" for himself. Adams played a large, if often unappreciated, role in the creation of the nation. He served on the committee to draft the Declaration of Independence in 1776, and he promoted the idea of a new U.S. constitution while serving as

ambassador to England in 1787. Perhaps Adams's most lasting contribution is as author of the Massachusetts state constitution, ratified in 1780. It is the oldest written constitution still in operation in the world. That document establishes "a government of laws, and not of men."

The Senate shall chuse their other Officers, and also a President pro tempore, in the Absence of the Vice President, or when he shall exercise the Office of President of the United States.

Another Senate officer is the president pro tempore, also known as the president pro tem, who presides when the vice president is absent. The president pro tem is third in the line of succession to the presidency, after the vice president and the Speaker of the House. However, the president pro tem is mainly a ceremonial office. The political head of the Senate is the majority leader, who is elected by the political party with the majority of Senate seats. The majority leader determines legislative strategy and is the most influential officer in the Senate.

The Senate shall have the sole Power to try all Impeachments. When sitting for that Purpose, they shall be on Oath or Affirmation. When the President of the United States is tried, the Chief Justice shall preside: And no Person shall be convicted without the Concurrence of two thirds of the Members present.

Once the House has impeached an official, by a majority vote, the Senate determines if that person is guilty or innocent of the charges. The proceeding is not a criminal trial, so different rules apply, as established by the Senate. The House appoints "managers," who act as prosecutors, and the accused may be represented by counsel. Senators must take a special oath for an impeachment trial, but they are not technically jurors. Senators are not allowed to speak during the trial, but they can present written questions for a witness to the presiding officer. Once the evidence has been presented, the senators deliberate in closed session and then vote in open session.

Some scholars question how much discretion the Senate has in its power "to try all impeachments." The Senate might decide not to pursue a full trial, despite impeachment by the House. Such an abbreviated procedure was proposed during the impeachment trial of President Bill Clinton in 1999, but it failed to pass. The Senate has never declined to proceed with a trial once the House has impeached an official. The Senate has relied on a committee's recommendations in the impeachment trial of a judge, and the Supreme Court upheld that process in *Nixon v. United States* (1993). The vice president officiates at all impeachment trials except when the president is accused. In that case, the chief justice presides. Otherwise, the vice president might possibly influence the outcome of the trial in order to become president. An impeached official must be found guilty by two-thirds of the senators present to be convicted.

Judgment in Cases of Impeachment shall not extend further than to removal from Office, and disqualification to hold and enjoy any Office of honor, Trust or Profit under the United States: but the Party convicted shall nevertheless be liable and subject to Indictment, Trial, Judgment and Punishment, according to Law.

If convicted by the Senate, an impeached official is automatically removed from office. In a separate proceeding, the Senate can also vote to disqualify that official from holding any future federal office. The House has impeached sixteen federal officials as of 2001, but only seven of those—all federal judges—were convicted by the Senate. Only two of those judges were disqualified from future office. In fact, one impeached and convicted federal judge, Alcee Hastings, was elected to Congress in 1992. Whether the Senate convicts or acquits, an impeached official can still be prosecuted under any criminal law that applies. Such prosecution does not violate the Fifth Amendment's prohibition of double jeopardy, or twice prosecuting a person for the same offense, because impeachment is not a criminal proceeding.

SECTION. 4. The Times, Places and Manner of holding Elections for Senators and Representatives, shall be prescribed in each State by the Legislature thereof; but the Congress may at any time by Law make or alter such Regulations, except as to the Places of chusing Senators.

Congress has the power to regulate the times, places, and manner of elections for senators and representatives. While the states set the basic qualifications for voting in federal elections, Congress may determine the procedures under which such votes are cast. For example, in 1872 Congress set the date for federal elections as the first Tuesday after the first Monday in November. Section 4 says that Congress may not alter the places of choosing senators, but this language refers mainly to the selection of senators in state legislatures, which was changed by the Seventeenth Amendment. Some states have argued that Section 4 allows them to impose term limits on federal legislators. However, the Supreme Court ruled in *U.S. Term Limits v. Thornton* (1995) that such requirements are unconstitutional changes in the qualifications for office, not in the procedures by which legislators are elected.

The Congress shall assemble at least once in every Year, and such Meeting shall be *on the first Monday in December,* unless they shall by Law appoint a different Day.

At the time of the American Revolution, the King of England had the arbitrary power to convene or dissolve Parliament at will. There were no guarantees that the people's representatives could meet and conduct business. The Declaration of Independence cites this abuse as one of the justifications for revolution. Therefore, the Constitution specifies that Congress must meet a least once a year. The actual date of that meeting has now been changed by the Twentieth Amendment to January 3, unless Congress sets a different day by law.

SECTION. 5. Each House shall be the Judge of the Elections, Returns and Qualifications of its own Members,…

For many years, both the House and the Senate exercised the power to refuse to seat duly elected legislators, even though they met the constitutional qualifications for office. In 1919, for example, the House denied a seat to a member of the Socialist Party from Wisconsin who had been convicted of espionage—an offense that at the time included opposing U.S. entry into World War I. However, in *Powell v. McCormack* (1969), the Supreme Court ruled that Congress could not, by a majority vote, refuse membership to a candidate who met the qualifications for office set forth in the Constitution. The case involved Rep. Adam Clayton Powell, Jr., an African American who had represented Harlem for more than twenty years. A congressional investigation determined that Powell had misused federal funds, and the House refused to seat him in 1967. The Supreme Court held that the appropriate recourse in such a case was expulsion, which required a two-thirds vote. The Court refused to retroactively convert the House's vote to refuse to seat Powell, even though by more than a two-thirds margin, into a vote to expel. And under House rules, a member could only be expelled during the same term in which the offense was committed.

…and a Majority of each shall constitute a Quorum to do Business; but a smaller Number may adjourn from day to day, and may be

quorum

the number of members in a group required to be present to carry out official business

authorized to compel the Attendance of absent Members, in such Manner, and under such Penalties as each House may provide.

In any legislative body, a minimum number, known as a **quorum,** must be present in order to conduct official business. The Constitution establishes a majority in either house as a quorum. If enough members are not present on the floor of a house to do business, a quorum call can be issued to compel attendance. If the Constitution did not specify a quorum, then a small number of legislators could pass laws affecting the entire nation.

A Catastrophe the Framers Could Not Have Foreseen *Norman Ornstein*

During the Cold War, a constitutional amendment was proposed to provide for the possibility of an attack on the Capitol. Congressional scholar Norman Ornstein renewed the call for such an amendment after the terrorist attacks of September 11, 2001.

What if United Flight 93—the plane that crash landed near Pittsburgh—had crashed into the Capitol dome on Sept. 11 at 9:30 or 10 A.M.? Both chambers of Congress were filled with lawmakers that morning. Hundreds might have been killed or incapacitated. The horror of such an attack would soon be punctuated by an

additional horror—a Congress unable to meet or act for months, because of constitutional provisions that do not contemplate a disaster of this dimension.

The problem is twofold: First is a provision in Article I that defines the number of members in each body required to be present to pass laws as a majority. Parliamentarians define this quorum as a majority of those elected, sworn in, *and living.* But a massive terrorist attack might leave sizable numbers alive but incapacitated....

In the Senate, where vacancies can be filled either by special elections or guber-

natorial appointments, governors could step in quickly. But the Constitution says vacancies in the House of Representatives can be filled only by special election. The past six special elections have taken between three and six months.

The possibility of months without a Congress, at the worst possible time, is unacceptable. The answer is a constitutional amendment to allow for governors to make interim emergency appointments. This would keep the basic structure our founders envisioned in place but also account for a catastrophe the framers could not have foreseen.

Each House may determine the Rules of its Proceedings, punish its Members for disorderly Behaviour, and, with the Concurrence of two thirds, expel a Member.

Section 5 deals with many of the housekeeping requirements of Congress, the nuts and bolts of doing business. Most legislatures follow certain rules of parliamentary procedure, and Section 5 gives each house of Congress the power to set its own rules. The variances in these rules can dramatically affect legislative strategy.

The Senate, for instance, has a long history of allowing unlimited debate on bills before a vote can be called. Some senators take advantage of this rule to kill legislation. They give long and irrelevant speeches to prevent a vote on a bill. This practice, known as a **filibuster,** derives from the Dutch word for pirate—and the Senate floor is essentially taken over by a few senators who "talk a bill to death." However, in 1917 the Senate adopted a rule of **cloture,** which now limits debate if supported by sixty senators. In effect, this means that a bill must have sixty allies in the Senate to guarantee passage, not just a mere majority. Because of its larger size, the House of Representatives began to limit debate in 1841.

Section 5 makes no mention of committees, yet they are the principal means by which Congress carries out its work. Proposed legislation is assigned to one or more committees, such as Finance or Agriculture, according to its subject matter. The bill must in most cases be approved by a committee in order to be voted on by the entire legislative body. Through its committees, Congress also exercises its power to investigate matters of proposed legislation. The Constitution does not specifically mention the power to conduct investigations, although Congress has done so since 1792. In *Watkins v. United States* (1957), the Supreme Court recognized investigation as an inherent power of Congress.

Each house of Congress can punish, or censure, its members for "disorderly" behavior. However, debate on the floor of Congress has not always been civil. This was especially true before the Civil War, when dueling was common. Legislators often carried arms, and during one debate thirty members of the House drew guns. Perhaps the most famous confrontation in the House was in 1798 when Rep. Roger Griswold of Connecticut used a hickory stick to attack Rep. Matthew Lyon of Vermont,

filibuster

unlimited and often irrelevant debate on a bill designed to prevent a vote on its passage

cloture

a procedural motion to end debate on a bill

"**Congress in session is Congress on public exhibition, whilst Congress in its committee-rooms is Congress at work.**"
—Woodrow Wilson

This engraving, entitled Congressional Pugilists, *depicts the 1798 brawl of Rep. Matthew Lyon and Rep. Roger Griswold on the floor of the House. The dispute began when Lyon spit tobacco juice on Griswold in response to his charge of cowardice.*

who retaliated with fire tongs. And on the Senate floor in 1856, abolitionist Sen. Charles Sumner of Massachusetts was seriously beaten by a proslavery member of the House of Representatives.

A member of Congress cannot be impeached, so expulsion is the only way a legislator can be removed from office. Section 5 requires a two-thirds vote for expulsion. The Supreme Court has ruled that expulsion does not have to be based on a criminal offense, but that "the right to expel extends to all cases where the offence is such as . . . is inconsistent with the trust and duty of a Member."

The Line Between Investigation and Persecution
Edward R. Murrow

Perhaps the most controversial congressional investigations were led in the 1950s by Sen. Joseph McCarthy (R-Wisc.), who branded many Americans as communists. On his television program See It Now, *legendary journalist Edward R. Murrow criticized Sen. McCarthy in March 1954. McCarthy was censured by the Senate later that year.*

No one familiar with the history of this country can deny that congressional committees are useful. It is necessary to investigate before legislating.

But the line between investigation and persecution is a very fine one, and the junior senator from Wisconsin has stepped over it repeatedly. His primary achievement has been in confusing the public mind as between the internal and external threat of Communism. We must not confuse dissent with disloyalty. We must remember always that accusation is not proof and that conviction depends upon evidence and due process of law. We will not walk in fear, one of another. We will not be driven by fear

into an age of unreason....

We proclaim ourselves, as indeed we are, the defenders of freedom—what's left of it—but we cannot defend freedom abroad by deserting it at home. The actions of the junior senator from Wisconsin have caused alarm and dismay amongst our allies abroad and given considerable comfort to our enemies. And whose fault is it? Not really his; he didn't create this situation of fear, he merely exploited it and rather successfully. Cassius was right. "The fault, dear Brutus, is not in our stars but in ourselves."

Each House shall keep a Journal of its Proceedings, and from time to time publish the same, excepting such Parts as may in their Judgment require Secrecy; and the Yeas and Nays of the Members of either House on any question shall, at the Desire of one fifth of those Present, be entered on the Journal.

The Constitution requires each house to keep an official record of its proceedings, including votes on legislation. Such a journal makes it easier for the public to know exactly what action Congress has taken, although certain parts may be kept secret. This journal should not be confused with the *Congressional Record*—a voluminous publication that includes floor speeches (and many that were never actually delivered), correspondence from constituents, and edited revisions of unwise remarks. Although published by Congress, it is neither the official nor actual record.

Neither House, during the Session of Congress, shall, without the Consent of the other, adjourn for more than three days, nor to any other Place than that in which the two Houses shall be sitting.
When Congress is in session, both houses have to coordinate their schedules. Otherwise, either house could delay action on a controversial measure by adjourning. Also, the nation's capital moved several times during the Revolutionary War, and the framers of the Constitution wanted to ensure that joint action of both houses was required to relocate the capital.

SECTION. 6. The Senators and Representatives shall receive a Compensation for their Services, to be ascertained by Law, and paid out of the Treasury of the United States.
Members of Congress are paid by the U.S. government, not the state they represent, which helps create a national identity for legislators. However, many Americans objected to the fact that Congress could vote itself a pay raise without review. In 1789, one of the twelve amendments submitted by Congress to the states in what became the Bill of Rights dealt with congressional pay raises. It prevented an increase in salaries from taking effect until after the next election of representatives. This amendment failed to be ratified for more than 200 years, until it became the Twenty-seventh Amendment in 1992.

They shall in all Cases, except Treason, Felony and Breach of the Peace, be privileged from Arrest during their Attendance at the Session of their respective Houses, and in going to and returning from the same; and for any Speech or Debate in either House, they shall not be questioned in any other Place.
This part of Section 6 gives federal legislators two kinds of immunity. The first has become somewhat obsolete. During session, members of Congress are privileged from civil arrest, which was more common when the Constitution was adopted. However, they are not privileged from arrest for criminal acts—including both misdemeanors and felonies. The second type of immunity involves punishment for remarks made as part of the legislative process. In England, the king had fined members of Parliament for libel if he disagreed with their speeches. The Speech or Debate Clause prevents a member of Congress from being sued for official actions that are essential to the deliberations of Congress, beyond just formal debate. However, the Supreme Court ruled in *Hutchinson v. Proxmire* (1979) that a "Golden Fleece Award" given by Senator William Proxmire to recipients of government waste was not protected by the Speech or Debate Clause because it was disseminated in press releases and constituent newsletters.

No Senator or Representative shall, during the Time for which he was elected, be appointed to any civil Office under the Authority of the United States, which shall have been created, or the Emoluments whereof shall have been encreased during such time; and no Person holding any Office under the United States, shall be a Member of either House during his Continuance in Office.

This provision in Section 6 prevents a member of Congress from assuming a federal office that was created during his or her term, or for which the salary was increased. Thus, a legislator cannot directly benefit from such executive appointments. In some cases, Congress has temporarily reduced the salaries of certain offices so that legislators who had voted for raises could be appointed.

More important, Section 6 illustrates the constitutional principle of separation of powers. It prohibits any member of Congress from simultaneously holding an office in the executive or judicial branches. This is in direct contrast to the parliamentary system of government–in which members of the legislature also serve as executive officials, including the prime minister (or chief executive) and the cabinet.

SECTION. 7. All Bills for raising Revenue shall originate in the House of Representatives; but the Senate may propose or concur with Amendments as on other Bills.

As one way of linking taxation with representation, the Constitution requires that revenue bills must originate in the House of Representatives, which is closer to the people than the Senate. However, the Senate may amend such bills, so the practical consequences of this provision in Section 7 are negligible. It applies only to those statutes that raise taxes in general, not that designate funds for special purposes or create fines.

"With Congress, every time they make a joke it's a law. And every time they make a law it's a joke."

—Will Rogers

Every Bill which shall have passed the House of Representatives and the Senate, shall, before it becomes a Law, be presented to the President of the United States: If he approve he shall sign it, but if not he shall return it, with his Objections to that House in which it shall have originated, who shall enter the Objections at large on their Journal, and proceed to reconsider it. If after such Reconsideration two thirds of that House shall agree to pass the Bill, it shall be sent, together with the Objections, to the other House, by which it shall likewise be reconsidered, and if approved by two thirds of that House, it shall become a Law. But in all such Cases the Votes of both Houses shall be determined by yeas and Nays, and the Names of the Persons voting for and against the Bill shall be entered on the Journal of each House respectively. If any Bill shall not be returned by the President

within ten Days (Sundays excepted) after it shall have been presented to him, the Same shall be a Law, in like Manner as if he had signed it, unless the Congress by their Adjournment prevent its Return, in which Case it shall not be a Law.

Section 7 describes how a bill becomes a law. The legislative process is fraught with such conflict and compromise that it is often said, in a phrase attributed to Prussian statesman Otto von Bismarck: "If you like laws and sausages, you should never watch either one being made." Section 7 does not say specifically how legislation passes the House or the Senate—no provision is made for a majority vote, for instance. Such details are left up to each house in establishing its own rules under Section 5 of Article I. However, before a bill is sent to the president, the House of Representatives and the Senate have to pass identical versions. If there are differences, both chambers appoint members of a **conference committee,** which proposes a compromise bill.

Section 7 includes several examples of checks and balances. It gives the president the power to **veto,** or reject, legislation passed by Congress. Congress can override the president's veto by a two-thirds vote of each house, but this is done rarely. The president has only ten days in which to veto a bill or it becomes law automatically. Similarly, if Congress adjourns during that ten days, the bill dies if the president does not sign it—a tactic known as a **pocket veto.**

Many presidents have advocated a **line item veto,** exercised by most state governors, to allow them to reject specific provisions in a bill rather than the whole thing. They believe such a power will help them combat wasteful programs that benefit only a few Americans at the expense of the many. Congress passed a Line Item Veto Act in 1996, but the Supreme Court ruled it unconstitutional in *Clinton v. New York* (1998). Efforts to pass a constitutional amendment for a line item veto have thus far failed.

Every Order, Resolution, or Vote to which the Concurrence of the Senate and House of Representatives may be necessary (except on a question of Adjournment) shall be presented to the President of the United

conference committee

a joint committee of both houses of Congress that proposes compromise legislation when there are disagreements on bills

veto

the president's power to reject a bill passed by Congress

pocket veto

the power of the president to prevent passage of a bill by refusing to sign it during an adjournment of Congress

line item veto

the power to reject specific provisions in a law without defeating the entire bill

Andrew Jackson used his veto power so often that congressional opponents referred to him as "King Andrew the First."

KINDA PINCHES
ACROSS THE TOES—
GIMME A SIZE
LARGER.

VAST PRESIDENTIAL AUTHORITY

CONGRESS

This cartoon from the Truman administration demonstrates the ambivalent nature of power sharing between Congress and the president.

States; and before the Same shall take Effect, shall be approved by him, or being disapproved by him, shall be repassed by two thirds of the Senate and House of Representatives, according to the Rules and Limitations prescribed in the Case of a Bill.
This provision in Section 7 is known as the Presentment Clause. It ensures that the president participates in the legislative process, whether or not the law in question is labeled a bill or a resolution. However, the Presentment Clause does not apply to proposed constitutional amendments, which do not have to be approved by the president before they are sent to the states for ratification.

With the growth of the regulatory state during the New Deal, Congress tried to limit the rule-making power of the executive branch through the **legislative veto.** Under this practice, Congress reserved the right to disapprove executive branch regulations without formally passing a law subject to the president's veto. Almost 200 laws included some form of legislative veto by 1983. That year the Supreme Court held in *Immigration and Naturalization Service v. Chadha* that the legislative veto violates the Presentment Clause. Once Congress delegates its legislative authority to an executive branch agency, said the Court, it cannot overturn that agency's regulations without passing another law that must be approved by the president.

SECTION. 8. The Congress shall have Power...
Section 8 of the Constitution sets forth the **enumerated powers** of Congress, those that are specifically listed as belonging to the national government. Congress may also exercise **implied powers,** which can be inferred from the enumerated powers—such as the power to draft people into the armed services as part of raising an army. In addition, the national

The Constitution Between Friends

The president and Congress share lawmaking power under the Constitution. This can often lead to conflict between the two branches, as illustrated by an anecdote attributed to President Grover Cleveland. The president refused to approve a bill sponsored by a member of Congress who belonged to the Tammany Hall political machine. When the politician inquired why, the president said that he thought the bill was unconstitutional. Replied the politician: "What's the Constitution between friends?"

government has **inherent powers,** which stem from a nation's sovereignty and do not have to be granted by the Constitution. These powers include regulating immigration and conducting foreign affairs.

...To lay and collect Taxes, Duties, Imposts and Excises, to pay the Debts and provide for the common Defence and general Welfare of the United States; but all Duties, Imposts and Excises shall be uniform throughout the United States;...

The first power listed in Section 8 is the power to tax. Under the Articles of Confederation, Congress could not lay or collect taxes and had to request

Uncle Sam solicits volunteers during World War I.

funds from the states. Often they did not comply. As a result, the nation was deeply in debt after the Revolutionary War. Congress needed the power to tax in order for the U.S. government to survive.

Congress may use the power to tax not only to raise revenue, but also to regulate economic activity. This was not always the case. In *Bailey v. Drexel Furniture Company* (1922), the Supreme Court struck down a tax on companies that used child labor, holding that only states could regulate employment. Since the New Deal, however, the Court has refused to inquire about the motives of Congress in passing tax laws.

In addition to the power to tax, Congress also has the power to spend. Section 8 authorizes Congress to provide for the common defense and general welfare, echoing phrases from the Preamble. The Supreme Court has ruled that this spending power is broad. Congress can use its spending power to encourage certain activities by the states, as a condition of receiving federal funds. For example, Congress passed a law in 1984 to withhold highway funding from states that did not raise the minimum drinking age to twenty-one.

The power to tax under Section 8 does not include the income tax, which was authorized in 1913 by the Sixteenth Amendment. Under Section 8, all indirect taxes such as **duties, imposts,** and **excises** must be uniform throughout the United States and cannot vary from state to state.

legislative veto

the practice by which Congress voids actions of executive branch agencies or officials

enumerated powers

the powers of the national government specifically listed in the Constitution

implied powers

those powers not specifically listed in the Constitution that can be inferred from the enumerated powers

inherent powers

those powers that belong to the government of a sovereign state

duties

taxes on imports

imposts

taxes on imports or general taxes

excises

taxes on domestic consumption of goods and services

To borrow Money on the credit of the United States;

The Constitution does not limit the amount of debt that the United States may incur. Congress borrows money by issuing government securities, such as bonds and Treasury certificates. High deficit spending during the 1980s and 1990s led to increased public support for a constitutional amendment to require a balanced budget. However, that impetus subsided during the economic boom of the late 1990s, which yielded budget surpluses.

To regulate Commerce with foreign Nations, and among the several States, and with the Indian Tribes;

The Commerce Clause has become the greatest source of federal power under the Constitution. Congress had no power to regulate commerce under the Articles of Confederation, and the states acted in a variety of ways to restrict the flow of commerce between one another. The first Supreme Court case to deal with the Commerce Clause involved the power of states to grant monopolies over steamboat navigation in their waterways. In that case, *Gibbons v. Ogden* (1824), Chief Justice John Marshall defined the commerce power broadly to include transportation, rather than limiting it to buying and selling, and struck down New York's monopoly for steamboats. This ruling increased the power of Congress to regulate interstate commerce and create a national economy.

However, from the 1890s to the 1930s, the Supreme Court consistently limited the ability of Congress to regulate the economy using the commerce power. Critics charged that Congress was using the commerce power to pass laws on social welfare, an area traditionally reserved to the states. In *United States v. E.C. Knight Company* (1895), the Court held that manufacturing was not part of interstate commerce and could not be regulated under the Sherman Antitrust Act. Similarly, the Court ruled in *Hammer v. Dagenhart* (1918) that the commerce power did not authorize Congress to prohibit child labor. The Supreme Court also struck down the National Industrial Recovery Act (NIRA), a centerpiece of the New Deal legislation, as an unconstitutional use of the commerce power in *Schechter Poultry Corporation v. United States* (1935).

But in 1937, the Supreme Court began to uphold New Deal economic programs as a valid exercise of the commerce power. Some scholars speculate that this change came because President Franklin Roosevelt, frustrated by the Court's previous rulings, proposed a "court-packing" plan to expand the Court with his own nominees. For several decades the Court routinely supported the federal government's exercise of the commerce power. In *United States v. Darby Lumber Company* (1941), for example, the Court overturned *Hammer* and ruled that Congress had the power to regulate wages and hours of workers engaged in interstate commerce.

The Supreme Court even upheld the use of the commerce power to justify the Civil Rights Act of 1964, which forbade racial discrimination in public accommodations—such as hotels and restaurants—that were privately owned. Previous court rulings had established that Congress could not prohibit private discrimination under the Fourteenth Amendment. However, because hotels affected interstate commerce, the Supreme Court upheld the ban on discrimination in those facilities in *Heart of Atlanta Motel v. United States* (1964).

But the Court signaled a major shift in its application of the Commerce Clause in *United States v. Lopez* (1995). The Court held that Congress had not shown a sufficient connection with interstate commerce when it passed a 1990 law creating gun-free school zones. And in *United States v. Morrison* (2000), the Supreme Court again struck down a statute passed under Commerce Clause authority. The Court ruled that the Violence Against Women Act, which allowed victims of gender-based violence to sue for damages in federal court, did not bear a sufficient relationship to interstate commerce to be upheld, despite the fact-finding record of Congress to the contrary.

Besides regulating trade between states, the Commerce Clause is also the principal source of federal authority regarding Native Americans. The Supreme Court defined the legal status of Indian tribes in *Cherokee Nation v. Georgia* (1831), in which Georgia tried to exercise jurisdiction over Cherokee land and people. As one of the "Five Civilized Tribes," the Cherokees had adopted white people's laws and customs, including owning slaves. Chief Justice John Marshall held for the Court's majority that Indian tribes were "domestic dependent nations," and the next year in *Worcester v. Georgia* struck down Georgia's regulation of the Cherokees as unconstitutional under the Commerce and Treaty Clauses.

President Andrew Jackson refused to enforce the decision. Under the federal Indian Removal Act, the Cherokees (along with the Choctaws, Chickasaws, Creeks, and Seminoles) were forcibly marched from their homes in the Southeast to new lands in the West. About four thousand Cherokees died on the Trail of Tears to present-day Oklahoma.

Native Americans in the West fared little better. In 1867, all tribes were forced to live on reservations and abandon their traditional way of life. Uprisings were all eventually defeated. Almost three hundred years of "Indian Wars" ended with the massacre of two hundred Sioux at Wounded Knee, South Dakota, in 1890.

Since 1871, Congress has ceased making treaties with Indian tribes, although previous treaties remain in force. American Indians were given U.S. citizenship in 1924, and they remain dual citizens of both the United States and their tribe. In 1968, Congress passed the Indian Civil Rights Act,

> "If it is interstate commerce that feels the pinch, it does not matter how local the operation that applies the squeeze."
>
> —Justice Robert H. Jackson

Chief Joseph led his Nez Perce tribe on a thousand-mile march from Oregon to Montana in 1877, trying to escape to Canada, but they surrendered and were sent to Oklahoma.

"My heart is sick and sad.... I will fight no more forever."

—Chief Joseph

which made certain provisions in the Bill of Rights applicable to tribal governments. As of the 2000 census, less than one percent of the U.S. population is Native American.

To establish an uniform Rule of Naturalization, and uniform Laws on the subject of Bankruptcies throughout the United States;
The original Constitution did not define citizenship. Only when the Fourteenth Amendment was added in 1868 did the Constitution promise citizenship to "all persons born or naturalized" in the United States— although that did not include Native Americans. Section 8 does give

The Constitution Put Beyond Their Reach

Protest of the Cherokee Nation

In 1836, the Cherokees sent a written protest to Congress, opposing removal from their native lands and noting the futility of their attempts to live under the Constitution.

The Cherokee were happy and prosperous under a scrupulous observance of treaty stipulations by the government of the United States, and from the fostering hand extended over them they made rapid advances in civilization, morals, and in the arts and sciences. Little did they anticipate that when taught to think and feel as the American citizen, and to have with him a common interest, they were to be *despoiled by their guardian,*

to become strangers and wanderers in the land of their fathers, forced to return to the savage life, and to seek a new home in the wilds of the far west....

For more than *seven long years* have the Cherokee people been driven into the necessity of contending for their just rights, and they have struggled against fearful odds.... Their resources and means of defense have been seized and withheld. The treaties, laws, and Constitution of the United States, their bulwark and only citadel of refuge, put beyond their reach; unfortunately for them, the protecting arm of the commander-in-chief of these

fortresses has been withdrawn from them. The judgments of the judiciary branch of the government in support of their rights have been disregarded and prostrated; and their petitions for relief, from time to time before Congress, have been unheeded....

The Cherokees cannot resist the power of the United States, and should they be driven from their native land, then they will look in melancholy sadness upon the golden chain presented by President Washington to the Cherokee people as emblematical of the brightness and purity of the friendship between the United States and the Cherokee Nation.

Congress the power to enact laws governing immigration and naturalization. In 1882, Congress passed the Chinese Exclusion Act, the first federal law to restrict immigration.

Until recently, the Supreme Court had held that Congress's power over immigration was plenary, or absolute. However, the Court ruled in *Zadvydas v. Davis* (2001) that, once inside the United States, both legal and illegal immigrants are protected by the Due Process Clause of the Fifth Amendment. Therefore, the Immigration and Naturalization Service could not detain indefinitely deportable immigrants who could not return to their home states.

Section 8 also gives Congress the power to regulate bankruptcies, which offer legal relief for creditors unable to pay their debts. Section 10 of Article I specifically prohibits states from passing laws impairing the obligation of contracts, although some states did enact bankruptcy codes in the absence of federal legislation.

To coin Money, regulate the Value thereof, and of foreign Coin, and fix the Standard of Weights and Measures;

To provide for the Punishment of counterfeiting the Securities and current Coin of the United States;

These two clauses of Section 8 both deal with the power to coin money. Congress has the exclusive power to coin money, which is prohibited to the states in Section 10. Under the Articles of Confederation, both the states and Congress could issue currency, which created an uncertain economy. The framers of the Constitution did not want Congress to have the power to issue paper money, but the government did so in 1862. At first, the Supreme Court struck down such action in 1870, but then it reversed itself in 1871, in what became known as the *Legal Tender Cases.* "Legal tender" means that Congress could require creditors to accept payment in paper money. Congress also has the power to punish counterfeiting of coin, paper money, and securities such as stocks and bonds.

To establish Post Offices and post Roads;

The postal power includes the authority to ensure the speedy delivery and security of the mail. The Supreme Court upheld the use of federal troops under this power to put down a railroad strike in the case of *In re Debs* (1895). Congress can also ban harmful materials from the mail, such as fraudulent advertisements. However, the postal service may not violate the First Amendment by intercepting nonobscene materials based on their political viewpoint.

To promote the Progress of Science and useful Arts, by securing for limited Times to Authors and Inventors the exclusive Right to their respective Writings and Discoveries;

This provision in Section 8 allows Congress to protect copyrights and patents. Copyrights allow the creator of literary or artistic works to retain exclusive right to copies of their work. Patents offer inventors the exclusive right to make and sell their inventions. The purpose of these protections of intellectual property is to encourage innovation and creativity in American society. Both copyrights and patents are set for limited times, after which the creations become part of the public domain. Some critics believe that Congress has extended the life of patents and copyrights to the public detriment. For instance, a pharmaceutical company's renewed patent can keep a cheaper generic drug off the market.

Brain-dead and Un-American *Ted Nugent*

Rock star Ted Nugent argued in the Wall Street Journal *that Napster, in which recordings were shared for free over the Internet, violated both copyright law and common sense.*

Common sense is alive and well in America if you're not stoned, drunk, greedy or just plain stupid. To think that anyone could even argue that Napster has the right to give away an artist's product is ridiculous.

Hey, I have a good idea! I'll just stand outside the local grocery store and offer its food free to the public. It doesn't matter if the owner took the risk, pays all the taxes and overhead, struggles with a bureaucratic land-mine field of regulations and laws, invests his warrior work ethic in bucketsful of sweat day after day, and basically busts his butt to provide a quality service and jobs for the community. Hell, no. I'll just make that decision for him, thank you, and give away his products and hard-earned money. Who does he think he is anyway?

The same applies to recording artists. We invest sweat and blood and millions of dollars creating musical products. It takes years of insane sacrifice and grueling tour schedules and intense effort. To think a third party should be allowed to give away our product for zero compensation is brain-dead and un-American.

To constitute Tribunals inferior to the supreme Court;

Congress can create lower courts beneath the Supreme Court, such as federal district and appellate courts. These courts are subject to the requirements in Article III that judges have lifetime appointments and cannot have their salaries reduced while in office. However, Congress has also created legislative courts that exercise special jurisdiction under Article I. They hear cases on specific topics—such as the military, tax, and bankruptcy. Judges in Article I courts do not have the protections of Article III judges.

To define and punish Piracies and Felonies committed on the high Seas, and Offences against the Law of Nations;

This provision gives Congress the power to punish piracy and other crimes on the high seas, one of the few times the Constitution expressly allows Congress to enact criminal laws. Section 8 also suggests that the United States will adhere to the law of nations, at least in certain respects. Congress has the power to make crimes of international law also punishable under the law of the United States.

To declare War, grant Letters of Marque and Reprisal, and make Rules concerning Captures on Land and Water;

An early draft of the Constitution gave Congress the power to "make" war, not just "declare" it. But in the end, the framers decided to split the war powers between the Congress and the president. Congress declares war, and then the president as commander-in-chief makes the necessary military decisions. However, Congress has declared war only five times, but U.S. forces were involved in many more armed conflicts.

In the modern era, the Korean War and Vietnam War cost thousands of American lives, even though Congress never officially declared war. These wars led to criticism of the executive branch for sending American troops to battle without clear congressional approval. In 1973, Congress passed the War Powers Act to limit the president's ability to commit soldiers to hostile areas—and to reassert its role in the early stages of war making. Under the act, the president must give notice to Congress of military deployment in armed conflict and remove the troops after sixty days, with a possible thirty-day extension, unless Congress authorizes the use of force. Many presidents regard the War Powers Act as unconstitutional, but the Supreme Court has refused to rule on the issue.

The power to grant **letters of marque and reprisal** is a holdover from the days of sailing ships. Such a letter would authorize private vessels to attack the shipping of an enemy nation without being punished as a pirate by their own country. The sailors on these vessels were also known as privateers.

Congress also has the power to seize the property of aliens from hostile foreign nations. The Supreme Court upheld the confiscation of property owned by German corporations during both world wars. Such property does not have to be actively used in warfare against the United States.

In addition to issuing a formal declaration of war, Congress has the power to regulate the war-time economy. During World War I, Congress authorized the president to take over factories and railroads. In World War II, Congress regulated consumer prices and rationing, and it allowed the president to seize factories during labor disputes. These war powers of Congress can carry on even once peace is declared, as long as a national

letters of marque and reprisal

authorization to attack the shipping of an enemy state without being punished as a pirate emergency continues to exist. However, in a 1947 labor law Congress refused to allow the president to seize industries during strikes, and as a result the Supreme Court struck down such action by President Harry Truman during the Korean War.

To raise and support Armies, but no Appropriation of Money to that Use shall be for a longer Term than two Years;

To provide and maintain a Navy;

These two clauses in Section 8 allow Congress to raise and maintain a professional military. At the time of the Revolutionary War, Americans detested a standing army that consisted of career soldiers. Such armies, loyal to the king, would be more likely to fire on unruly colonists than their neighbors in the local militia. The militia consisted of citizen-soldiers who kept their jobs in the community and drilled as part-time warriors. Under the Articles of Confederation, only the states could raise armies, and they were responsible for recruiting forces in the Continental Army. One of the most controversial provisions of the Constitution was its authorization of a standing army. Section 8 limits funding for the military to two-year terms.

Linked to the power to raise armies is the ability to pass conscription laws, which began during the Civil War. The Supreme Court upheld the draft during World War I. Although Congress ended the draft in 1973, it renewed draft registration in 1980. In *Rostker v. Goldberg* (1981), the Supreme Court held that Congress could lawfully exclude women from draft registration because they were not eligible for combat service.

To make Rules for the Government and Regulation of the land and naval Forces;

The members of the armed forces operate under a separate system of law and regulations than civilians. If they are accused of crimes, they are prosecuted under the Uniform Code of Military Justice, and they do not receive certain protections in the Bill of Rights. For instance, the Fifth Amendment specifically excludes members of the military from the right to a grand jury indictment. The Supreme Court has upheld other restrictions on constitutional rights when applied to the military. Commanders can prohibit the distribution of political literature by civilians on military bases, and soldiers do not have to be allowed to wear religious headgear such as yarmulkes.

To provide for calling forth the Militia to execute the Laws of the Union, suppress Insurrections and repel Invasions;

To provide for organizing, arming, and disciplining, the Militia, and for governing such Part of them as may be employed in the Service of the United States, reserving to the States respectively, the Appointment of the Officers, and the Authority of training the Militia according to the discipline prescribed by Congress;

Section 8 contains two clauses that give Congress authority over the militia, a part-time army that is organized by individual states. Congress has delegated to the president the power to call forth the militia. The militias remained under state control until 1916, when Congress passed a law making them part of the national government. Now the state militias are known as the National Guard, and they can be called into full-time duty in the U.S. armed forces.

To exercise exclusive Legislation in all Cases whatsoever, over such District (not exceeding ten Miles square) as may, by Cession of particular States, and the Acceptance of Congress, become the Seat of the Government of the United States, and to exercise like Authority over all Places purchased by the Consent of the Legislature of the State in which the Same shall be, for the Erection of Forts, Magazines, Arsenals, dock-Yards, and other needful Buildings;—And

The framers of the Constitution agreed that the nation's capital should be located in a district independent of state government and subject only to federal control. In part, this decision was based on the experience of the Continental Congress in 1783, which was meeting in Philadelphia. Unpaid soldiers from the Continental Army threatened to storm Congress, and the local and state officials refused to offer protection.

After ratification of the Constitution, Americans disagreed about where to locate the permanent capital. New York was the first capital, but only for a year, after which it moved to Philadelphia for ten years. In 1790, Alexander Hamilton and Thomas Jefferson struck a deal whereby the capital would move to the South, to a new District of Columbia on the Potomac River created by the cession of lands from Maryland and Virginia. In exchange for a southern capital, Jefferson agreed to Hamilton's plan for the federal government to assume the Revolutionary War debts of the states. Construction began on new homes for the president and Congress, and in 1800 the capital moved for the last time.

In 1846, Congress gave back the Virginia portion of the District, only to see it become hostile territory during the Civil War. Maryland, too, threatened to secede, which would have made the nation's capital totally surrounded by Confederate territory. After the war, Congress appointed a committee to run the District government, implementing laws passed by Congress. It wasn't until 1973 that Congress approved a limited version of democratic self-rule for the District's residents.

In 1961, the Twenty-third Amendment gave District residents the right to vote in presidential elections, but they remain the only taxpaying U.S. citizens who do not have voting representation in Congress. In 1978, Congress passed a constitutional amendment to give the District congressional representation as though it were a state, but the states failed to ratify it. Some citizens continue to advocate D.C. statehood, while others believe that the residential areas should be returned to Maryland.

Much of the District of Columbia was still a rural area when this photograph was taken in 1890.

To make all Laws which shall be necessary and proper for carrying into Execution the foregoing Powers, and all other Powers vested by this Constitution in the Government of the United States, or in any Department or Officer thereof.

Under the Articles of Confederation, the national government had only those powers specifically listed. The Necessary and Proper Clause is the source of many of the implied powers of the national government. It is also known as the Elastic Clause, because it gives Congress the flexibility to carry out its other enumerated powers. From the beginning, Americans argued over how to interpret the Constitution in general, and this phrase in particular. Alexander Hamilton believed in a broad or loose construction of the Constitution, which would strengthen the new national government. Thomas Jefferson argued for a strict construction of the Constitution, which would limit the powers of the national government. Hamilton believed that Congress had the power to create a national bank; Jefferson did not.

In *McCulloch v. Maryland* (1819), the Supreme Court ruled that the Necessary and Proper Clause gave Congress the power to establish a national bank. Chief Justice John Marshall, in his opinion for the Court, supported a loose construction of the Constitution. He wrote that the Constitution, unlike a legal code, contained the broad outlines of government power, not every small detail. Said Marshall: "We must never forget that it is *a constitution* we are expounding." More than a hundred years later, Justice Felix Frankfurter called this the "most important single sentence in American constitutional law." Decisions throughout the Marshall Court (1801–35) established a broad interpretation of the powers of the national government while the Constitution was still in its infancy.

This view of the Necessary and Proper Clause largely prevails today. Although the Supreme Court under Chief Justice William Rehnquist has begun to curtail the powers of Congress, particularly in relationship to the states, the Elastic Clause remains the source of much federal power. Most criminal laws, for example, are based on Congress's authority under the Necessary and Proper Clause.

> **"The legislative department is everywhere extending the sphere of its activity and drawing all power into its impetuous vortex."**
>
> —James Madison

SECTION. 9. The Migration or Importation of such Persons as any of the States now existing shall think proper to admit, shall not be prohibited by the Congress prior to the Year one thousand eight hundred and eight, but a Tax or duty may be imposed on such Importation, not exceeding ten dollars for each Person.

Section 9 lists the limitations on the power of Congress. It forbids Congress to ban the importation of slaves before 1808. Many of the framers of the Constitution opposed the Atlantic slave trade as brutal, even though they owned slaves themselves. Congress did ban the importation of slaves in 1808, but it did not restrict the domestic slave trade.

About a half million of the approximately eleven million African slaves who arrived in the New World came to British North America and the United States. Most African slaves went to the sugar plantations of Brazil and the West Indies, where they died quickly. Benjamin Franklin decried the infliction of human suffering for such trivial tastes:

> Can the sweetening our tea, &c. with sugar be a circumstance of such absolute necessity? Can the petty pleasure thence arising to the taste compensate for so much misery produced among our fellow creatures, and such a constant butchery of the human species by this pestilential detestable traffic in the bodies and souls of men?

Filled with Horrors of Every Kind *Olaudah Equiano*

Kidnapped from his home in West Africa at the age of eleven, and sold as a slave to neighboring tribes, Olaudah Equiano describes the terrors aboard a slave ship headed for the New World.

I now saw myself deprived of all chance of returning to my native country, or even the least glimpse of hope of gaining the shore, which I now considered as friendly, and I even wished for my former slavery in preference to my present situation, which was filled with horrors of every kind, still heightened by my ignorance of what I was to undergo. I was not long suffered to indulge my grief; I was soon put down under the decks, and there I received such a salutation in my nostrils as I had never experienced in my life: so that, with the loathsomeness of the stench and crying together, I became so sick and low that I was not able to eat, nor had I the least desire to taste anything. I now wished for the last friend, death, to relieve me....

In the crowded conditions on board slave ships, about ten to twenty percent of the Africans died.

The Privilege of the Writ of Habeas Corpus shall not be suspended, unless when in Cases of Rebellion or Invasion the public Safety may require it.

The writ of **habeas corpus** is historically one of the earliest civil liberties, sometimes known as the Great Writ. The phrase in Latin means "having the body." When a writ of habeas corpus is issued, the officer who is in charge of a prisoner is required by court order to show cause why the prisoner is being held. Habeas corpus is a protection against arbitrary arrest.

Section 9 does allow habeas corpus to be suspended during times of rebellion or invasion, but it is unclear whether Congress or the president has the power to suspend the writ. During the Civil War, Abraham Lincoln suspended the writ without congressional approval, although Congress did later endorse his action.

However, the Supreme Court ruled in *Ex Parte Milligan* (1866) that the power to suspend habeas corpus did not include using military courts if the civilian courts were open. The Court held that "the Constitution of the United States is a law for rulers and people, equally in war and in peace, and covers with the shield of its protection all classes of men, at all times, and under all circumstances."

Today, habeas corpus is most often used by state prisoners to challenge their convictions in federal court. The Supreme Court and Congress have acted to limit habeas corpus appeals in death penalty cases. The Court ruled in 1996 that such restrictions did not amount to an unconstitutional suspension of habeas corpus.

No Bill of Attainder or ex post facto Law shall be passed.
This provision in Section 9 prohibits Congress from passing a **bill of attainder,** which inflicts punishment on a person through an act of legislation, without a trial. It also bars **ex post facto laws,** which make an action criminal after it is committed or retroactively increase the penalty for a crime.

No Capitation, or other direct, Tax shall be laid, *unless in Proportion to the Census or enumeration herein before directed to be taken.*
Section 9 requires that capitations or head taxes, along with other **direct taxes,** must be allocated according to population—which made the tax formula very complicated. Direct taxes are primarily taxes on property. The framers themselves were not entirely clear what a direct tax was, and the Supreme Court varied on its definition. In 1895, the Court ruled that the income tax was a direct tax, but that decision was voided by the Sixteenth Amendment in 1913.

No Tax or Duty shall be laid on Articles exported from any State.

No Preference shall be given by any Regulation of Commerce or Revenue to the Ports of one State over those of another; nor shall Vessels bound to, or from, one State, be obliged to enter, clear, or pay Duties in another.
These two provisions in Section 9 limit Congress's power to interfere with the commerce of the states. Congress cannot tax a state's exports, which was very important to the agricultural South when the Constitution was drafted. Also, Congress cannot favor certain ports. Neither can the states make one another pay duties on their vessels, as though they were from foreign countries, which was a problem under the Articles of Confederation.

No Money shall be drawn from the Treasury, but in Consequence of Appropriations made by Law; and a regular Statement and Account of the Receipts and Expenditures of all public Money shall be published from time to time.
All public expenditures must be authorized by statute. This limitation actually preserves the power of the legislative branch over the executive branch, which cannot spend money without an appropriation from Congress. Section 9 was violated, for example, when Lt. Col. Oliver North,

habeas corpus

a court order directing that an officer who has custody of a prisoner show cause why the prisoner is being held

bill of attainder

a legislative act that punishes a person without a trial

ex post facto laws

those that criminalize actions after the fact

direct taxes

most commonly, taxes based on the value of land, as opposed to those based on privileges or uses an executive branch employee, sold weapons to Iran and used the proceeds to finance the contras in Nicaragua during the 1980s.

No Title of Nobility shall be granted by the United States: And no Person holding any Office of Profit or Trust under them, shall, without the Consent of the Congress, accept of any present, Emolument, Office, or Title, of any kind whatever, from any King, Prince, or foreign State.

Section 9 also prohibits the U.S. government from granting titles of nobility, thus ensuring the democratic nature of the republic. It also forbids the president and other U.S. officials from accepting gifts from foreign governments without permission from Congress. The president usually accepts such gifts in trust for the American people, although a certain amount of gifts may be kept as personal mementos.

SECTION. 10. No State shall enter into any Treaty, Alliance, or Confederation; grant Letters of Marque and Reprisal; coin Money; emit Bills of Credit; make any Thing but gold and silver Coin a Tender in Payment of Debts; pass any Bill of Attainder, ex post facto Law, or Law impairing the Obligation of Contracts, or grant any Title of Nobility.

Section 10 sets forth limits on the powers of the states. States are forbidden to carry out foreign affairs or alliances, as a sovereign government would do. Nor can they coin money or issue paper currency. Like Congress, they cannot pass bills of attainder or ex post facto laws, or grant titles of nobility.

Additionally, the states may not pass laws that void contracts after the fact. The framers of the Constitution wanted to protect property rights, and they were concerned that some states might pass laws favoring debtors. In an important ruling on the Contract Clause, *Fletcher v. Peck* (1810), the Supreme Court held that a state could not revoke public land grants that had been obtained fraudulently. In 1827, the Court did allow states to pass bankruptcy laws, as long as they applied prospectively. In more modern cases, the Court is still willing to occasionally strike down laws under the Contract Clause, but it does not enjoy the same prominence as in the early days of the republic.

No State shall, without the Consent of the Congress, lay any Imposts or Duties on Imports or Exports, except what may be absolutely necessary for executing it's inspection Laws: and the net Produce of all Duties and Imposts, laid by any State on Imports or Exports, shall be for the Use of the Treasury of the United States; and all such Laws shall be subject to the Revision and Controul of the Congress.

This provision prevents states from regulating exports and imports, except for inspection laws. It also gives Congress the ultimate authority over trade with other nations and other states.

No State shall, without the Consent of Congress, lay any Duty of Tonnage, keep Troops, or Ships of War in time of Peace, enter into any Agreement or Compact with another State, or with a foreign Power, or engage in War, unless actually invaded, or in such imminent Danger as will not admit of delay.

Once again, Section 10 lists some of the prerogatives of sovereign governments that can no longer be exercised by the states. These include keeping a standing army and making war, except in case of invasion. The states also may not issue tonnage duties, which tax a vessel when it is brought into port or kept there. With congressional approval, states may enter into interstate compacts, which today have become an important way for states to cooperate in policy making.

> **"Congress is functioning the way the Founding Fathers intended—not very well."**
> —Rep. Barber B. Conable, Jr.

This earliest photograph of the Capitol was taken in 1846, before a larger dome and expanded wings were built.

The Temple of the People

Thomas Jefferson referred to the U.S. Capitol as "the first temple dedicated to the sovereignty of the people." When the seat of the nation's government moved to Washington, D.C., in 1800, only one wing of the Capitol had been built. The building was still under construction when the British burned it in 1814 during the invasion of Washington. The original Capitol was completed in 1825, topped by a modest dome.

With the westward expansion of the nation, and the admission of new states, came the need for an enlarged Capitol to contain the growing number of senators and representatives. By 1859, both houses had moved into expanded wings, and work began on a much larger dome. Crowning the new dome would be a statue of the allegorical figure Freedom. However, the design of her headdress— modeled after the cap of a freed

slave in ancient Rome—was vetoed by Jefferson Davis, the future president of the Confederacy. The Civil War erupted before the new dome was completed, but President Abraham Lincoln insisted that work continue as "a sign we intend the Union shall go on." Finally, in 1863, the statue of Freedom took her perch, but much of the work on the Capitol had been done by slaves.

ARTICLE II

SECTION. 1. The executive Power shall be vested in a President of the United States of America. He shall hold his Office during the Term of four Years, and, together with the Vice President, chosen for the same Term, be elected, as follows:

Each State shall appoint, in such Manner as the Legislature thereof may direct, a Number of Electors, equal to the whole Number of Senators and Representatives to which the State may be entitled in the Congress: but no Senator or Representative, or Person holding an Office of Trust or Profit under the United States, shall be appointed an Elector.

The Electors shall meet in their respective States, and vote by Ballot for two Persons, of whom one at least shall not be an Inhabitant of the same State with themselves. And they shall make a List of all the Persons voted for, and of the Number of Votes for each; which List they shall sign and certify, and transmit sealed to the Seat of the Government of the United States, directed to the President of the Senate. The President of the Senate shall, in the Presence of the Senate and House of Representatives, open all the Certificates, and the Votes shall then be counted. The Person having the greatest Number of Votes shall be the President, if such Number be a Majority of the whole Number of Electors appointed; and if there be more than one who have such Majority, and have an equal Number of Votes, then the House of Representatives shall immediately chuse by Ballot one of them for President; and if no Person have a Majority, then from the five highest on the List the said House shall in like Manner chuse the President. But in chusing the President, the Votes shall be taken by States, the Representation from each State having one Vote; A quorum for this purpose shall consist of a Member or Members from two thirds of the States, and a Majority of all the States shall be necessary to a Choice. In every Case, after the Choice of the President, the Person having the greatest Number of Votes of the Electors shall be the Vice President. But if there should remain two or more who have equal Votes, the Senate shall chuse from them by Ballot the Vice President.

The Congress may determine the Time of chusing the Electors, and the Day on which they shall give their Votes; which Day shall be the same throughout the United States.

No Person except a natural born Citizen, or a Citizen of the United States, at the time of the Adoption of this Constitution, shall be eligible to the Office of President; neither shall any Person be eligible to that

Office who shall not have attained to the Age of thirty five Years, and been fourteen Years a Resident within the United States.

In Case of the Removal of the President from Office, or of his Death, Resignation, or Inability to discharge the Powers and Duties of the said Office, the Same shall devolve on the Vice President, and the Congress may by Law provide for the Case of Removal, Death, Resignation or Inability, both of the President and Vice President, declaring what Officer shall then act as President, and such Officer shall act accordingly, until the Disability be removed, or a President shall be elected.

The President shall, at stated Times, receive for his Services, a Compensation, which shall neither be increased nor diminished during the Period for which he shall have been elected, and he shall not receive within that Period any other Emolument from the United States, or any of them.

Before he enter on the Execution of his Office, he shall take the following Oath or Affirmation:—"I do solemnly swear (or affirm) that I will faithfully execute the Office of President of the United States, and will to the best of my Ability, preserve, protect and defend the Constitution of the United States."

SECTION. 2. The President shall be Commander in Chief of the Army and Navy of the United States, and of the Militia of the several States, when called into the actual Service of the United States; he may require the Opinion, in writing, of the principal Officer in each of the executive Departments, upon any Subject relating to the Duties of their respective Offices, and he shall have Power to grant Reprieves and Pardons for Offences against the United States, except in Cases of Impeachment.

He shall have Power, by and with the Advice and Consent of the Senate, to make Treaties, provided two thirds of the Senators present concur; and he shall nominate, and by and with the Advice and Consent of the Senate, shall appoint Ambassadors, other public Ministers and Consuls, Judges of the supreme Court, and all other Officers of the United States, whose Appointments are not herein otherwise provided for, and which shall be established by Law: but the Congress may by Law vest the Appointment of such inferior Officers, as they think proper, in the President alone, in the Courts of Law, or in the Heads of Departments.

The President shall have Power to fill up all Vacancies that may happen during the Recess of the Senate, by granting Commissions which shall expire at the End of their next Session.

SECTION. 3. He shall from time to time give to the Congress Information of the State of the Union, and recommend to their Consideration such Measures as he shall judge necessary and expedient; he may, on extraordinary Occasions, convene both Houses, or either of them, and in Case of Disagreement between them, with Respect to the Time of Adjournment, he may adjourn them to such Time as he shall think proper; he shall receive Ambassadors and other public Ministers; he shall take Care that the Laws be faithfully executed, and shall Commission all the Officers of the United States.

SECTION. 4. The President, Vice President and all civil Officers of the United States, shall be removed from Office on Impeachment for, and Conviction of, Treason, Bribery, or other high Crimes and Misdemeanors.

ARTICLE II: THE EXECUTIVE BRANCH

The duty of the executive branch is to enforce the laws. As a result of increasing federal regulation, the executive is by far the largest branch of government. It consists not only of the president, the vice president, and the cabinet officers, but also more than three million civilian and military employees. The primary responsibility of the president, and the entire executive branch, is best expressed in Section 3 of Article II: "He shall take care that the laws be faithfully executed."

Article II focuses almost exclusively on the president. It sets forth how the president is to be selected, through the electoral college. Article II also describes presidential powers—among them commanding the armed forces, negotiating treaties, and nominating justices of the Supreme Court. And, if the president has committed "high crimes and misdemeanors," Article II allows him or her to be impeached and removed from office.

SECTION. 1. The executive Power shall be vested in a President of the United States of America.

Alexander Hamilton wrote in *Federalist* 70 that "energy in the executive" was the definition of good government. But Americans have been highly ambivalent about the use of executive power. Having overthrown a king, they were not eager to re-create his likeness. Yet the lack of an efficient executive caused many to oppose the Articles of Confederation.

Under the Articles, there was no separate executive branch of government. The Congress appointed a president from its members– who acted as a presiding officer, not a chief executive. Technically, John Hanson of Maryland served as the first president of the United States in 1781. The Confederation Congress carried out the business of government through executive departments and appointed civil officers to administer them.

During the Constitutional Convention in 1787, the composition of the executive branch was one of the most contentious subjects. Some delegates advocated a plural executive, which Congress could increase or decrease at will. Others insisted that, despite the example of the British monarchy, a single executive would best prevent tyranny. After lengthy debate, the delegates finally agreed on one "president of the United States of America."

Still, Americans debated the proper role of the president. Roger Sherman, a delegate to the Constitutional Convention from Connecticut, argued that the executive was "nothing more than an institution for carrying the will of the Legislature into effect." According to this view, the president was little more than a clerk. Thomas Jefferson feared the opposite. He wrote to John Adams after the Constitutional Convention ended: "Their president seems a bad edition of a Polish king." Jefferson worried that the new president, like the Polish king, would be elected for life.

Some Americans had speculated that George Washington would become king after the Revolutionary War. But Washington steadfastly refused any overtures of unelected leadership. In 1783 he quelled a revolt among his unpaid officers, convincing them to remain loyal to their country. Later that year, after peace was secured, he voluntarily resigned his commission as commander in chief of the Continental Army–a rare act among victorious generals. Washington's refusal to grasp power helped pave the way for a stronger executive under the Constitution.

Article II does not define the exact nature of the president's powers. Unlike Article I, which limits the powers of Congress to those "herein granted," Article II vests the president with the entire "executive power." Presidents themselves have disagreed about whether Article II includes certain inherent powers not specifically listed. In general, the Supreme Court has upheld the principle that the president has some inherent powers that do not need to be specifically mentioned in the Constitution, especially regarding foreign policy.

The Supreme Court did rule in *United States v. Nixon* (1974) that the president's need for confidential communications, known as **executive privilege,** was constitutionally based. However, the Court also held that executive privilege in general does not outweigh the demand for evidence in a criminal trial, if national security issues are not involved. Unless President Richard Nixon claimed that he would be violating military or

executive privilege
doctrine that the president does not have to share certain information with Congress or the judiciary

diplomatic secrets, held the Court, he had to turn over tape recordings of his White House conversations for use in the Watergate prosecution.

The Supreme Court has also held that Article II gives the president "absolute immunity from damages liability" for his official acts. But the Court unanimously ruled in *Clinton v. Jones* (1997) that the president can be sued while in office for actions unrelated to his official conduct.

Some scholars believe that the president has acquired too much power in the modern era, overshadowing the role that the Constitution assigns to Congress. Historian Arthur Schlesinger, Jr., wrote that during the era of Watergate and the Vietnam War "the constitutional presidency…has become the imperial presidency." However, in the wake of President Nixon's resignation, former president Gerald Ford remarked in 1980: "We have not an imperial presidency, but an imperiled presidency."

Other presidents have experienced the limitations of the president's powers. In 1952, Harry Truman said of his successor, General Dwight Eisenhower, who had commanded the Allied forces in World War II: "He'll sit here, and he'll say 'Do this! Do that!' *And nothing will happen.* Poor Ike–it won't be a bit like the Army. He'll find it very frustrating." Truman summarized his own frustration this way: "I sit here all day trying to persuade people to do the things they ought to have sense enough to do without my persuading them…. That's all the powers of the President amount to."

> "The president is at liberty, both in law and conscience, to be as big a man as he can."
>
> —Woodrow Wilson

Speaking of Sanctuaries . . .

Critics accused Richard Nixon of hiding behind executive privilege.

He shall hold his Office during the Term of four Years,…

The framers of the Constitution considered several terms of office for the president. Some believed that the president should serve a single term, from seven to twenty years. Alexander Hamilton opposed such a method, arguing that the president would become a "monster" unaccountable to others and "continually tempted…to subvert the Government." In *Federalist* 72, Hamilton maintained that barring the president from being reelected "would be a diminution of the inducements to good behavior." Pennsylvania delegate Gouverneur Morris concurred, saying that such a provision encouraged the president to "make hay while the sun shines."

The original Constitution set no limit on the number of terms that a president could be reelected, but George Washington established the practice of serving only two terms. That precedent held until 1940, when

Franklin Delano Roosevelt ran for his third term. After Roosevelt died during his fourth term as president, Congress proposed the Twenty-second Amendment, which restricted a president to two full terms—or ten years if filling the unexpired term of another president. The amendment was ratified in 1951.

Energy in the Executive *Alexander Hamilton*

In Federalist *70, Alexander Hamilton maintains that a strong executive is essential to good government.*

There is an idea, which is not without its advocates, that a vigorous executive is inconsistent with the genius of republican government.... Energy in the executive is a leading character in the definition of good government. It is essential to the protection of the community against foreign attacks; it is not less essential to the steady administration of the laws; to the protection of property against those irregular and high-handed combinations which sometimes interrupt the ordinary course of justice; to the security of liberty against the enterprises and assaults of ambition, of faction, and of anarchy. Every man the least conversant in Roman history knows how often that republic was obliged to take refuge in the absolute power of a single man....

A feeble executive implies a feeble execution of the government. A feeble execution is but another phrase for a bad execution; and a government ill executed, whatever it may be in theory, must be, in practice, a bad government.

Alexander Hamilton was the first secretary of the treasury.

...and, together with the Vice President, chosen for the same Term, be elected, as follows:

The vice presidency "isn't worth a bucket of warm spit." Thus said John Nance Garner of Texas, vice president to Franklin Delano Roosevelt. Allegedly, Garner used a more colorful term and reporters sanitized the expression for print. The framers of the Constitution gave scant thought to the role of the vice president, who—as second-place finisher in the electoral college—was originally little more than the runner up in a beauty pageant. Roger Sherman of Connecticut argued that, beyond his role as president of the Senate, the vice president "would be without employment."

However, other concerns about the vice presidency arose during the debate over the Twelfth Amendment, which required separate balloting for the president and vice president. Opponents of the amendment argued that under such a system, in which the two candidates ran for office as part of one ticket, little care would be given to the qualifications of the vice president. "They will seek a man of moderate talents," said one senator during the debate over the amendment, "whose ambition is bounded by that office, and whose influence will aid them in electing the President."

Each State shall appoint, in such Manner as the Legislature thereof may direct, a Number of Electors, equal to the whole Number of Senators and Representatives to which the State may be entitled in the Congress: but no Senator or Representative, or Person holding an Office of Trust or Profit under the United States, shall be appointed an Elector.

> "In America, anyone can become president. That's one of the risks you take."
>
> —Adlai Stevenson

The method of selecting the president was resolved late in the Constitutional Convention. The delegates disagreed over whether the president should be chosen by the legislature or by popular election. George Mason, a delegate from Virginia and author of that state's bill of rights, argued that "it would be as unnatural to refer the choice of a proper character for chief magistrate to the people as it would to refer a trial of colors to a blind man."

The framers agreed on a compromise for choosing the president: the electoral college. Each state would appoint electors, equal to the number of its congressional delegation, who would then vote for president. The underlying assumption of the electoral college was that, in a nation as large as America, the citizenry would not be able to make an informed choice. Instead, elite electors would choose the president in a deliberative atmosphere, free from intrigue and coercion. One problem with this theory was that the electoral college did not meet as one body, but rather as delegations in their respective states. To ensure the independence of the president, no member of Congress or federal officeholder was allowed to serve as an elector. But the electoral college never operated as the framers intended, quickly becoming a mere rubber stamp–in most cases–for the popular vote.

"YOU THINK THIS ELECTION COULD BE DECIDED BY A FIVE-TO-FOUR VOTE?"

©2000 HERBLOCK

However, Article II clearly vests the power to select the president in the states, not the people. There is no constitutional right for individual citizens to vote for president. The framers of the Constitution chose not to establish a national standard for voter eligibility or participation in presidential elections. Individual states can choose their electors through a popular election–or not. Beginning with Pennsylvania in 1788, an increasing number of states gradually allowed citizens to vote for presidential electors. Now all states do.

But can a state reclaim its power to choose electors once it delegates that choice to a popular vote? The 2000 presidential election highlighted this question, when the Florida legislature considered selecting its own slate of electors—if the Florida Supreme Court's decision to order a hand recount of ballots overturned George Bush's initial victory in the machine recount. In the U.S. Supreme Court case that ensued, *Bush v. Gore* (2000), a majority of the Court stated that under Article II a legislature could take back the power to appoint electors at any time. The Court also ruled that the hand recount procedure treated voters unequally and violated the Fourteenth Amendment. The Supreme Court ordered the hand recount of Florida ballots to stop. For the first time in American history, a U.S. Supreme Court decision determined the winner of a presidential election.

The 2000 election, where George W. Bush lost the popular vote but won the presidency, once again raised challenges to the electoral college. Some scholars believe that the electoral college is an outdated relic of slavery and anti-democratic forces. They argue that a constitutional amendment to establish the direct election of the president by the people is more consistent with the democratic system of "one person, one vote." Under the current electoral college system, one electoral vote represents 232,000 people in South Dakota, whereas in New York it represents 550,000. But supporters of the electoral college contend that it is essential to preserving the role of the states in the federal system—similar to the states' equal representation in the Senate, regardless of population. Without the electoral college, they argue, candidates would pay attention only to national issues, and regional differences would disappear.

The Supreme Court issued its opinion in Bush v. Gore *faster than any other case in its history.*

One possible solution to the electoral college dilemma is to award extra electoral votes to the winner of the popular election. Proponents of this "national bonus" plan argue that it preserves a role for small states and thus is more likely than direct election to become a constitutional amendment. Such amendments must be approved by three-fourths of the states, and small states would probably block ratification of an amendment to abolish the electoral college entirely. Indeed, reform of the electoral college has been the most frequently proposed constitutional amendment, but it has never received the necessary two-thirds majority to pass Congress and then be submitted to the states for ratification.

Another proposed reform to the electoral college is to award electoral votes by congressional district, with two additional votes awarded to the statewide winner–as do Nebraska and Maine. All other states in the 2000 election used the "winner take all" system of awarding electoral votes, which can further distort the difference between the popular and the electoral vote. Still another alternative is to award electoral votes proportionally according to the popular vote–meaning that third parties would have more power to shape coalition governments, as in many European nations.

Because Article II awards electoral votes to states, millions of American citizens are not eligible to vote for president. Citizens of U.S. territories such as Puerto Rico and Guam cannot officially vote in presidential elections. The Twenty-third Amendment gave the District of Columbia three electoral votes, as though it were a state, but Congress–not the local government–determines how those electors are chosen.

A Starbucks-ification of Our Political Life Charles Fried

According to Harvard law professor Charles Fried, the electoral college ensures that national issues do not overshadow regional differences.

We could become a more centralized state, like France. A constitutional amendment to elect the president by the plurality of the popular vote would redirect the candidates' attention to national audiences. National issues would drive out any attention to local concerns or personalities. National television would play a larger role than it does now. And this would lead to a further Starbucks-ification of our political life, where every locality and region would slowly homogenize with every other into one undifferentiated mass.

The Electors shall meet in their respective States, and vote by Ballot for two Persons, of whom one at least shall not be an Inhabitant of the same State with themselves. And they shall make a List of all the Persons voted for, and of the Number of Votes for each; which List they shall sign and certify, and transmit sealed to the Seat of the Government of the United States, directed to the President of the Senate. The President of the Senate shall, in the Presence of the Senate and House of Representatives, open all the Certificates, and the Votes shall then be counted. The Person having the greatest Number of Votes shall be the President, if such Number be a Majority of the whole Number of Electors appointed; and if there be more than one who have such Majority, and have an equal Number of Votes, then the House of Representatives shall immediately chuse by Ballot one of them for President; and if no Person have a Majority, then from the five highest on the List the said House shall in like Manner chuse the President. But in

chusing the President, the Votes shall be taken by States, the Representation from each State having one Vote; A quorum for this purpose shall consist of a Member or Members from two thirds of the States, and a Majority of all the States shall be necessary to a Choice. In every Case, after the Choice of the President, the Person having the greatest Number of Votes of the Electors shall be the Vice President. But if there should remain two or more who have equal Votes, the Senate shall chuse from them by Ballot the Vice President.
The actual procedure by which the electors cast their votes for president—indicated in italics above—was changed by the Twelfth Amendment in 1804. The framers of the Constitution, acting before the rise of political parties, saw no problem with having the runner-up in the presidential election serve as vice president. But in the election of 1796, Thomas Jefferson, a Democratic-Republican, became the vice president of his political rival John Adams, a Federalist. In the election of 1800, both political parties offered a slate of two candidates, but because the electoral vote did not distinguish between president and vice president, the result was a tie. Thomas Jefferson and his running mate, Aaron Burr, received the same number of electoral votes, requiring the House of Representatives to choose the president. Surprisingly, Burr refused to remove himself from consideration, and after thirty-six ballots the House elected Jefferson—only two weeks before his inauguration. As a result, the Twelfth Amendment provided for separate balloting procedures for the president and vice president. In the event that a candidate did not achieve a majority of the electoral votes, the House of Representatives would select the president and the Senate would select the vice president.

Many of the delegates to the Constitutional Convention in 1787 believed that, other than George Washington, a presidential candidate would rarely receive a majority of electoral votes. They thought of the electoral college as a nominating committee, and debated intensely whether the House of Representatives or the Senate should select the president when no majority prevailed in the electoral college. The framers chose the House, but then assigned each state's delegation an equal vote when selecting the president.

Political parties soon overtook the nominating function for presidential candidates, and the electoral college most often determined the winner of the election. In fact, the House of Representatives chose the president only twice: in 1800 and 1824. The framers' vision of an independent body of electors quickly vanished. Political parties offered their own slate of electors in the popular election, pledged to vote for the party's candidate. Rarely, a "faithless elector" did not vote as the party instructed, and several states passed laws binding an elector to the result of the popular vote. The constitutionality of such laws remains unclear, but the Supreme Court has ruled that political parties may require loyalty pledges from potential

"No man who ever held the office of President would congratulate a friend on obtaining it."
—John Adams, upon election of his son

electors. Today, most states do not even list the names of the electors on their presidential ballots.

Under the electoral college system, the winner of the popular vote for president has been defeated at least four–and possibly five–times: 1824, 1876, 1888, 1960, and 2000. In 1824, Andrew Jackson received the plurality of popular votes but not a majority of the electoral college. The House of Representatives then selected as president John Quincy Adams, who placed second in the popular vote. However, not all the candidates appeared on the ballots in all the states, and in several states there was no popular vote because the legislature chose the electors.

The Constitution does not specify what should happen if electoral votes are challenged. In 1876, four states submitted two sets of electoral votes, and Congress established an electoral commission to determine which votes should be counted. Democrat Samuel Tilden had defeated Republican Rutherford B. Hayes in the popular vote and was only one electoral vote shy of victory, but the electoral commission awarded all four contested states to Hayes. Congress placated southern Democrats by promising to end Reconstruction. As a result of the 1876 election, Congress enacted procedures to review contested electoral votes.

In 1888, President Grover Cleveland won the popular vote, but was defeated in the electoral college by Benjamin Harrison. Cleveland was elected again in 1892, becoming the only president to serve nonsequential terms. In 1960, John F. Kennedy won the electoral college by a wide margin, but depending on how Alabama's electors are credited, may well have lost the popular vote. Alabama elected a slate of eleven unpledged Democratic electors in 1960, only five of whom voted for Kennedy. If those electors are prorated, then Richard Nixon won the popular vote by one-tenth of one percent. In the 2000 presidential election, Al Gore defeated George Bush in the popular vote by about five hundred thousand votes–or half of one percent of the total votes cast–but lost the electoral college.

Despite a newspaper's erroneous projection of his defeat, President Harry Truman won reelection in 1948 by a comfortable margin in both the popular vote and the electoral college.

The Congress may determine the Time of chusing the Electors, and the Day on which they shall give their Votes; which Day shall be the same throughout the United States.

By federal statute, the first Tuesday after the first Monday in November is election day. Every four years, presidential electors are chosen on that day. Federal law also requires that the electors cast their own votes for presidential candidates on the first Monday after the second Wednesday in December. Congress has set January 6 as the date that the electoral votes

Where's the Party?

In his farewell address of 1796, George Washington warned the nation "against the baneful effects of the spirit of party." Little did he know that political parties, although nowhere mentioned in the Constitution, would soon dominate the selection of the president. Nor did the framers of the Constitution expect that candidates would actively campaign for the presidency. During the first century of presidential elections, the ruling ethos was that "the office should seek the man, rather than the man seek the office." But with the increased role of political parties and professional campaigns came increased costs. In the words of Mark Hanna, a Republican who managed William McKinley's presidential campaign: "There are two things important in politics. The first is money, and I can't remember what the second one is." In the 2000 election, presidential candidates received more than $500 million in public and private funds— almost a 25 percent increase from 1996.

Political parties now serve the nominating function that the framers of the Constitution expected to be fulfilled by the electoral college.

are counted before a joint session of Congress.

After the controversial election of 1876, Congress established procedures for challenging electoral votes. Under this system, states that had certified electors by December 12 would have a "safe harbor" against challenge, unless both houses of Congress agreed to the challenge. Based on this deadline, the Supreme Court in *Bush v. Gore* (2000) refused to mandate a hand recount of the Florida presidential ballots. However, many other states did not certify their electors by that date in the 2000 election.

For a variety of reasons, about 2.5 million ballots (2 percent of the votes cast) were not counted in the 2000 presidential election. As a result, many states and Congress considered measures to update voting technology. Kathleen Sullivan of Stanford Law School has proposed a constitutional amendment that would give Congress the power to set national standards for presidential elections and ballots.

No Person except a natural born Citizen, or a Citizen of the United States, at the time of the Adoption of this Constitution, shall be eligible to the Office of President; neither shall any Person be eligible to that Office who shall not have attained to the Age of thirty five Years, and been fourteen Years a Resident within the United States. This clause of Article II states the minimum qualifications for the president. The president must be a natural-born, not naturalized, U.S. citizen. Thus, even though Congress has made the secretary of state part of the line of succession to become president after the vice president, Henry Kissinger and Madeleine Albright would not have been eligible. There is a question whether a child born abroad of U.S. citizens, who is regarded as a natural-born citizen under federal law, would also be qualified to be president under the Constitution. The president must be at least thirty-five years old and have lived in the United States for fourteen years. However, as in the case of Herbert Hoover, those fourteen years do not have to be consecutive or immediately precede the presidential election.

Your Vote Does Not Count *Rep. John Lewis*

A veteran of the civil rights movement, Rep. John Lewis (D-Ga.) opposed any attempt to prevent votes from being counted during the 2000 election.

The history of the vote in America is a history of conflict, of struggling for the principle of one person, one vote. Friends of mine died for this principle. I was beaten and jailed because I stood up for it. For millions [of African Americans] like me, the struggle for the right to vote is not mere history; it is experience....

Our Constitution does not reserve this right to Americans who can decipher a confusing ballot. A great nation should not deny the right because a tiny piece of paper stubbornly clings to a ballot. We dishonor the sacrifice of those who fought for this right when we spend countless hours trying to keep a ballot, a vote, a voice, from being heard.

Immediately after the [2000] elections, analysts told us that this experience would teach us that every vote counts. I fear . . . the opposite.

If you were confused by a butterfly ballot, your vote does not count. If the military neglected to postmark your absentee ballot, your vote does not count. If your ballot has a dimpled, hanging, or pregnant chad, your vote does not count. Unless there are drastic changes in the way votes are being tallied, these are the lessons we will learn in Florida.

In Case of the Removal of the President from Office, or of his Death, Resignation, or Inability to discharge the Powers and Duties of the said Office, the Same shall devolve on the Vice President, and the Congress may by Law provide for the Case of Removal, Death, Resignation or Inability, both of the President and Vice President, declaring what Officer shall then

Who Are We Really Voting For? *Arthur Miller*

In a 2001 address sponsored by the National Endowment for the Humanities, playwright Arthur Miller observes that acting has become essential to political leadership.

Political leaders everywhere have come to understand that to govern they must learn how to act…. [W]ho are we really voting for? The self-possessed character who projects dignity, exemplary morals, and enough forthright courage to lead us through war or depression, or the person who is simply good at creating a counterfeit with the help of professional coaching, executive tailoring, and that whole armory of pretense that the groomed president can now employ? Are we allowed anymore to know what is going on not merely in the candidate's facial expression and his choice of suit but also in his head? Unfortunately…this is something we are not told until the auditioning ends and he is securely in office…. As with most actors, any resemblance between the man and the role is purely accidental.

act as President, and such Officer shall act accordingly, until the Disability be removed, or a President shall be elected.

This part of Article II was changed by the Twenty-fifth Amendment in 1967. Originally, it was unclear whether the vice president actually became president when a predecessor died, or merely "acted" as president until another president was elected. John Tyler ended the debate by assuming the title of president when William Henry Harrison became the first president to die in office in 1841. The Twenty-fifth Amendment clearly states that the vice president becomes president upon the death of his predecessor. The amendment also sets forth the procedures under which a presidential disability is determined.

The White House was draped in black bunting to mourn the assassination of President James Garfield in 1881. Three other presidents were killed in office: Abraham Lincoln in 1865; William McKinley in 1901; and John F. Kennedy in 1963.

If both the president and the vice president are unable to fill the office, Congress can specify the order of succession among the remaining federal officers. Next in line by federal statute are the Speaker of the House of Representatives, the president pro tempore of the Senate, and the secretary of state, followed by the other cabinet officers in chronological order by the date their departments were created. This person is then the acting president until another one is elected. He or she must meet the same qualifications as the president, and must resign any other federal office. At least one cabinet secretary is always absent from the State of the Union address, to ensure a successor to the presidency in the event of a terrorist attack on the joint session of Congress.

The President shall, at stated Times, receive for his Services, a Compensation, which shall neither be increased nor diminished during the Period for which he shall have been elected, and he shall not receive within that Period any other Emolument from the United States, or any of them.

The president is guaranteed a fixed salary while in office, in order to maintain the independence of the executive branch from Congress—either through threats or bribes. However, the president must not receive additional "perks" from the federal government or an individual state, beyond legitimate expenses. George Washington refused to accept a salary, although he was awarded $25,000 to cover his expenses. Since 1789, the president's salary has been raised five times. In 2001, the president's paycheck increased from $200,000 to $400,000.

Before he enter on the Execution of his Office, he shall take the following Oath or Affirmation:—"I do solemnly swear (or affirm) that I will faithfully execute the Office of President of the United States, and will to the best of my Ability, preserve, protect and defend the Constitution of the United States."

The president has a sworn duty to defend the U.S. Constitution. According to some presidents, such as Andrew Jackson, this oath of office gives the president an independent authority to evaluate the constitutionality of laws. Therefore, even though the Supreme Court had upheld a national bank as constitutional, Jackson vetoed a law chartering such a bank.

George Washington added the words "so help me God" and the practice of swearing the oath upon a Bible. The chief justice of the United States traditionally administers the president's oath of office, at least since the inauguration of John Adams. Depending on the circumstances, the chief justice is not always available. Lyndon Johnson took the oath of office from a justice of the peace on *Air Force One,* with the body of slain President John F. Kennedy aboard.

President George Washington began the tradition of an inauguration ceremony in 1789. But he did not look forward to it. A few weeks before his inauguration, Washington wrote: "My movements to the chair of Government will be accompanied with feelings not unlike those of a

John F. Kennedy plays with his children in the Oval Office, the president's ceremonial office. It is part of the West Wing, an extension of the White House built in 1902.

culprit who is going to the place of his execution, so unwilling am I, in the evening of a life nearly consumed in public cares to quit a peaceful abode for an ocean of difficulties." Presidents since then have been more enthusiastic, and their inaugural addresses have become part of America's literary heritage.

Thomas Jefferson sought to heal the division of partisan politics, at least in his inauguration speech in 1801. "We are all Republicans, we are all Federalists," he said, but his defeated opponent John Adams would not stay for the ceremony. Abraham Lincoln's second inaugural address at the close of the Civil War sought to "bind up the nation's wounds" and offer reconciliation "with malice toward none, with charity for all." During the despair of the Great Depression, Franklin Roosevelt promised the country that "the only thing we have to fear is fear itself." And at the dawn of the space age, John F. Kennedy admonished his fellow Americans: "Ask not what your country can do for you—ask what you can do for your country."

SECTION. 2. The President shall be Commander in Chief of the Army and Navy of the United States, and of the Militia of the several States, when called into the actual Service of the United States;...

Section 2 of Article II lists the powers of the president. First among these is the president's role as commander-in-chief of the military—both the U.S. armed forces and the state militias, known today as the National Guard. This provision is designed to ensure civilian control of the military. Although several former generals have served as president, they had previously resigned their military commissions.

George Washington, shown here reviewing troops during the Whiskey Rebellion in 1794, was the only president actually to lead troops into combat while in office. Washington later pardoned the leaders of the rebellion.

The president is commander-in-chief of the armed forces, but Congress has the sole power to declare war and to raise and support armies. According to the framers, an important advantage of this system was that it would delay a decision to go to war. However, since World War II, presidents have repeatedly sent American troops into combat without a declaration of war by Congress. Some scholars argue that, in an era of nuclear weapons, the president does not have enough time to consult Congress before deploying troops to protect national security. But in 1973, after prolonged American involvement in Korea and Vietnam without declarations of war, Congress passed the War Powers Resolution—over a veto by President Richard Nixon. Among other provisions, this law limited the power of the president to deploy combat troops for more than sixty days without the approval of Congress.

Many presidents have regarded the War Powers Resolution as unconstitutional. The courts have ruled that the law involves a "political question" between the executive and legislative branches and refused to intervene. In practice, the law has not curtailed short-term use of combat troops by the president. At the last minute, Congress did approve the deployment of combat forces in the 1991 Persian Gulf War, but President George H. W. Bush did not believe such authorization was necessary. In 2001, Congress also approved the use of military force, under the terms of the War Powers Act, in Afghanistan against the terrorist network responsible for attacks against New York and Washington.

The president's emergency powers as commander-in-chief have not been limited just to the use of armed forces. During the Civil War, Abraham Lincoln argued that he was authorized to suspend the writ of habeas corpus, a constitutional right that protects citizens from arbitrary arrest. Asked Lincoln in a special session of Congress on July 4, 1861: "Are all the laws, but one, to go unexecuted, and the government itself go to pieces, lest that one be violated?" Congress then passed a law allowing the suspension of habeas corpus during the Civil War, as provided in Article I.

Woodrow Wilson and Franklin Roosevelt both claimed that emergency powers gave them the ability to regulate the economy during wartime. Franklin Roosevelt also issued an executive order during World War II that allowed the internment in concentration camps of 120,000 Japanese Americans, two-thirds of whom were natural-born U.S. citizens. The Supreme Court upheld this action as a valid use of the president's wartime powers in *Korematsu v. United States* (1944). Critics of the decision believe that the president's powers when the nation is at war should not include measures that would be unconstitutional during peace. But as Francis

Without Congressional Participation *John Hart Ely*

Constitutional scholar John Hart Ely argues that both Congress and the courts have abdicated their responsibility to preserve the constitutional role of Congress in warmaking.

Contrary to the words and unmistakable purpose of the Constitution, contrary as well to reasonably consistent practice

from the dawn of the republic to the mid-twentieth century, . . . decisions [to go to war] have been made throughout the Cold War period by the executive, without significant congressional participation (or judicial willingness to insist on such participation). It is common to style this shift a usurpation, but that

oversimplifies to the point of misstatement. It's true our Cold War presidents generally wanted it that way, but Congress (and the courts) ceded the ground without a fight. In fact, . . . the legislative surrender was a self-interested one: Accountability is pretty frightening stuff.

Biddle, FDR's attorney general who opposed internment, concluded: "The Constitution has not greatly bothered any wartime president."

...he may require the Opinion, in writing, of the principal Officer in each of the executive Departments, upon any Subject relating to the Duties of their respective Offices,...

The heads of the executive departments—such as State, Treasury, and Agriculture—are commonly referred to as the president's **cabinet.** This group of advisors serves at the pleasure of the president, and its influence varies according to each administration. George Washington relied heavily on his cabinet members; Andrew Jackson virtually ignored them. Instead, Jackson relied on informal advisors he referred to as his Kitchen Cabinet.

The executive branch is by far the largest branch of the federal government. Besides the secretaries of the fourteen executive departments, the executive branch includes 1.8 million civilian employees (excluding the U.S. Postal Service, an independent agency) and 1.4 million active-duty members of the armed forces. The employees of the executive branch are known collectively as the **bureaucracy.**

... and he shall have Power to grant Reprieves and Pardons for Offences against the United States, except in Cases of Impeachment.

The president has the power to pardon all federal criminal offenses. The pardon may be issued after the crime has been committed, but before any formal charges have been filed. Thus, President Gerald R. Ford pardoned Richard Nixon on September 8, 1974–barely one month after Nixon resigned the presidency in the face of certain impeachment–for any crimes he might have committed while in office. President Ford believed that such a pardon, although extremely controversial, would spare the nation a prolonged ordeal in the criminal prosecution of Nixon. President Bill Clinton also faced criticism about pardons made as he was leaving office in 2001. A president's discretion over pardons is unreviewable by Congress or the courts, but it is illegal to give or receive a bribe in exchange for favorable treatment by government officials.

He shall have Power, by and with the Advice and Consent of the Senate, to make Treaties, provided two thirds of the Senators present concur;...

The strains of the Vietnam War show on President Lyndon Johnson, as he listens to a tape recording from the front lines by his son-in-law, Capt. Chuck Robb.

cabinet
the president's selected advisors, usually consisting of the heads of the executive departments

bureaucracy
a large and complex administrative organization

An early draft of the Constitution would have given the power to make treaties to the Senate alone, but that was changed with the creation of the presidency. It is the sole responsibility of the president to negotiate treaties with foreign nations, but such treaties do not become binding on the United States without the **advice and consent** of the Senate. They must be ratified by two-thirds of the senators present (assuming a quorum). At the end of World War I, President Woodrow Wilson persuaded other nations to agree to his Fourteen Points—a comprehensive plan for peace that included the creation of a League of Nations. The Senate failed to approve the treaty, however, and many historians believe this action may have contributed to World War II.

To avoid conflict with the Senate, presidents have increasingly relied upon executive agreements to achieve foreign policy goals. These agreements with other nations do not require the approval of the Senate, but their distinction from treaties has not been clearly established. Some examples of executive agreements include the 1945 Yalta agreement to divide Germany among the Allied nations, and the 1980 agreement with Iran to end the hostage crisis.

President George Bush meets with his advisors in the Cabinet Room. George Washington's cabinet got its name from the small room it met in during a crisis with the French government.

Another unclear area is the extent to which a president can reinterpret or refuse to enforce a treaty. For example, in 1979, President Jimmy Carter terminated a mutual defense treaty with Taiwan in order to recognize the People's Republic of China. Senator Barry Goldwater contested that decision in federal court, but the Supreme Court refused to rule on the merits of the issue.

…and he shall nominate, and by and with the Advice and Consent of the Senate, shall appoint Ambassadors, other public Ministers and Consuls, Judges of the supreme Court, and all other Officers of the

United States, whose Appointments are not herein otherwise provided for, and which shall be established by Law: but the Congress may by Law vest the Appointment of such inferior Officers, as they think proper, in the President alone, in the Courts of Law, or in the Heads of Departments.

The president's power to make appointments is subject to the advice and consent of the Senate. Experts disagree as to the extent of the Senate's power to reject presidential appointments. Some say that the president's discretion to choose members of the cabinet and other high-ranking executive branch officials should be unfettered. But because judges represent an independent branch of government and have life tenure, certain commentators argue that the Senate has both the prerogative and the duty to inquire into the political leanings of judicial nominees.

President Ronald Reagan's unsuccessful nomination of Judge Robert Bork to the U.S. Supreme Court in 1987 sparked enormous controversy about the proper role of the Senate in Supreme Court appointments. Bork's opponents argued that his judicial philosophy was extremist and would reverse abortion rights for women and affirmative action for minorities. To these senators, the U.S. Constitution required their independent assessment of Bork's fitness to serve on the nation's highest court. They pointed out that the Senate had previously rejected Supreme Court nominees because of political differences, beginning with George Washington's nomination of John Rutledge to be chief justice in 1795. Judge Bork's supporters believed he had been unfairly pilloried because of

advice and consent

the constitutional power of the Senate to approve treaties and presidential appointments

---

A Senate Taboo *Senator Charles E. Schumer*

Throughout American history, argues Senator Charles E. Schumer (D-N.Y.), the Senate has considered the political values of judicial nominees.

For one reason or another, examining the ideologies of judicial nominees has become something of a Senate taboo. In part out of a fear of being labeled partisan, senators have driven legitimate consideration and discussion of ideology underground. The not-so-dirty little secret of the Senate is that

we do consider ideology, but privately....

During our nation's first century, the Senate rejected one out of every four Supreme Court nominees. But since Judge Robert Bork's nomination was defeated in 1987 largely because of his positions on abortion, civil rights, and civil liberties, ideology has played more of a behind-the-scenes role in nomination hearings. It would be best for the Senate, the president's nominees, and the country if we return to a

more open and rational debate about ideology when we consider nominees....

If the president uses ideology in deciding whom to nominate to the bench, the Senate, as part of its responsibility to advise and consent, should do the same in deciding whom to confirm. Pretending that ideology doesn't matter—or, even worse, doesn't exist—is exactly the opposite of what the Senate should do.

his conservative political philosophy, despite his prestigious legal accomplishments. They coined the term *Borked* to describe the politicization of the judicial appointment process. These senators argued that nominees should only be rejected if they were clearly unqualified for the job, not because certain senators opposed them politically.

Judges are appointed for life, but the president can remove members of the executive branch from office. A dispute with Congress over this power of removal led to the impeachment of President Andrew Johnson in 1868. In general, the Supreme Court has ruled that in order to "take care that the laws be faithfully executed," as required by Section 3 of Article II, the president must have the power to fire subordinates.

George Washington: First in the Hearts of His Countrymen

It is difficult to overestimate the importance of George Washington (1732–1799) in the formation of the United States, as a nation and a government. Washington's victory as commander-in-chief of the Continental Army during the Revolutionary War wrested America's independence from Great Britain. By presiding over the Constitutional Convention in 1787, he helped create a more stable form of governance, and he served as a model for the newly created executive branch. During his administration, Washington sought to keep the various factions of American politics working together as a cohesive whole. When Washington died in 1799, Revolutionary War hero Henry "Light-Horse Harry" Lee wrote a tribute that was delivered by future chief justice John Marshall on the floor of the House of Representatives: "First in war, first in peace, first in the hearts of his countrymen."

The President shall have Power to fill up all Vacancies that may happen during the Recess of the Senate, by granting Commissions which shall expire at the End of their next Session.

The president can grant a recess appointment if the Senate is not in session—excluding holidays and temporary adjournments. Sometimes the president uses this power when deadlocked with the Senate over a controversial nominee. Recess appointments are temporary and expire at the end of the Senate's next session. President George Washington gave a recess appointment to John Rutledge to be chief justice of the United States in 1795. However, Rutledge was rejected by the Senate because of his criticism of the Jay Treaty, despite being a former justice on the Supreme Court and a Federalist ally of Washington.

SECTION. 3. He shall from time to time give to the Congress Information of the State of the Union, and recommend to their Consideration such Measures as he shall judge necessary and expedient; he may, on extraordinary Occasions, convene both Houses, or either of them, and in Case of Disagreement between them, with Respect to the Time of Adjournment, he may adjourn them to such Time as he shall think proper;…

By tradition, the president delivers the State of the Union address before a joint session of Congress, after it convenes each January. Thomas Jefferson sent written reports to Congress, but since Woodrow Wilson, presidents have appeared in person. The State of the Union often includes the president's legislative program for the coming year.

> "Congressional supremacy is…a constitutional fact: there is little a president can do if a determined congressional majority opposes it."
>
> —George Will

The president has no authority to introduce legislation on Capitol Hill. However, as the leader of his or her political party, the president has great influence over the Congress. Consequently, the president is often regarded as the initiator of national legislative agendas, even though he must rely on individual members of Congress to enact such a program. According to presidential scholar Richard Neustadt: "The President and Congress are at once so independent and so intertwined that neither can be said to govern save as both do." Another way the president influences the legislative process is by convening a special session of Congress. Thus far, the president has never adjourned a session of Congress.

…he shall receive Ambassadors and other public Ministers;…

The president is the nation's chief diplomat and the sole representative of the country when dealing with foreign powers. Other nations are not allowed to lobby Congress directly, for example. The president's power to receive ambassadors is also the power to recognize foreign governments.

Members of the first Japanese delegation to the United States were photographed by Mathew Brady in 1860.

...he shall take Care that the Laws be faithfully executed,...

The Take Care Clause of Article II is the source of much of the president's power. It expresses the fundamental mission of the executive branch: to enforce the law. The Supreme Court has ruled that this clause justifies the president to take sweeping action to carry out the law: "If the emergency arises, the army of the nation, and all its militia, are at the service of the nation, to compel obedience to its laws."

Five presidents attended the funeral of Richard Nixon in 1994. Before Nixon died, five former presidents were alive at the same time—which had not happened previously in American history since the Civil War.

The president can also exercise a quasi-legislative function by issuing executive orders. These regulations have the force of law—at least until Congress enacts conflicting legislation, the courts overrule them, or a later president rescinds them. In 1948, President Harry Truman used an executive order to ban segregation in the armed forces. Since 1789, more than 15,000 executive orders have been issued.

The president has a certain amount of discretion in terms of how vigorously he or she will enforce particular laws. Depending on their political views, administrations have varied in their enforcement of civil rights laws or abortion regulations, for example. During the 1970s, President Richard Nixon impounded—or refused to spend—funds for programs of which he disapproved. Critics charged that this action exceeded the president's power, because the funds had been properly appropriated by Congress. The Supreme Court has not ruled on the constitutionality of impoundment, but Congress has passed laws restricting its use.

...and shall Commission all the Officers of the United States.

Even when a nominee has been approved by the Senate, the president can still refuse to complete the process by giving that person a commission. Without a commission, the appointee cannot assume office. Several modern attorneys general have interpreted this phrase of Article II to acknowledge the right of the president not to deliver commissions, even once he or she has signed them, although the Supreme Court decided differently in *Marbury v. Madison* (1803).

SECTION. 4. The President, Vice President and all civil Officers of the United States, shall be removed from Office on Impeachment for, and Conviction of, Treason, Bribery, or other high Crimes and Misdemeanors.

Impeachment is the process by which a civil officer of the United States is charged with wrongdoing. Under the Constitution, the House of Representatives has the sole power of impeachment, and the Senate has the responsibility to try the charges and remove guilty parties from office.

Section 4 of Article II establishes who may be impeached and upon what grounds. The delegates at the Constitutional Convention debated whether the president should be impeachable. Benjamin Franklin reminded them that, in societies where the executive could not be impeached, he was often assassinated. Section 4 applies to executive branch officials and federal judges, but not to members of Congress. In a separate procedure, Article I, Section 5 allows each house of Congress to expel a member upon a two-thirds vote. The Supreme Court has ruled that the impeachment process is not subject to judicial review and therefore cannot be appealed to the courts.

Impeachment is not a criminal proceeding, and its punishment is limited only to removal from office. However, experts disagree whether an officeholder must be guilty of a criminal offense in order to be impeached. Section 4 refers to "treason, bribery, or other high crimes and

Mrs. President

The President's spouse is not mentioned in the Constitution, but she has often been crucial to her husband's popularity—and at times played an important role in policy making. Abigail Adams was so influential with her husband, John, that her enemies referred to her as "Mrs. President." Eleanor Roosevelt pioneered the role of the activist first lady—mobilizing public support through press conferences, radio broadcasts, and a syndicated newspaper column. Hillary Rodham Clinton became the first first lady to be elected to office representing New York in the U.S. Senate.

Could Mrs. President ever become Madam President instead? Eleanor Roosevelt offered this answer in 1940: "At present the answer is emphatically 'No.' It will be a long time before a woman will have any chance of nomination or election." In 1984, Geraldine Ferraro became the first woman nominated to a major party ticket as vice president. *Newsweek* columnist Eleanor Clift predicts that, as evidenced by the President 2000 Barbie doll, a woman president is not far off: "Fantasy will nudge politics to catch up with real life."

Abigail Adams, wife of the second president, was known for her strong viewpoints and political influence with her husband.

misdemeanors." Some argue that the phrase "high crimes and misdemeanors" implies serious crimes, like treason and bribery, that threaten the security of the nation. Others believe it can include malfeasance in office that might not otherwise be a crime. The danger is that if Americans do not agree on the standard for impeachment, then judges or presidents might be removed from office merely because they are politically unpopular.

Indeed, the first controversial impeachment, that of Supreme Court Justice Samuel Chase in 1804, became a battleground between Federalists and Democratic-Republicans–the nation's earliest political parties. As a trial judge, Chase made inflammatory political speeches to juries and even actively campaigned for President John Adams while serving on the Supreme Court. Thomas Jefferson, who defeated Adams in the 1800 election, expressed a personal interest in the impeachment of Chase. Chase's defenders argued that his actions, while intemperate, were not illegal and therefore not impeachable. His acquittal by the Senate in 1805 was widely regarded as preserving the independence of the judicial branch.

Of the sixteen federal officials impeached as of 2001, most were judges. Thus far, only federal judges have been convicted and removed from office. Two presidents were impeached, and one president resigned when faced with certain impeachment. In 1868 Andrew Johnson, a southern Democrat, became the first president to be impeached–as part of a conflict with the Radical Republicans over Reconstruction. Johnson fired his secretary of war, Edwin Stanton, a political ally of the Radical Republicans, despite the recently passed Tenure of Office Act. That law forbade the president from removing, without the Senate's consent, a federal official whose appointment had been confirmed by the Senate. Johnson regarded the act as unconstitutional. Some members of the Senate apparently agreed, and he was acquitted by one vote.

President Richard Nixon avoided impeachment in 1974 by resigning, the first president ever to do so. In July, the House Judiciary Committee approved articles of impeachment against Nixon that charged him, among other offenses, with obstruction of justice by covering up White House involvement in a burglary at the Democratic National Committee headquarters. As articulated by Republican senator Howard Baker, the issue was: "What did the president know and when did he know it?" The Supreme Court's unanimous ruling in *United States v. Nixon* forced the president to release tape recordings of White House conversations considered to be a "smoking gun" of his guilt, and he resigned on August 9.

The House of Representatives impeached President Bill Clinton on December 19, 1998. It accused Clinton of perjury in his grand jury testimony about a sexual relationship with Monica Lewinsky, a White

House intern, and of obstructing justice by concealing evidence of the affair. Clinton's grand jury testimony was related to a sexual harassment lawsuit by Paula Jones, who had worked for Clinton when he was governor of Arkansas. In 1997, the Supreme Court unanimously ruled that Clinton could not delay the Jones lawsuit until after he left the presidency.

Under federal law, former judge Kenneth Starr had been appointed as an independent counsel to investigate Clinton's involvement in an Arkansas real estate development known as Whitewater. Starr also investigated the Lewinsky affair. Starr convened a federal grand jury to gather evidence of whether the president had perjured himself about Lewinsky in his deposition in the Jones lawsuit. The House's impeachment charges were based on President Clinton's testimony before Starr's grand jury, not his deposition in the underlying Jones case.

Although Clinton admitted to the nation that he had been misleading about his relationship with Lewinsky, he maintained that his grand jury answers did not meet the legal definition of perjury. According to Rep. Barney Frank, a Democrat, the issue was: "What did the president touch and when did he touch it?" Democrats also argued that even if the president were guilty of perjury, it related to a private consensual affair and did not affect his duties as president. Republicans countered that perjury by the president undermined the rule of law and violated his constitutional responsibility to "take care that the laws be faithfully executed."

On February 12, 1999–voting largely along party lines–half the Senate found President Clinton guilty of the charges, but he was acquitted because the Constitution requires a two-thirds vote for removal. In January 2001,

> **"It depends on what the meaning of the word 'is' is."**
>
> —Bill Clinton

What Did the President Touch and When Did He Touch It? *Rep. Barney Frank*

To Rep. Barney Frank (D-Mass.), censure by Congress would have been a more appropriate punishment for President Clinton than impeachment.

What did the president touch and when did he touch it? I mean, that was the big account of perjury, was that Bill Clinton acknowledged that she had performed oral sex on him but he denied that he touched her breasts or vagina. To impeach the president of the United States because he admitted that the woman sucked him, but he denied that he touched her....

I think it would have been better for the House to have done censure and not gone to the Senate. And one of their arguments was censure doesn't mean anything. It's just a slap on the wrist....

I reminded people that I myself had been reprimanded [because of involvement with a male prostitute].... And what I said was "Look, you all, some of you are saying this doesn't mean anything. I know it means something. I was reprimanded, I know what it meant to me. And I don't see how anybody who ever served here can say a reprimand from this place doesn't mean anything. It memorializes the fact that you behaved very badly."...

President Clinton settled a lawsuit seeking to disbar him in Arkansas. He signed a court order in which he agreed that some of the answers in his Jones deposition were false, but he did not admit to perjury. He accepted a five-year suspension of his license to practice law in Arkansas and paid a $25,000 fine. As part of that agreement, the federal independent counsel closed his investigation of the president, having found no evidence of impeachable offenses in the Whitewater scandal and declining to prosecute the president for perjury.

Under This Roof

The president's home is also the seat of the executive branch of government. Once called the President's Palace or the Executive Mansion, today it is known as the White House. This title became popular when the building was repainted after the British burned it in 1814, although some sources referred to it as the White House even earlier. Theodore Roosevelt made the name official in 1901.

George Washington was the only president who never lived in the White House, although he planned its design and location. John Adams moved from the capital in Philadelphia to the still unfinished White House in November 1800. His wife,

This earliest known photograph of the White House was taken in 1846 by John Plumbe, Jr.

Abigail, would use what is now the East Room for drying her laundry. After spending his first night in his new home, Adams wrote a letter to Abigail that gave the White House its trademark benediction: "I pray Heaven to bestow the best of blessings on this house, and on all that shall hereafter inhabit it. May none but honest and wise men ever rule under this roof!"

ARTICLE III

SECTION. 1. The judicial Power of the United States shall be vested in one supreme Court, and in such inferior Courts as the Congress may from time to time ordain and establish. The Judges, both of the supreme and inferior Courts, shall hold their Offices during good Behaviour, and shall, at stated Times, receive for their Services, a Compensation, which shall not be diminished during their Continuance in Office.

SECTION. 2. The judicial Power shall extend to all Cases, in Law and Equity, arising under this Constitution, the Laws of the United States, and Treaties made, or which shall be made, under their Authority;—to all Cases affecting Ambassadors, other public Ministers and Consuls;—to all Cases of admiralty and maritime Jurisdiction;—to Controversies to which the United States shall be a Party;—to Controversies between two or more States;—between a State and Citizens of another State;—between Citizens of different States,—between Citizens of the same State claiming Lands under Grants of different States, and between a State, or the Citizens thereof, and foreign States, Citizens or Subjects.

In all Cases affecting Ambassadors, other public Ministers and Consuls, and those in which a State shall be Party, the supreme Court shall have original Jurisdiction. In all the other Cases before mentioned, the supreme Court shall have appellate Jurisdiction, both as to Law and Fact, with such Exceptions, and under such Regulations as the Congress shall make.

The Trial of all Crimes, except in Cases of Impeachment, shall be by Jury; and such Trial shall be held in the State where the said Crimes shall have been committed; but when not committed within any State, the Trial shall be at such Place or Places as the Congress may by Law have directed.

SECTION. 3. Treason against the United States, shall consist only in levying War against them, or in adhering to their Enemies, giving them Aid and Comfort. No Person shall be convicted of Treason unless on the Testimony of two Witnesses to the same overt Act, or on Confession in open Court.

The Congress shall have Power to declare the Punishment of Treason, but no Attainder of Treason shall work Corruption of Blood, or Forfeiture except during the Life of the Person attainted.

ARTICLE III: THE JUDICIAL BRANCH

judicial review

the power of the courts to declare a law or an act of the executive unconstitutional

The duty of the judicial branch is to interpret the laws. Or, in the words of Chief Justice John Marshall, "to say what the law is." Article III has been interpreted by the Supreme Court to give the judiciary the power to declare acts of the president or Congress unconstitutional. This power, known as **judicial review,** gives American courts much more influence than in other countries.

Article III is the shortest, and least specific, of the constitutional provisions establishing the three branches of government. The framers of the Constitution spent far less time—and debate—on the judiciary than Congress or the president. Yet the power of unelected judges to overturn laws in a democracy has become one of the most controversial issues in American government.

SECTION. 1. The judicial power of the United States,...

What is the nature of the judicial power? Article III doesn't really say. There was no national judiciary under the Articles of Confederation, so the framers of the Constitution were working from scratch. The essence of the judicial power is to interpret the laws. However, Article III makes no mention of judicial review, the third branch's greatest power. Several of the framers implied the idea of judicial review in their comments at the Constitutional Convention—although it was not specifically debated. But as Alexander Hamilton made clear in *Federalist* 78, the power of judicial review was anticipated even before the Constitution was ratified. Hamilton declared that the judiciary was the "least dangerous" branch of government, because it had neither the legislature's power of the purse nor the executive's power of the sword—it had "neither force nor will but merely judgment." However, many Americans throughout history have disagreed with Hamilton, because unelected judges have the power to overturn the decisions of elected officials. And yet, argued Hamilton, even though unelected, the judiciary was the true guardian of the ultimate will of the people: the Constitution.

In *Marbury v. Madison* (1803), the Supreme Court established the power of judicial review for federal judges. In that case, Chief Justice John Marshall faced the consequences of his own carelessness as secretary of state under President John Adams. (Today, Marshall would have been forced to recuse himself due to a conflict of interest.) Marshall had neglected to deliver several last-minute judicial commissions Adams issued as he was leaving office. The new secretary of state, James Madison—appointed by Marshall's political and constitutional adversary, Thomas Jefferson—refused to honor some of these "midnight appointments."

Now a frustrated office seeker, William Marbury brought suit under the Judiciary Act of 1789 to force Madison to deliver his commission as justice of the peace for the District of Columbia. Under the terms of the act, Marbury could go straight to the Supreme Court as part of its original jurisdiction, rather than appealing through the lower courts. However, as Chief Justice Marshall and a unanimous Court declared, Congress could not amend the original jurisdiction of the Supreme Court–as set forth in Section 2 of Article III–without amending the Constitution. For the first time, an act of Congress was declared unconstitutional by the judiciary.

In *Marbury,* Chief Justice Marshall wrote: "It is, emphatically, the province and duty of the judicial department, to say what the law is." Did Marshall mean that judges, through judicial review, have the final word on the meaning of the Constitution? This question sparked debate even in Marshall's time, although public reaction to the *Marbury* decision was favorable overall. Both Jefferson and James Madison argued in the Virginia and Kentucky resolutions, passed to oppose a 1798 federal law prohibiting criticism of the government, that states had the power to declare acts of Congress unconstitutional. Similarly, President Andrew Jackson asserted his power of constitutional interpretation by refusing to carry out a Supreme Court decision about the Cherokee Nation, allegedly saying: "John Marshall has made his decision, now let him enforce it." Abraham Lincoln also argued in his first inaugural address that the *Dred Scott v. Sandford* (1857) decision did not settle forever U.S. policy on the question of slavery in the federal territories.

The Supreme Court did not explicitly declare itself to be the final authority on the meaning of the Constitution until *Cooper v. Aaron* (1958). In that case, the Court denied the power of the governor of Arkansas to oppose its desegregation decision in *Brown v. Board of Education* (1954). The unanimous Court said in *Cooper* that the *Marbury* decision had established the principle that "the federal judiciary is supreme in the exposition of the law of the Constitution." The court reiterated its position as "ultimate interpreter of the Constitution" in *Baker v. Carr* (1962) and *United States v. Nixon* (1974).

Some scholars believe that the process of constitutional interpretation is more dynamic than merely following Supreme Court decisions. As law professor Cass Sunstein wrote in his book *The Partial Constitution:*

> The Constitution does not mean only what the judges say it means.... Its meaning to Congress, the President, state government, and citizens in general has been more important than its meaning within the narrow confines of the Supreme Court building.

"We are under a Constitution, but the Constitution is what the judges say it is."
—Charles Evans Hughes

Of course, the people have the final say about the meaning of the Constitution through their power to amend it. But that is a very difficult process. Until such amendment, the American system of judicial review gives judges a unique degree of power. In the words of historian Gordon Wood: "I do not know of any country in the world where judges wield as much power in shaping the contours of life as they do in the United States."

The Least Dangerous Branch *Alexander Hamilton*

In Federalist 78, Alexander Hamilton argues that the judiciary is the least dangerous branch to democracy, and that courts are the true defenders of the will of the people.

Whoever attentively considers the different departments of power must perceive that, in a government in which they are separated from each other, the judiciary from the nature of its functions, will always be the least dangerous to the political rights of the Constitution; because it will be least in a capacity to annoy or injure them. The executive not only dispenses the honors but holds the sword of the community. The legislature not only commands the purse but prescribes the rules by which the duties and rights of every citizen are to be regulated. The judiciary, on the contrary, has no influence over either the sword or the purse; no direction either of the strength or of the wealth of the society, and can take no active resolution whatever. It may truly be said to have neither FORCE nor WILL but merely judgment; and must ultimately depend upon the aid of the executive arm even for the efficacy of its judgments....

The complete independence of the courts of justice is peculiarly essential in a limited Constitution. By a limited Constitution, I understand one which contains certain specified exceptions to the legislative authority; such, for instance, as that it shall pass no bills of attainder, no *ex post facto* laws, and the like. Limitations of this kind can be preserved in practice no other way than through the medium of the courts of justice, whose duty it must be to declare all acts contrary to the manifest tenor of the Constitution void. Without this, all the reservations of particular rights or privileges would amount to nothing....

...shall be vested in one supreme Court, and in such inferior courts as the Congress may from time to time ordain and establish.

The Supreme Court is the only court established by the Constitution. All lower federal courts are created by Congress. Today these courts include federal district courts, which hear cases at the trial level, and U.S. appellate courts, which hear the first level of appeals in the federal system. Final appeals are heard by the Supreme Court, consequently known as the court of last resort.

The Supreme Court got off to a shaky start. President George Washington had a hard time filling the six seats on the first Supreme Court. Justices resented the duty to ride circuit, which required them to travel to hear trial court cases—some more than a thousand miles yearly—in an era of dangerous roads and rowdy inns. Not until 1891, when Congress created the federal appellate courts, were the justices relieved of this burden. John Jay, the first chief justice, resigned to take the more prestigious job of governor of New York. Other prominent Americans, such as Alexander Hamilton and Patrick Henry, refused nominations to be chief justice. But with the appointment of John Marshall as chief justice in 1801, the Court began to assume its place as an equal branch of government and a more desirable career choice.

Nothing in the Constitution requires that the Supreme Court consist of nine justices. The exact number is determined by Congress and has varied from the original six allowed in 1789 to a high of ten authorized in 1863. After the Civil War, the number of justices settled at nine, until the Great Depression. When an aging and recalcitrant Court refused to uphold the constitutionality of New Deal legislation, President Franklin Roosevelt proposed that a new justice be added for each member of the Court aged seventy and older—supposedly to help with the workload. This plan would have raised the Court's total to fifteen. Reaction to Roosevelt's "court-packing" plan was intensely negative, because it was seen as a direct attack on the independence of the judiciary. But while the bill was being considered by Congress it became moot. One of the opposition justices began voting with Roosevelt, a move later dubbed by future justice Abe Fortas as "the switch in time that saved the nine." In 1948, a federal law set the size of the Supreme Court at eight associate justices and one chief justice.

The Constitution also does not specify what the qualifications of a Supreme Court justice should be. There are no requirements of minimum age or length of citizenship, as with the president and members of Congress. Before 1957, not all the justices even had law degrees, because until World War I most lawyers trained through apprenticeships instead of law schools. Several leading justices had no prior judicial experience—including John Marshall, Earl Warren, and Felix Frankfurter. Although the greatest legal minds can become Supreme court justices, so can political cronies of the president. In defending President Richard Nixon's nomination of Judge Harrold Carswell to the Supreme Court, Senator Roman Hruska remarked: "Even if he is mediocre, there are a lot of mediocre judges and people and lawyers. They are entitled to a little representation, aren't they?" Carswell's nomination was defeated.

The Supreme Court begins each annual term of hearing cases on the first Monday in October. The dates of the Court's term are set by Congress and have varied in the past. Now the Court's term begins in October and ends in June. The most controversial decisions are usually issued in June.

The chief justice is the only judicial officer mentioned in the Constitution, which states in Article I that the chief justice shall preside over the impeachment trial of the President. The chief justice is the head of the entire judicial branch, not just the Supreme Court. Therefore his or her proper title is chief justice of the United States—not chief justice of the

"We are not final because we are infallible, but we are infallible only because we are final."

— Justice Robert H. Jackson

John Jay refused a second nomination as chief justice because he thought the office lacked prestige.

Supreme Court. The chief justice administers all U.S. courts created under Article III–including ninety-four federal district courts, thirteen appellate courts, and the Supreme Court.

The Judges, both of the supreme and inferior Courts, shall hold their Offices during good Behaviour, and shall at stated Times, receive for their Services, a Compensation, which shall not be diminished during their Continuance in Office.

The great democratic dilemma of the Constitution is the power that is given to unelected judges. On the one hand, Americans rely on judges who are independent of the political process to protect minority rights. On the other hand, such independent judges also limit majority rule, the essence of democracy. Under Article III, judges serve "during good Behaviour"–a life term that can be ended only by impeachment.

In the Declaration of Independence, Thomas Jefferson criticized King George III for, among other things, making "judges dependent on his will

From Potato Hole to Temple of Karnak

The Supreme Court had no permanent home when the U.S. capital moved to Washington, D.C., in 1800. The Court first met in a committee room of the new Capitol building, then occupied the Senate's former chambers on the ground floor in 1810. This room was so dark and dank that the *New York Tribune* referred to it as a "potato hole." When the British burned the Capitol in 1814, the Supreme Court again met in temporary quarters until its chamber was restored in 1819. Then in 1860, the Court moved directly upstairs to the newly vacated Senate chambers, where it stayed for seventy-five years until 1935. Chief Justice William Howard Taft—the only former U.S. president to serve on the Supreme Court—argued that, as a separate branch of government, the Court needed its own building independent of

From 1810 to 1860, the Supreme Court met in this ground-floor chamber of the U.S. Capitol.

the Congress. Others thought the proposed design too ostentatious. When the Supreme Court finally moved into its new quarters across the street from the Capitol, one justice remarked that the Court would become "nine black beetles in the Temple of Karnak." But the inscription on the pediment of the new building became the Supreme Court's motto: "Equal Justice Under Law."

alone for the tenure of their offices and the amount and payment of their salaries." But after Jefferson served as president, and struggled with Chief Justice John Marshall over interpretations of the Constitution, he questioned the life tenure of judges: "A judiciary independent of a king or executive alone, is a good thing; but independence of the will of the nation is a solecism, at least in a republican government." Even today, some citizens and constitutional scholars believe that federal judges should serve fixed terms, rather than have unlimited lifetime tenure.

The proper role of an unelected judiciary has been one of the most controversial constitutional issues in American history. How are judges to apply the law in a way that is consistent with democratic self-government? How do they interpret law and not make law? Justice Oliver Wendell Holmes, Jr., believed that judges should not second-guess the opinions of the majority, as expressed in laws enacted by the legislature, unless the Constitution clearly prohibited such action. To Holmes, the mere fact that a judge disagreed with the wisdom of a law was not sufficient to make it unconstitutional.

Holmes's point of view is known as **judicial restraint.** Under this philosophy, judges must show great deference to popularly elected legislatures and previous court decisions—and thus be slow to make drastic changes in public policy. Advocates of **judicial activism,** however, believe that judges play an important role in public policy and are less reluctant to overturn laws and precedents. Judicial activism and judicial restraint are not linked to political philosophy. A judge can be a liberal politically and still exercise judicial restraint; similarly, a conservative judge can issue activist decisions.

Linked to the question of judicial activism are various theories about how judges should interpret the Constitution. Advocates of **strict construction**—among them Thomas Jefferson—believe that judges should limit themselves to narrow interpretations of the Constitution's text and avoid enlarging the powers of government. Proponents of broad or **loose construction**—as was Chief Justice John Marshall—maintain that the Constitution gives general guidance about basic principles but allows "play in the joints" for government to adapt to specific crises. As Chief Justice Marshall wrote in *McCulloch v. Maryland* (1819), "We must never forget that it is *a constitution* we are expounding," rather than a wordy legal code that details all contingencies.

President Richard Nixon renewed the debate over strict construction with his judicial nominees in the 1970s. During the 2000 presidential campaign, George W. Bush also promised to appoint "strict constructionists" to the Supreme Court, citing Justices Antonin Scalia and Clarence Thomas as examples. Justice Scalia, however, resists that label. "I

judicial restraint

philosophy under which judges avoid overturning statutes and precedents

judicial activism

philosophy under which judges do not avoid overturning statutes and precedents

strict construction

policy of construing the Constitution's text narrowly to limit government power

loose construction

policy of construing the Constitution's text broadly to allow flexible government power am not a strict constructionist, and no one ought to be," he says. "A text should not be construed strictly, and it should not be construed leniently; it should be construed reasonably, to contain all that it fairly means." Justice Scalia refers to himself as a "textualist" or "originalist" who relies on the original meaning of the words in the Constitiution rather than the intent of the framers who wrote the constitution.

"WE WERE TOLD THEY WERE 'STRICT CONSTRUCTIONISTS'"

Justice Scalia opposes interpreting the Constitution as an evolving document, which he believes gives unelected judges too much power. He wrote in his book *A Matter of Interpretation:* "The ascendant school of constitutional interpretation affirms the existence of what is called The Living Constitution, a body of law that (unlike normal statutes) grows and changes from age to age, in order to meet the needs of a changing society. And it is judges who determine those needs and 'find' that changing law."

A leading proponent of the "framers' intent" school of constitutional interpretation is Judge Robert Bork, a former federal appellate judge and Supreme Court nominee. Bork believes that, as demonstrated by his own confirmation hearings before the Senate in 1987, the law is becoming politicized, and judges are too often reading their own personal preferences into the Constitution, rather than following the intent of its framers. Critics of this judicial philosophy argue that the framers' intent is impossible to determine. They point out that the framers had varying opinions on the meaning of the Constitution, as did the members of the state conventions who ratified it.

Another theory of judicial review, put forward by constitutional scholar John Hart Ely in his book *Democracy and Distrust,* argues that courts should act as referees in the political process to ensure equal representation. Beyond that, says Ely, in order to be consistent with democracy, judges should leave the protection of substantive rights that are not specifically mentioned in the Constitution to majority rule.

"If my fellow citizens want to go to hell, I will help them. It's my job."

—Justice Oliver Wendell Holmes

A Meaning That Does Not Change *Justice Clarence Thomas*

In a 2001 speech to the American Enterprise Institute, Justice Clarence Thomas argued that upholding the framers' intent is the only judicial philosophy consistent with a written Constitution.

When interpreting the Constitution and statutes, judges should seek the original understanding of the provision's text, if the meaning of that text is not readily apparent.

This approach works in several ways to reduce judicial discretion and to maintain judicial impartiality. First, by tethering their analysis to the understanding of those who drafted and ratified the text, modern judges are prevented from substituting their own preferences for the Constitution.

Clarence Thomas was appointed to the Supreme Court in 1991.

Second, it places the authority for creating the legal rules in the hands of the people and their representatives, rather than in the hands of the judiciary. The Constitution means what the delegates of the Philadelphia Convention and of the state ratifying conventions understood it to mean, not what we judges think it should mean.

Third, this approach recognizes the basic principle of a *written* Constitution. "We the People" adopted a written Constitution precisely because it has a fixed meaning, a meaning that does not change. Otherwise we would have adopted the British approach of an unwritten, evolving constitution. Aside from amendment according to Article V, the Constitution's meaning cannot be updated, or changed, or altered by the Supreme Court, the Congress, or the President.

The Constitution Made Me Do It *Laurence H. Tribe*

A critic of the framer's intent philosophy, Laurence Tribe of Harvard Law School believes that judicial decisions are inherently political because judges must always make value choices.

Should the peculiar opinions held…by men who have been dead for two centuries always trump contemporary insights into what the living Constitution means and ought to mean? Should we permit others to rule us from the grave…through

hidden beliefs and premises perhaps deliberately left unstated?…

The most serious flaw in both slavish adherence to the constitutional text and the inevitably inconclusive inquiry into the intent of those who wrote it is…that they abdicate responsibility for the choices that constitutional courts *necessarily* make. The Supreme Court just cannot avoid the painful duty of exercising judgment so as to give concrete meaning to the fluid

Constitution, because the constitutional rules and precepts that it is charged with administering lack that certainty which permits anything resembling automatic application. Strict constructionism in all its variants is thus built on [the] myth…that the Supreme Court does not make law, but finds law ready-made by others…. But disclaimers that "the Constitution made me do it" are rarely more persuasive than those that blame the devil.

SECTION. 2. The judicial Power shall extend to all Cases, in Law and Equity, arising under this Constitution, the Laws of the United States, and Treaties made, or which shall be made, under their Authority;— to all Cases affecting Ambassadors, other public Ministers and Consuls;—to all Cases of admiralty and maritime Jurisdiction;—to Controversies to which the United States shall be a Party;—to Controversies between two or more States;—*between a State and Citizens of another State;*—between Citizens of different States;— between Citizens of the same State claiming Lands under Grants of different States, *and between a State, or the Citizens thereof, and foreign States, Citizens or Subjects.*

jurisdiction

the legal authority of a court to hear and decide a case

Section 2 of Article III defines the **jurisdiction** of the federal courts. This provision of the Constitution, along with laws passed by Congress, gives courts the legal power to decide certain types of cases. *The Wizard of Oz* illustrates one kind of jurisdiction. In that movie, the Wicked Witch of the West threatens Dorothy, who has just arrived in Munchkin Land. Glinda, the Good Witch of the North, responds with a laugh: "Rubbish! You have no power here. Begone—before somebody drops a house on you, too!" Like the Wicked Witch of the West, the federal courts have geographic limits. The United States and its territories are divided into local judicial districts for trial cases, which are grouped into regional circuits for appellate review.

Besides geography, the jurisdiction of the federal courts is also limited by subject matter. The federal courts can hear cases "arising under" the Constitution, U.S. laws, and treaties with foreign nations—as well as cases involving diplomats and the law of the sea. The federal courts also have jurisdiction over cases involving certain parties, such as the United States government or citizens of different states. The goal of this provision of Article III was to avoid the possibility of prejudice by state courts against the federal government or citizens of other states. To lighten the workload of the federal courts, Congress in 1988 required that cases between citizens of different states—known as diversity jurisdiction—must involve a minimum dispute of more than $50,000.

The Constitution allows courts only to hear "cases or controversies." This means that, despite their training in law school, judges do not rule on hypothetical cases. The case must be a real dispute between actual litigants. Moreover, the courts do not give **advisory opinions** to the president or other government officials, telling them in advance whether a particular action is constitutional. Several proposals to allow such advisory opinions were specifically rejected by the Constitutional Convention. In 1793, President George Washington sought the opinion of the Supreme Court on several questions of international law, but the Court refused to answer them

advisory opinions

determinations by the Supreme Court whether future actions of the president or Congress would be constitutional on the grounds of separation of powers.

The portion of this section of Article III that appears in italics has been overturned by the Eleventh Amendment. Originally, this provision in the Constitution allowed a state to be sued by citizens of another state, as the Supreme Court held in *Chisholm v. Georgia* (1793). That case was the first of four Supreme Court rulings that were subsequently overturned by constitutional amendments.

In all Cases affecting Ambassadors, other public Ministers and Consuls, and those in which a State shall be Party, the supreme Court shall have original Jurisdiction. In all the other Cases before mentioned, the supreme Court shall have appellate Jurisdiction, both as to Law and Fact, with such Exceptions, and under such Regulations as the Congress shall make.

The word *jurisdiction* literally means the power "to say what the law is." Chief Justice John Marshall asserted that power on behalf of the federal courts in *Marbury v. Madison* (1803). Marshall based his decision on this clause in Article III that sets forth the Supreme Court's **original jurisdiction**–the types of cases it can hear directly, not through appeals from lower courts. As the Court pointed out in *Marbury,* Congress has the power to change the **appellate jurisdiction** of the Supreme Court, but its original jurisdiction can be altered only by constitutional amendment.

Since 1925, Congress has gradually eliminated most mandatory appeals to the Supreme Court, so the Court's workload is almost entirely discretionary. By far most cases involve a petition for a **writ of certiorari.** These appeals may be filed by parties in federal or state court cases in which a federal question of law is involved. If four justices agree to issue the

original jurisdiction

cases that a court can hear directly, rather than through appeals

appellate jurisdiction

cases based on appeals from lower courts

writ of certiorari

an order issued by the U.S. Supreme Court that directs a lower court to transmit records for a case that it will hear on appeal

The Supreme Court justices in the 2001–2002 term were, from left to right: Antonin Scalia, Ruth Bader Ginsburg, John Paul Stevens, David Souter, William Rehnquist, Clarence Thomas, Sandra Day O'Connor, Stephen Breyer, and Anthony Kennedy.

writ of certiorari, the case will be heard by the Supreme Court. Cases most likely to be accepted for review are those on an issue where the lower appellate courts have issued conflicting rulings. In the 2001–2002 term, the Supreme Court received more than 7,000 petitions for certiorari, but issued written opinions in only seventy-six cases.

In 1868, Congress acted to limit the jurisdiction of the Supreme Court to hear a case regarding the writ of habeas corpus, a court order that prevents arbitrary arrest. The Supreme Court upheld the law the next year, although Congress repealed the law in 1884. Since that time, however, experts have debated how far Congress can go to eliminate the appellate jurisdiction of the Court. Congress has considered, but not enacted, legislation to restrict Supreme Court jurisdiction regarding school prayer, abortion, and criminal procedure. In 1996, the Supreme Court upheld the Antiterrorism and Effective Death Penalty Act, which restricted but did not eliminate habeas corpus appeals to the Supreme Court.

John Marshall: The Great Chief Justice

John Marshall (1755–1835) is universally regarded as the greatest chief justice, both because of the quality and length of his tenure. Marshall was the fourth person to serve as chief justice, and his opinions established the broad powers of the national government. Chief Justice Marshall worked hard to eliminate the practice of seriatim opinions, in which each justice separately gave the reasoning for his ruling—as was the English custom. Instead,

Marshall instituted an "opinion of the court," which reflected the reasoning of the entire majority. And during Marshall's thirty-four years as chief justice, by far most decisions were unanimous. When Marshall died in Philadelphia, the Liberty Bell cracked while tolling his death.

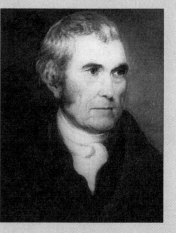

John Marshall served for thirty-four years (1801–1835), the longest term of any chief justice.

The Trial of all Crimes, except in Cases of Impeachment, shall be by Jury; and such Trial shall be held in the State where the said Crimes shall have been committed; but when not committed within any State, the Trial shall be at such Place or Places as the Congress may by Law have directed.

Trial by jury is one of the few individual rights protected in the original Constitution. Before the Bill of Rights was added in 1791, the Constitution mainly set forth the structure of government and did not guarantee many civil liberties. But juries were so vital to Americans that they are now specified four times in the Constitution: for deciding criminal cases in

Article III; for screening criminal charges (grand juries) in the Fifth Amendment; again for deciding criminal cases in the Sixth Amendment, along with other fair trial guarantees; and for deciding civil cases in the Seventh Amendment.

Juries involve lay citizens in the dispensation of justice, rather than relying solely on professional judges. As Thomas Jefferson said, the jury means a trial "by the people themselves." Thus, to many Americans, juries are essential to self-government. However, other Americans criticize the jury system, both in criminal and civil trials, as being unreliable and unfair. These arguments are discussed in the chapters on the Fifth, Sixth, and Seventh Amendments.

> "It is almost impossible to exaggerate the jury's importance in the constitutional design."
>
> —Akhil Reed Amar

A Wise Old Woman *Justice Sandra Day O'Connor*

Like Shakespeare's Portia, Justice Sandra Day O'Connor has blazed new paths for women in the law. But she challenges the view that women judges judge differently than men.

In my own time, and in my own life, I've witnessed the revolution in the legal profession that has resulted in women representing...over forty percent of law school graduates.... I myself, after graduating near the top of my class at Stanford Law School, was unable to obtain a position at any national law firm, except as a legal secretary. Yet I have since had the privilege of serving as a state senator, a state judge, and a Supreme Court justice....

The new presence of women in the law has prompted many feminist commentators to ask whether women have made a difference to the profession, whether women have different

Sandra Day O'Connor became the first woman to be appointed to the Supreme Court in 1981.

styles, aptitudes, or liabilities.... One author has even concluded that my opinions differ in a peculiarly feminine way from those of my colleagues.

The gender differences cited currently are surprisingly similar to stereotypes from years past.... Women judges are more likely to emphasize context and deemphasize the general principles. Women judges are more compassionate. And so forth....

Asking whether women attorneys speak with a "different voice" than men do is a question that is both dangerous and unanswerable. It sets up again the polarity between the feminine virtues of homemaking and the masculine virtues of breadwinning. It threatens, indeed, to establish new categories of "women's work" to which women are confined and from which men are excluded.

Do women judges decide cases differently by virtue of being women? I would echo the answer of my colleague, Justice Jeanne Coyne of the Supreme Court of Oklahoma, who responded that "a wise old man and a wise old woman reach the same conclusion."

Julius and Ethel Rosenberg prepare for transport to prison after they were convicted of espionage.

attainder

the forfeiture of rights and property by a person convicted of treason

corruption of blood

revoking the inheritance of the descendants of a treasonous person

SECTION. 3. Treason against the United States, shall consist only in levying War against them, or in adhering to their Enemies, giving them Aid and Comfort. No Person shall be convicted of Treason unless on the Testimony of two Witnesses to the same overt Act, or on Confession in open Court.

The Congress shall have Power to declare the Punishment of Treason, but no Attainder of Treason shall work Corruption of Blood, or Forfeiture except during the Life of the Person attainted.

Treason is the only crime defined in the Constitution. In England, treason charges had been used to punish criticism of the government. To avoid such abuse, the framers of the Constitution established very specific elements of the crime that must be proved–and the standard of evidence for that proof. Furthermore, although an **attainder** of treason could deprive a traitor of his assets, Congress could not punish the heirs of a traitor by revoking their inheritance–a practice known as **corruption of blood.**

The definition of treason was tested early in the republic. President Thomas Jefferson sought to prosecute his former vice president and political adversary, Aaron Burr, for treason in 1807. Burr was accused of organizing an expedition of men with aims of attacking Spanish lands west of the Mississippi, and possibly New Orleans. The alleged conspiracy took place in Ohio, where the men first gathered, although Burr was not present. But in a declaration to Congress, Jefferson announced that Burr's "guilt is placed beyond question."

Burr was tried in federal court at Richmond, Virginia, with Chief Justice John Marshall serving in his capacity as circuit court judge. In his rulings on the evidence, Marshall construed the definition of treason very narrowly, requiring that two witnesses must testify that Burr was actually involved in levying war, not just conspiracy. Based on Marshall's rulings, the jury acquitted Burr of all charges.

Because of the high standard of proof for treason, convictions have been rare in U.S. history–and those who were convicted were frequently pardoned. Participants in the Whiskey Rebellion of 1794 were pardoned, as were southern combatants during the Civil War. It was not until 1947 that the Supreme Court acted to uphold a treason conviction.

But the U.S. government prosecuted disloyal citizens on other grounds–and with less proof than required for treason. In 1917, Congress passed the Espionage Act, making it illegal to convey unauthorized information on national defense. In 1951, Julius and Ethel Rosenberg–both devoted members of the American Communist Party–were convicted under the Espionage Act for conspiring to transmit atomic secrets to the Soviet Union. When the Supreme Court refused to hear their appeals, they were both executed on June 19, 1953. After the Cold War ended, evidence from U.S. and Soviet intelligence files implicated Julius as a spy, but it appears that Ethel was only tangentially involved.

My Country Versus Me *Wen Ho Lee*

In March 1999, scientist Wen Ho Lee was accused of stealing nuclear secrets for China from the Los Alamos National Laboratory. In September 2000, Lee pled guilty to a felony count of mishandling classified material, but he was never proven to be a spy. In his book My Country Versus Me, *Lee describes his treatment by the FBI.*

The federal marshals took me away in handcuffs to the Santa Fe County Adult Correctional Facility. I was in a transport van, just me and the guards. In my mind, so many questions and thoughts were swirling. What was going to happen next? Could the government find a way to kill me in prison? I figured that if they didn't kill me, one day I would get out....

My family didn't even know where I was—the judge didn't tell them or my lawyers where I would be imprisoned. I was allowed to make one phone call my first night in jail. I called my wife and told her I was in Santa Fe and that I would be okay. That was the only call I was allowed to make to my family for the entire month to come. My wife sounded frightened, and told me that my family members were all very anxious, not knowing where I was or what was happening to me. They remembered that the FBI had threatened execution, "like the Rosenbergs," and they were in a panic. It was terrible to make them worry so. I knew it was deliberate, the FBI and U.S. attorney's way of putting pressure on them, to torture them too....

Sitting alone in solitary confinement with a light bulb burning continuously, I sometimes felt like I must have

Wen Ho Lee denies he ever spied or stole U.S. nuclear secrets for China.

made a mistake and should not have come to America in 1964 for my Ph.D. I must have done something terrible to have ended up like this. As I sat in jail, I had to conclude that no matter how smart you are, no matter how hard you work, a Chinese person, an Asian person like me, will never be accepted. We will always be foreigners.

ARTICLE IV

SECTION. 1. Full Faith and Credit shall be given in each State to the public Acts, Records, and judicial Proceedings of every other State. And the Congress may by general Laws prescribe the Manner in which such Acts, Records and Proceedings shall be proved, and the Effect thereof.

SECTION. 2. The Citizens of each State shall be entitled to all Privileges and Immunities of Citizens in the several States.

A Person charged in any State with Treason, Felony, or other Crime, who shall flee from Justice, and be found in another State, shall on Demand of the executive Authority of the State from which he fled, be delivered up, to be removed to the State having Jurisdiction of the Crime.

No Person held to Service or Labour in one State, under the Laws thereof, escaping into another, shall, in Consequence of any Law or Regulation therein, be discharged from such Service or Labour, but shall be delivered up on Claim of the Party to whom such Service or Labour may be due.

SECTION. 3. New States may be admitted by the Congress into this Union; but no new State shall be formed or erected within the Jurisdiction of any other State; nor any State be formed by the Junction of two or more States, or Parts of States, without the Consent of the Legislatures of the States concerned as well as of the Congress.

The Congress shall have Power to dispose of and make all needful Rules and Regulations respecting the Territory or other Property belonging to the United States; and nothing in this Constitution shall be so construed as to Prejudice any Claims of the United States, or of any particular State.

SECTION. 4. The United States shall guarantee to every State in this Union a Republican Form of Government, and shall protect each of them against Invasion; and on Application of the Legislature, or of the Executive (when the Legislature cannot be convened), against domestic Violence.

ARTICLE IV: FULL FAITH AND CREDIT

Article IV governs the relationships among the states. Under the Articles of Confederation, the states treated one another like independent sovereign nations, but under the Constitution states had to respect one another's court decisions and laws. From marriage and divorce, to criminal prosecutions, to the status of slaves, the states were bound to acknowledge the validity of another state's laws even when they disagreed with the outcome.

SECTION. 1. Full Faith and Credit shall be given in each State to the public Acts, Records, and judicial Proceedings of every other State. And the Congress may by general Laws prescribe the Manner in which such Acts, Records and Proceedings shall be proved, and the Effect thereof.

This section of Article IV, known as the Full Faith and Credit Clause, requires states to respect one another's civil laws, records, and court rulings. It also allows Congress to establish standards to validate such official acts, as well as regulate "the effect thereof." Under the full faith and credit doctrine, if a person loses a lawsuit in California but later moves to Maryland, the Maryland court must enforce the California judgment. However, states are allowed to make certain exceptions for "public policy" reasons. For instance, states may refuse to recognize marriages that involve incest or polygamy.

Perhaps the most controversial issue under the Full Faith and Credit Clause is whether a state must recognize a same-sex marriage or civil union performed in another state. In 1993, the Hawaii Supreme Court held that a restriction on homosexual marriage could violate the state constitution's equal protection clause. In response, Congress passed the Defense of Marriage Act (DOMA) in 1996, which defined marriage under federal law as a contract between a man and a woman and allowed states to refuse to recognize same-sex marriages from other states. Hawaii voters amended their state constitution in 1998 to allow legislators to prohibit gay marriages. However, in 2000 Vermont became the first state to pass a law creating civil unions for same-sex partners, which would extend many of the legal benefits of marriage.

> "I think we go beyond the Constitution here.... I'm not homophobic; I'm not a bigot,... and I love my daughter. I simply can't handle it yet."
>
> —Rep. Sonny Bono, on gay marriage

Carolyn Conrad, right, and Kathleen Peterson were the first same-sex couple to file for a civil union in Vermont.

Opponents of gay marriage have proposed a Federal Marriage Amendment to forestall any constitutional problems under the Full Faith and Credit Clause. There are questions about the validity of the DOMA, since Congress has never before acted to restrict a state's legal proceedings under Article IV. Moreover, gay rights advocates may challenge DOMA as illegal discrimination prohibited by the Fourteenth Amendment's guarantee of equal protection of the laws. Under the Federal Marriage Amendment, marriage is defined as the union between a man and a woman, and states are not required to recognize civil unions.

To Nationalize Same-Sex Unions *Robert Bork*

Former federal judge and Supreme Court nominee Robert Bork argues that a constitutional amendment is the only way to bar homosexual marriage in unwilling states, given the Full Faith and Credit Clause of Article IV.

Many court watchers believe that...the U.S. Supreme Court will hold that there is a constitutional right to homosexual marriage, just as that court invented a right to abortion. The chosen instrument will be the Equal Protection Clause of the Fourteenth Amendment. After all, if state law forbids Fred to marry

Henry, aren't they denied equal protection when the law permits Tom and Jane to marry?...

To head off the seemingly inexorable march of the courts toward the radical redefinition of marriage, the Alliance for Marriage has put forward the proposed Federal Marriage Amendment: "Marriage in the United States shall consist only of the union of a man and a woman. Neither this Constitution or the constitution of any state, nor state or federal law, shall be construed to require that marital status or the legal incidents thereof be conferred upon unmarried couples or groups."...

Activists are already trying to nationalize same-sex unions: same-sex couples will travel to any state that allows them to marry or have civil unions, relying on the constitutional requirement that states give full faith and credit to the judgments of other states to validate their status in their home states. They will attack the constitutionality of the federal Defense of Marriage Act, which seeks to block this. One way or another, federalism is going to be overridden. The only question is whether the general rule will permit or prohibit the marriage of same-sex couples.

Section. 2. The Citizens of each State shall be entitled to all Privileges and Immunities of Citizens in the several States.

This section of Article IV, known as the Privileges and Immunities Clause, prohibits states from discriminating against citizens of other states without justification. For instance, the Supreme Court has ruled that Alaska could not limit jobs on its oil pipeline to state residents. Also, states may not deny nonresidents admission to the bar to practice law. But states are allowed to charge higher tuition to out-of-state students, because local citizens have paid taxes to support public universities. The Supreme Court has ruled that Section 2 is related to the Commerce Clause in Article I, because it "was intended to create a national economic union." However, the Court has not defined exactly what rights are included under this clause.

A Person charged in any State with Treason, Felony, or other Crime, who shall flee from Justice, and be found in another State, shall on Demand of the executive Authority of the State from which he fled, be delivered up, to be removed to the State having Jurisdiction of the Crime.

Article IV provides for **extradition,** which allows the governor of a state in which a person has been accused or convicted of a crime to demand custody of a fugitive from another state. In 1861, the Supreme Court held that it did not have the power to coerce a state to comply with extradition. Therefore, governors have at times refused to extradite certain fugitives. But in 1987, the Supreme Court ruled that federal courts could order governors to comply with the extradition provisions in Article IV. Asylum states may not inquire into the validity of a fugitive's arrest or the conditions of punishment in the demanding state.

extradition
the surrender by one state to another of a person accused or convicted of a crime in the other state

No Person held to Service or Labour in one State, under the Laws thereof, escaping into another, shall, in Consequence of any Law or Regulation therein, be discharged from such Service or Labour, but shall be delivered up on Claim of the Party to whom such Service or Labour may be due.

This provision in Article IV, known as the Fugitive Slave Clause, was overturned by the Thirteenth Amendment's ban on slavery. A source of much friction between northern and southern states, the Fugitive Slave Clause allowed slaveholders or their agents to go into free states to capture escaped slaves. Congress enacted a Fugitive Slave Act in 1793 that allowed federal magistrates in free states to certify alleged runaways for removal to slave states–although normally extradition would be a matter of state law. To protect its free black citizens from kidnapping by slave catchers, Pennsylvania passed a personal liberty statute, but the Supreme Court declared the law unconstitutional in 1842.

Congress approved a much harsher version of the Fugitive Slave Act in 1850, which denied accused slaves the right to trial by jury and other due process guarantees. Under this law, more than nine hundred alleged fugitives were returned to southern states from 1850 to 1861. According to historian John Hope Franklin, there is no exact count of runaway slaves, but he estimates a minimum of fifty thousand attempts were made annually as of 1860. Young men in their twenties ran away most frequently–and repeatedly–but only a tiny percentage of the escapes were successful.

The Funeral of Liberty
Charles E. Stevens

Anthony Burns escaped from slavery only to be returned by federal troops.

At times the Fugitive Slave Act had to be enforced by federal troops. Bostonian Charles E. Stevens describes the scene in 1854 when three platoons of Marines with loaded cannon—arrayed against fifty thousand onlookers—transported Anthony Burns to the ship that would take him to Virginia and slavery.

It was the first time that the armed power of the United States had ever been arrayed against the people of Massachusetts. Men who witnessed the sight, and reflected upon its cause, were made painfully to recognize the fact, before unfelt, that they were subjects of two governments....

The route from the courthouse to the wharf had by this time become thronged with a countless multitude.... At different points along the route were displayed symbols significant of the prevailing sentiment.... From a window opposite the Old State House was suspended a coffin, upon which was the legend, "The Funeral of Liberty."...
Along this Via Dolorosa, with its cloud of witnesses, the column now began to move.... In its progress, it went past the Old State House.... Just below, it passed over the ground where, in the massacre of 1770, fell Attucks, the first Negro martyr in the cause of American liberty.

SECTION. 3. New States may be admitted by the Congress into this Union; but no new State shall be formed or erected within the Jurisdiction of any other State; nor any State be formed by the Junction of two or more States, or Parts of States, without the Consent of the Legislatures of the States concerned as well as of the Congress.
Section 3 provides for the admission of new states to the Union. Under the Articles of Confederation, the western land claims of some of the original thirteen states were organized into the Northwest Territory in 1787. This land eventually became the states of Ohio, Indiana, Illinois, Michigan, and Wisconsin. According to the Northwest Ordinance, these states were to be admitted to the Union on an equal political basis with the original states. The Supreme Court upheld this principle in 1911—ruling that Congress could not, as part of legislation admitting Oklahoma to the Union, prohibit the state from moving its capital.

New states cannot be formed out of the territory of other states without their consent, as well as the approval of Congress. Five states have been created from preexisting states. Vermont was admitted from New York in 1791; Kentucky from Virginia in 1792; Tennessee from North Carolina in 1796; and Maine from Massachusetts in 1820. In 1863, the western counties of Virginia that wanted to remain in the Union formed a rump legislature, which approved the creation of West Virginia. After the Civil War, Virginia finally agreed to the split.

Most of the fifty states were territories before they became states. Under this model, citizens in a territory petition to be admitted to the Union. Next, the president and Congress authorize the territory to draft a constitution, which must also be approved by a majority of both houses and the president. Then the new state is admitted to the Union.

Residents of the District of Columbia voted in 1980 to seek statehood, and they held a constitutional convention in 1982. But when the House of Representatives voted on the petition for statehood in 1993, it was overwhelmingly defeated. A proposed constitutional amendment that would have treated D.C. as though it were a state expired without being ratified in 1985.

The Congress shall have Power to dispose of and make all needful Rules and Regulations respecting the Territory or other Property belonging to the United States; and nothing in this Constitution shall be so construed as to Prejudice any Claims of the United States, or of any particular State.

Congress has legislative power over all U.S. property and territory. Under Supreme Court rulings, Congress may legislate directly for a territory, or Congress may delegate its power to a territorial legislature. This exercise of authority is limited by the Bill of Rights, however. The Supreme Court held in *Dred Scott v. Sandford* (1857) that Congress could not forbid slavery in the western territories of the United States because such action deprived slaveholders of their right to property without due process of law, in violation of the Fifth Amendment.

But complete constitutional rights do not apply to every federal territory. The Supreme Court ruled in the *Insular Cases* (1901) that the Constitution does not always follow the flag. The Court distinguished between incorporated territories, which receive full constitutional rights because they may become states, and unincorporated territories, which will never become states and thus are guaranteed only certain fundamental rights such as free speech and fair trial.

SECTION. 4. The United States shall guarantee to every State in this Union a Republican Form of Government,...

This provision in Article IV is known as the Guarantee Clause, and it says that the United States will ensure that every state has a "republican form of government." What is a republic? James Madison answered in *Federalist* 39 that a republic is "a government which derives all its powers directly or indirectly from the great body of the people." To the framers, a republic that consisted of representative institutions was vastly superior to a democracy in which the people ruled directly—such as in ancient Greece, which the framers regarded as mob rule. However, the framers did not specifically define the elements of a republican government in Article IV, nor did they state which branch of the federal government was responsible for enforcing it.

The Supreme Court has consistently ruled that most issues raised under the Guarantee Clause are political questions that must be resolved by Congress, not the judicial branch. In *Luther v. Borden* (1849), the Court refused to decide which of two competing governments in Rhode Island was legitimately elected. Similarly, when Oregon adopted the initiative and referendum, elements of direct democracy, the Court declined in 1912 to declare these measures a violation of the Guarantee Clause. But constitutional scholar John Hart Ely has argued in his book *Democracy and Distrust* that the Guarantee Clause, rather than the Fourteenth Amendment, provides the best justification for legislative reapportionment under the principle of "one person, one vote."

Benjamin Franklin: The First American

Printer, inventor, and diplomat— Benjamin Franklin (1706–1790) embodied American genius. Of humble birth in Boston, Franklin was celebrated by European nobility as one of the greatest scientists of his age. "Doctor Franklin," as he became known in America, was the elder statesman who convinced France to finance the American Revolution. He also provided intellectual gravitas, and pithy wit, at the Constitutional Convention. Franklin helped create an American identity in 1754 by proposing the Albany Plan of Union, which extended far beyond previous regional plans for colonial cooperation. Franklin contrasted the weak and divided stance of the colonies with the success of the Iroquois Confederacy: "It would be a very strange thing if six nations of ignorant savages should be capable of forming a scheme for such an union, and be able to execute it in such a manner as that it has subsisted for ages, and appears indissoluble; and yet that a like union should be impracticable for ten or a dozen English colonies, to whom it is more necessary, and must be more advantageous." Although the Albany Plan of Union failed, Franklin nursed a nation into independence.

...and shall protect each of them against Invasion; and on Application of the Legislature, or of the Executive (when the Legislature cannot be convened), against domestic Violence.

A revolt of debt-ridden farmers and Revolutionary War veterans in western Massachusetts from the summer of 1786 to early 1787, known as Shays' Rebellion, remained fresh in the minds of many of the delegates at the Constitutional Convention. Thus, the framers included a provision in Article IV that the federal government would protect states against invasion or domestic violence, upon request. Another concern, particularly for southern delegates, was the possibility of slave revolts. From 1800 to 1831, there were four major slave rebellions. In 1800, a blacksmith named Gabriel led a march on Richmond. In 1811, a free Haitian and hundreds of slaves marched on New Orleans. Former slave Denmark Vesey plotted to capture Charleston, South Carolina, in 1822. The most notorious rebellion was led by Baptist preacher Nat Turner in Virginia in 1831, during which more than fifty whites were killed. All the rebellions ultimately failed and hundreds of slaves were executed. Federal authorities never intervened.

The rebellion of Nat Turner in 1831 caused great fear among southern whites.

ARTICLE V

The Congress, whenever two thirds of both Houses shall deem it necessary, shall propose Amendments to this Constitution, or, on the Application of the Legislatures of two thirds of the several States, shall call a Convention for proposing Amendments, which, in either Case, shall be valid to all Intents and Purposes, as Part of this Constitution, when ratified by the Legislatures of three fourths of the several States, or by Conventions in three fourths thereof, as the one or the other Mode of Ratification may be proposed by the Congress; Provided that no Amendment which may be made prior to the Year One thousand eight hundred and eight shall in any Manner affect the first and fourth Clauses in the Ninth Section of the first Article; and that no State, without its Consent, shall be deprived of its equal Suffrage in the Senate.

ARTICLE V: AMENDMENTS

O ne of the difficulties under the Articles of Confederation was that any amendments had to be approved unanimously by the states. That made change virtually impossible. Not a single amendment was ratified under the Articles. However, according to the Declaration of Independence, "it is the right of the people to alter or to abolish" a government that does not secure their rights. Through the amendment process, the Constitution made a bloody revolution less necessary because it made peaceful change possible. And without the promise that a bill of rights could be added under Article V, the states might not have ratified the Constitution at all.

The Congress, whenever two thirds of both Houses shall deem it necessary, shall propose Amendments to this Constitution, or, on the Application of the Legislatures of two thirds of the several States, shall call a Convention for proposing Amendments,...
There are two ways to propose constitutional amendments, but only one has ever been used. In all cases, Congress has passed a proposed amendment by a two-thirds vote of the members present—assuming a quorum—in both the House of Representatives and the Senate. The president's approval is not required. Under the second method, two-thirds

of the states must petition Congress to call a constitutional convention.

The framers wanted to provide the states an outlet in case Congress refused to consider a proposed amendment. However, many legal experts question whether a constitutional convention, once called, could be limited to a particular topic. They point to the 1787 Constitutional Convention–which created a new constitution instead of amending the Articles of Confederation–as an example. But other scholars respond that a constitutional convention only has the power to propose amendments; it is still up to the states to ratify such change.

Thomas Jefferson: To Secure These Rights

No one in the founding generation was more committed to individual rights than Thomas Jefferson (1743–1826). His Declaration of Independence asserted that all people were endowed with "certain unalienable rights." (Jefferson wrote "inalienable," but an error in transcription changed the phrase for posterity.) The very purpose of government, the Declaration continued, was "to secure these rights." Thus, Jefferson was deeply dismayed to learn that the new Constitution did not contain a bill of rights, and from his post in France as U.S. ambassador he lobbied James Madison to add one. Jefferson wrote Madison in 1787: "A bill of rights is what the people are entitled to against every government on earth." Like many of the founders, Jefferson owned slaves while at the same time proclaiming that "all men are created equal." This contradiction became one that the nation could not endure.

...which, in either Case, shall be valid to all Intents and Purposes, as Part of this Constitution, when ratified by the Legislatures of three fourths of the several States, or by Conventions in three fourths thereof, as the one or the other Mode of Ratification may be proposed by the Congress;...

Two methods are also prescribed for **ratification** of amendments. A proposed amendment becomes part of the Constitution when it is approved by the legislatures or ratifying conventions of three-fourths of the states. Congress determines which method of ratification shall be used. Only the Twenty-first Amendment, which repealed Prohibition, has been ratified by state conventions.

Other issues about ratification involve the timing of such decisions by the states. Beginning with the Eighteenth Amendment, Congress included in most proposed amendments a deadline by which states must ratify it. In *Dillon v. Gloss* (1921), the Supreme Court upheld the power of Congress to set such deadlines, although it is not specifically mentioned in Article V. However, the Court in that case also ruled that state ratifications should be contemporaneous with the proposed amendment. It specifically cited as no longer valid two amendments that had been submitted as part of the Bill of

ratification

approval of the U.S. Constitution or its amendments by state conventions or legislatures

The ERA failed to be ratified, although both first ladies Betty Ford and Rosalyn Carter supported it.

"I wish the Constitution which is offered had been made more perfect, but I sincerely believe it is the best that could be obtained at this time; and... a constitutional door is opened for amendment hereafter."

—George Washington

Rights in 1789 but failed ratification by enough states. One of those amendments, which prohibited a pay raise for Congress from taking effect before an intervening election, was ratified by the necessary thirty-eighth state in 1992. Despite the Supreme Court's previous ruling, both the executive branch and Congress certified the Twenty-seventh Amendment as valid–even though more than 200 years had passed since it was first ratified by a state.

A related issue is whether Congress can extend the deadline for ratification of an amendment. This issue arose with the Equal Rights Amendment (ERA), which contained a ratification deadline of seven years in its authorizing legislation–not in the actual amendment itself. Congress then extended the deadline by three years, by only a majority vote. A lower federal court struck down such action by Congress, but before the Supreme Court could rule on the issue the extended deadline expired without any additional state ratifications, making the question moot.

Some of the states that had ratified the ERA later tried to rescind their ratifications. Similarly, states had rescinded their ratifications of the Fourteenth Amendment, but Congress refused to recognize such actions. However, Congress did recognize a state that first rejected, then later approved, a constitutional amendment. In *Coleman v. Miller* (1939), the Supreme Court dealt with these issues, but inconclusively. The Court held that at least some of the issues around the ratification process are nonjusticiable–meaning that a court has no authority to review them. Generally, most scholars believe that Congress, and not the Court, should determine the validity of a state's ratification, that states may not rescind ratification, and that states may later approve an amendment even after they first disapproved it.

Provided that no Amendment which may be made prior to the Year One thousand eight hundred and eight shall in any Manner affect the first and fourth Clauses in the Ninth Section of the first Article; and that no State, without its Consent, shall be deprived of its equal Suffrage in the Senate.

There are three amendments that, under Article V, may not be added to the Constitution. The first two are related to slavery. Article V prohibits an amendment banning the slave trade before 1808, a power that Section 9 of Article I also denies to Congress. In addition, an amendment could not be passed before 1808 that changed limitations on direct or capitation taxes. Such taxes imposed a greater burden on slaveholders. The passage of time, as well as the Thirteenth and Sixteenth Amendments, have made these provisions in Article V moot.

However, one limitation remains. Under Article V, no amendment to the Constitution may deny a state of equal representation in the Senate. As the United States increases in population, this restriction becomes more controversial. For instance, as of the 2000 census, the most populous state, California, had about 34 million residents; the least populous state, Wyoming, had half a million. Nonetheless, both states receive two votes in the Senate. This disproportionate representation does not correspond with the principle of "one person, one vote" that the Supreme Court has applied to both houses of state legislatures and to the U.S. House of Representatives. Yet Article V prohibits an amendment to make the Senate more representative of population. Many citizens believe that it is important to preserve the role of the states in American government, thus creating a system of federalism that is unique to the United States.

Congress passed an amendment banning child labor in 1924, but it failed ratification.

But in his book *The Frozen Republic: How the Constitution is Paralyzing Democracy,* Daniel Lazare advocates a scenario in which California threatens to leave the Union in order to make U.S. government more democratic.

Lazare asserts that "We the People" have the ultimate amending power under the Constitution and–just like the framers in 1787–can change a form of government that no longer works.

Similarly, Akhil Reed Amar of Yale Law School believes that the amending process in Article V applies only to governmental bodies, such as the Congress and state legislatures, not the people themselves. He maintains that the Constitution reserves to the people, acting directly, the right to pass amendments through a national initiative process, by a simple majority vote.

Some scholars also argue that there are inherent limits in the amendment process, not specifically spelled out in Article V. For instance, political scientist Walter F. Murphy of Princeton claims that judges should be able to refuse to enforce an amendment, such as one legalizing racial discrimination, that contradicts other basic constitutional values. However, the Supreme Court has consistently refused to recognize any limits on the content of constitutional amendments. Other scholars believe that the Constitution has been informally amended through Supreme Court decisions and major historical events such as the Civil War and the Great Depression.

Almost Amendments

More than 11,000 constitutional amendments have been introduced in Congress since 1789. Of these, only thirty–three received the necessary two-thirds vote and were submitted to the states for ratification. Six of those have never been ratified:

Reapportionment Amendment (1789). As the U.S. population grew, this amendment would have allowed Congress to decide on the number of members in the House of Representatives, provided that the House was not smaller than two hundred members and not larger than one representative for every fifty thousand persons.

Titles of Nobility Amendment (1810). In addition to Article I's ban on titles of nobility for federal officials, this amendment would have stripped U.S. citizenship from any person who accepted such titles from foreign powers without the consent of Congress.

Corwin Amendment (1861). An attempt to avert the Civil War, this amendment—not opposed by incoming President Abraham Lincoln—would have irrevocably prevented Congress from interfering with a state's "domestic institutions," including slavery.

Child Labor Amendment (1924). Seeking to overturn a Supreme Court ruling, this amendment would have given Congress the power to limit and regulate child labor, which the Court later upheld in 1941.

Equal Rights Amendment (1972). This amendment would have prevented federal and state governments from denying men and women "equality of rights under the law."

D.C. Voting Rights Amendment (1978). In addition to repealing the Twenty-third Amendment, this amendment would have treated the District of Columbia as a state for the purposes of congressional representation, electoral votes, and amending the Constitution.

Article V makes the amending process difficult but not impossible. The framers were concerned that the Constitution be open to change, but not subject to the whims of a simple majority like an ordinary law. In *Federalist* 43, James Madison sets forth the balance that the framers sought to achieve in Article V: "It guards equally against that extreme facility, which would render the Constitution too mutable; and that extreme difficulty, which might perpetuate its discovered faults."

Keep Pace with the Times *Thomas Jefferson*

In an 1816 letter to a friend, Thomas Jefferson warned that constitutions must be amended in order to advance with the progress of human knowledge.

Some men look at constitutions with sanctimonious reverence, and deem them like the ark of the covenant, too sacred to be touched. They ascribe to men of the preceding age a wisdom more than human, and suppose what they did to be beyond amendment. I knew that age well; I belonged to it, and labored with it.... But I know also, that laws and institutions must go hand in hand with the progress of the human mind. As that becomes more developed, more enlightened, as new discoveries are made, new truths disclosed, and manners and opinions change with the change in circumstances, institutions must advance also, and keep pace with the times. We might as well require a man to wear still the coat which fitted him when a boy, as civilized society to remain ever under the regimen of their barbarous ancestors.

ARTICLE VI

All Debts contracted and Engagements entered into, before the Adoption of this Constitution, shall be as valid against the United States under this Constitution, as under the Confederation.

This Constitution, and the Laws of the United States which shall be made in Pursuance thereof; and all Treaties made, or which shall be made, under the Authority of the United States, shall be the supreme Law of the Land; and the Judges in every State shall be bound thereby, any Thing in the Constitution or Laws of any State to the Contrary notwithstanding.

The Senators and Representatives before mentioned, and the Members of the several State Legislatures, and all executive and judicial Officers, both of the United States and of the several States, shall be bound by Oath or Affirmation, to support this Constitution; but no religious Test shall ever be required as a Qualification to any Office or public Trust under the United States.

ARTICLE VI: THE SUPREME LAW OF THE LAND

federalism

a political system in which power is shared between the national and state governments

According to Article VI, the Constitution and laws of the United States are "the supreme law of the land." Both state and federal officials, including judges, must take an oath to support the Constitution, even if state law contradicts it. Unlike the Articles of Confederation, the Constitution trumps state power. However, the Constitution also protects the powers of the states in many ways. This system of **federalism,** in which the national and state governments share power, is a key feature of American government. Article VI also guarantees a measure of religious freedom by banning religious tests for public office.

All Debts contracted and Engagements entered into, before the Adoption of this Constitution, shall be as valid against the United States under this Constitution, as under the Confederation.
The framers did not want to in effect declare bankruptcy by creating a new government. Therefore, they included a provision in the Constitution to assure creditors that any debts incurred by the national government under

the Articles of Confederation would be honored under the Constitution. These Revolutionary War debts were considerable. In addition, many individual states still owed substantial sums for war expenses. After the Constitution went into effect, Alexander Hamilton made an agreement with Thomas Jefferson that the national government would assume the war debts of the states in exchange for locating the national capital on the Potomac River.

This Constitution, and the Laws of the United States which shall be made in Pursuance thereof; and all Treaties made, or which shall be made, under the Authority of the United States, shall be the supreme Law of the Land; and the Judges in every State shall be bound thereby, any Thing in the Constitution or Laws of any State to the Contrary notwithstanding.

This provision in Article VI is known as the Supremacy Clause. It establishes the Constitution, federal statutes, and U.S. treaties as "the supreme law of the land." The Constitution is the highest form of law in the American legal system. State judges are required to uphold the U.S. Constitution, even if state laws or constitutions conflict with it.

Treaties must comply with the Constitution. However, the treatymaking power of the U.S. government is broader than the lawmaking power of Congress. The Supreme Court ruled in *Missouri v. Holland* (1920) that

James Madison: The Father of the Constitution

Of great modesty and short stature, James Madison (1751–1836) was easily overlooked. But his philosophical mind and practical political sense made him indispensable to the infant nation. Madison's Virginia Plan, which he wisely asked Governor Edmund Randolph to introduce, became the foundation of the new Constitution devised at the Constitutional Convention in 1787. Yet Madison avoided praise for his creation. He wrote a friend in 1834: "You give me a credit to which I have no claim in calling me 'the writer of the Constitution of the U.S.' This was not like the fabled goddess of wisdom the offspring of a single brain. It ought to be regarded as the work of many heads and many hands." Perhaps Madison's greatest achievement was drafting the Bill of Rights and shepherding it through the First Congress, despite his belief that it was unnecessary. When Madison died in 1836, he was the last surviving delegate to the Constitutional Convention and, according to Madison's wishes, his notes of the convention proceedings were only to be published posthumously.

James Madison served as the fourth U.S. president.

pursuant to a treaty with Great Britain, the United States could regulate the hunting of migratory birds, even though Congress had no independent authority to pass such legislation.

The Senators and Representatives before mentioned, and the Members of the several State Legislatures, and all executive and judicial Officers, both of the United States and of the several States, shall be bound by Oath or Affirmation, to support this Constitution; but no religious Test shall ever be required as a Qualification to any Office or public Trust under the United States.

All state and federal officials must swear to uphold the Constitution. Some scholars argue that this requirement in Article VI gives Congress, the president, and the Supreme Court an equal power to interpret the Constitution. Members of the military and naturalized citizens must take an oath to defend the Constitution, but native-born civilians do not.

Article VI also bans religious tests for public office in the federal government. This was one of the few provisions in the original Constitution that protected civil liberties. During the ratification debates, some opponents of the Constitution argued that belief in God should be a requirement for office seekers. The Supreme Court extended the ban on religious tests to state governments, holding that they violated freedom of religion under the First Amendment, in *Torcaso v. Watkins* (1961).

Where All Religious Societies Are on an Equal Footing *Jonas Phillips*

Philadelphia merchant Jonas Phillips, a Jewish leader and Revolutionary War veteran, wrote a letter to the Constitutional Convention delegates in 1787 opposing religious tests for public office, although the public had not yet been told about the new Constitution.

I the subscriber being one of the people called Jews of the city of Philadelphia, a people scattered and dispersed among all nations, do behold with concern that among the laws in the Constitution of Pennsylvania there is a clause, sect. 10 to viz— I do acknowledge the scriptures of the old and new testament to be given by a divine inspiration. To swear and believe that the new testament was given by divine inspiration is absolutely against the religious principle of a Jew, and is against his conscience to take any such oath. By the above law a Jew is deprived of holding any public office or place of government.…

It is well known among all the citizens of the 13 united states that the Jews have been true and faithful Whigs, and during the late contest with England they have been foremost in aiding and assisting the states with their lives and fortunes, they have supported the cause, have bravely fought and bled for liberty which they cannot enjoy. Therefore if the honorable Convention shall in their wisdom think fit and alter the said oath…then the Israelites will think themselves happy to live under a government where all religious societies are on an equal footing.…

ARTICLE VII

The Ratification of the Conventions of nine States, shall be sufficient for the Establishment of this Constitution between the States so ratifying the Same.

Done in Convention by the Unanimous Consent of the States present the Seventeenth Day of September in the Year of our Lord one thousand seven hundred and Eighty seven and of the Independence of the United States of America the Twelfth In witness whereof We have hereunto subscribed our Names,

G°. Washington
Presidt and deputy from Virginia

Delaware
Geo: Read
Gunning Bedford jun
John Dickinson
Richard Bassett
Jaco: Broom

Maryland
James McHenry
Dan of St Thos. Jenifer
Danl. Carroll

Virginia
John Blair—
James Madison Jr.

North Carolina
Wm. Blount
Richd. Dobbs Spaight
Hu Williamson

South Carolina
J. Rutledge
Charles Cotesworth
Pinckney
Charles Pinckney
Pierce Butler

Georgia
William Few
Abr Baldwin

New Hampshire
John Langdon
Nicholas Gilman

Massachusetts
Nathaniel Gorham
Rufus King

Connecticut
Wm. Saml. Johnson
Roger Sherman

New York
Alexander Hamilton

New Jersey
Wil: Livingston
David Brearley
Wm. Paterson
Jona: Dayton

Pennsylvania
B Franklin
Thomas Mifflin
Robt. Morris
Geo. Clymer
Thos. FitzSimons
Jared Ingersoll
James Wilson
Gouv Morris

Attest William Jackson Secretary

ARTICLE VII: RATIFICATION

When the framers signed the Constitution on September 17, 1787, they still faced the arduous task of persuading the American people to agree with them. And the framers did not even agree among themselves. Only thirty-nine of the fifty-five delegates who attended the Constitutional Convention signed the final version of the Constitution. The nation quickly divided into two factions: the Federalists, who supported ratification of the Constitution, and the Antifederalists, who opposed it. Eventually the Federalists prevailed, once they had promised Americans that a bill of rights would be added to the Constitution as soon as the new Congress convened.

The Ratification of the Conventions of nine States, shall be sufficient for the Establishment of this Constitution between the States so ratifying the Same.

The framers specified that the Constitution would take effect when nine of the thirteen states ratified it. Under the Articles of Confederation, all the states had to approve before its provisions went into operation–which took four years, even during wartime. The framers wanted to ensure that a few holdout states–such as Rhode Island, which refused to send delegates to the Constitutional Convention–could not prevent the others from moving forward. Technically, this provision of the Constitution was illegal. The Articles of Confederation lawfully remained in effect unless all the states agreed to change it. But the new Constitution allowed a different form of government to usurp the Articles with only nine states approving. James Madison referred to this contradiction in *Federalist* 40 as the "most plausible" objection to the work of the convention, but few opponents of the Constitution raised it.

The framers also stipulated that ratification would not be done by the state legislatures, but by state conventions especially chosen for that purpose. Americans intensely debated the provisions of the new Constitution, filling newspapers with letters written under classical pseudonyms–as was the custom of the day. A series of eighty-five newspaper articles published under the pen name "Publius" greatly influenced the ratification debates in New York. Known collectively as *The Federalist Papers,* these essays were written mainly by James Madison and Alexander Hamilton, both delegates to the Constitutional Convention. *The Federalist Papers* have become the leading source of information about the intentions of the framers of the Constitution.

But the Constitution had eloquent critics as well. One of the most prominent was Richard Henry Lee of Virginia, who argued that supporters of the Constitution were abandoning the spirit of the American revolution. He wrote in 1788:

> It will be considered, I believe, as a most extraordinary epoch in the history of mankind, that in a few years there should be so essential a change in the minds of men. 'Tis really astonishing that the same people, who have just emerged from a long and cruel war in defence of liberty, should now agree to fix an elective despotism upon themselves and their posterity.

Even Daniel Carroll, who signed the Constitution as a delegate from Maryland, criticized the document as "the Continental Congress in two volumes instead of one."

"We must all rise or fall together."
—John Hancock

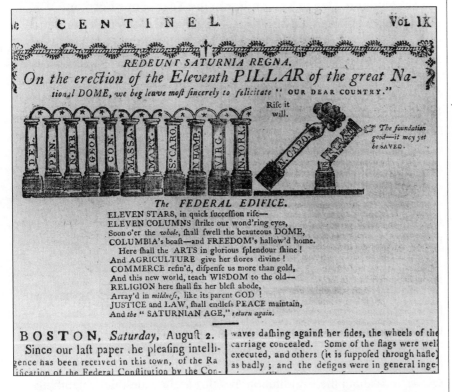

This drawing celebrates the ratification of the Constitution by eleven states, shown in order from left to right. North Carolina finally ratified the Constitution on November 21, 1789; Rhode Island ratified it on May 29, 1790.

The chief stumbling block to the Constitution became its lack of a bill of rights. Some states considered calling a new constitutional convention to remedy the problem. Of course, a second convention could easily throw out the work of the first, just as the framers had abandoned the Articles of Confederation. Consequently, the Federalists promised that the first Congress would add a bill of rights—even though they thought it was

> "To say...
> that a bad
> government
> must be
> established for
> fear of anarchy,
> is really saying
> that we must
> kill ourselves
> for fear of dying."
> —Richard Henry Lee

unnecessary because the Constitution created a government of limited powers. The question then became whether states would wait to ratify the Constitution until such a bill of rights was proposed. This created a chicken-and-the-egg dilemma: if enough states did not ratify with only the promise of subsequent amendments, the Constitution would not go into effect.

Delaware ratified the Constitution first, on December 7, 1787. New Hampshire became the necessary ninth state to ratify on June 21, 1788. However, even with nine states, the new union could not succeed without the participation of the large states of Virginia and New York. Virginia ratified the Constitution on June 25, 1788, and New York approved it on July 26, 1788. The Constitution took effect with the convening of the new Congress in March 1789.

Done in Convention by the Unanimous Consent of the States present the Seventeenth Day of September in the Year of our Lord one thousand seven hundred and Eighty seven and of the Independence of the United States of America the Twelfth In witness whereof We have hereunto subscribed our Names,

> "The truth
> is...that the
> Constitution is
> itself, in every
> rational sense,
> and to every
> useful purpose, a
> bill of rights."
> —Alexander
> Hamilton

G°. Washington
Presidt and deputy from Virginia

Several prominent delegates to the Constitutional Convention refused to support the final version of the Constitution. Edmund Randolph, governor of Virginia, had presented the Virginia Plan during the convention—which proposed that the Articles of Confederation be abandoned and a new constitution drafted instead. But he declined to endorse the end result. George Mason, author of the Virginia Declaration of Rights, also opposed the Constitution, principally because it lacked a bill of rights. Mason said that he would "sooner chop off his right hand than put it to the Constitution as it now stands."

Hoping to find a compromise, Benjamin Franklin suggested that the final wording of the Constitution read: "done in convention by the unanimous consent of the *states* present." That way, delegates could still sign the document as witnesses to the action of the convention, despite their individual objections. Franklin pointed out that he himself had reservations about the Constitution, but that as the oldest delegate, there had been many occasions in his life where he was certain he was right, then later changed his mind.

Nonetheless, three of the delegates still present—Randolph, Mason, and Elbridge Gerry of Massachusetts—did not sign. George Washington signed first, as president of the convention. The next day, he wrote the Marquis de Lafayette, referring to the new Constitution:

It is now a child of fortune, to be fostered by some and buffeted by others. What will be the general opinion on, or the reception of it, is not for me to decide, nor shall I say any thing for or against it: if it be good I suppose it will work its way good; if bad, it will recoil on the framers.

However, Washington did write letters to friends—knowing that these were seldom kept private—supporting the Constitution as the best effort that could be obtained at the time. Without Washington in the crucial role as president of the convention, even more Americans would have viewed the Constitution as a naked grab for power.

As it was, the outcome of the convention had been in doubt because it met in secrecy. The day after the convention ended, a Philadelphia matron queried Benjamin Franklin: "What have we got, a republic or a monarchy?" "A republic," answered Franklin, "if you can keep it."

> **"Our new Constitution is now established, and has an appearance that promises permanency; but in this world nothing can be said to be certain, except death and taxes."**
> —Benjamin Franklin

Though Every Other Blessing May Expire *Mercy Otis Warren*

Writing as "A Columbian Patriot" in 1788, Mercy Otis Warren opposed the ratification of the new Constitution by Massachusetts without the addition of a bill of rights.

The proposed constitution appears contradictory to the first principles which ought to govern mankind…. The very suggestion, that we ought to trust to the precarious hope of amendments and redress, after we have voluntarily fixed the shackles on our own necks should have awakened to a double degree of caution….

But it is a republican principle that the majority should rule; and if a spirit of moderation could be cultivated on both sides, till the voice of the people at large could be fairly heard it should be held sacred.—And if, on such a scrutiny, the proposed constitution should appear repugnant to their character and wishes…[w]ho would then have the effrontery to say, it ought not to be thrown out with indignation, however some respectable names have appeared to support it.—But if after all, on a dispassionate and fair discussion, the people generally give their voice for a voluntary dereliction of their privileges, let every individual who chooses the active scenes of life, strive to support the peace and unanimity of his country, though every other blessing may expire.

PART II:

AMENDMENTS TO THE CONSTITUTION OF THE UNITED STATES

A s George Washington predicted, the American people began the process of amending the Constitution almost as soon as its ink dried. These amendments were added in clusters. The first ten amendments, ratified in 1791, became known as the Bill of Rights. They protected the individual liberties that many Americans feared would be weakened under the new Constitution. Amendments Eleven and Twelve, which were adopted soon after the Bill of Rights, solved problems regarding state sovereignty and the electoral college that became apparent once the Constitution went into practice.

After a sixty-year gap came the Civil War Amendments, which radically transformed American society—freeing the slaves, securing equal protection of the laws, and extending suffrage to black men. Then after another forty years were added the amendments of the Progressive Era—the income tax, direct election of senators, Prohibition, and suffrage for women. Only two amendments—ending lame duck sessions and repealing Prohibition—were enacted during the traumatic years of the Great Depression and World War II. Since 1950, most amendments have focused on voting—limiting presidential terms, allowing residents of the District of Columbia to participate in presidential elections, banning the poll tax, and extending the vote to eighteen-year-olds. Two other amendments dealt with presidential disability and congressional pay raises.

Congress sent each state a copy of the Bill of Rights, with twelve proposed amendments. One was never ratified; another finally became the Twenty-seventh Amendment in 1992.

Considering its age, the U.S. Constitution has relatively few amendments—which is probably part of its success. For a constitution to have staying power, it must be above ordinary law, and therefore beyond the reach of mere majorities. Yet a constitution also must be flexible enough to adapt to crises without becoming obsolete. It is a difficult balance to maintain, as the failure of other constitutions demonstrates.

AMENDMENT I

Congress shall make no law respecting an establishment of religion, or prohibiting the free exercise thereof; or abridging the freedom of speech, or of the press; or the right of the people peaceably to assemble, and to petition the Government for a redress of grievances.

THE FIRST AMENDMENT: FREEDOM OF EXPRESSION

Some people say the rights protected by the First Amendment are the most important in the entire Bill of Rights, because they are listed before the other nine amendments. However, in the original version of the Bill of Rights, what is now the First Amendment came third–after proposed amendments on reapportionment and congressional pay raises. The states failed to ratify these amendments, moving the third amendment into first place.

Whatever its order in the original Bill of Rights, the First Amendment includes the rights many Americans hold most dear, and it forms the foundation of American democratic government. The five freedoms listed in the First Amendment–religion, speech, press, assembly, and petition–enable citizens to participate in the process of self-government. Together, these five rights are sometimes referred to as freedom of expression. Because the First Amendment protects the expression of deep convictions, it can also expose deep differences among the American people. Thus, the First Amendment is often at the center of the nation's most contentious debates. Without the freedoms in the First Amendment, it would be impossible for Americans to assert any other rights they have, thus making it the most important amendment in the Bill of Rights.

Congress shall make no law...

This first phrase in the First Amendment has several implications. By specifically referring to Congress, the Bill of Rights limits only the government or its agents, not private parties. This requirement that the government be involved in any claim under the Constitution or the Bill of Rights is known as **state action.** For example, freedom of speech does not protect employees of private companies who criticize their supervisors.

state action

the requirement that government or its agents must be involved in order for the Constitution or the Bill of Rights to apply

incorporation

process by which the Supreme Court applied the Bill of Rights to the states via the Fourteenth Amendment

Hugo Black was a U.S. senator when appointed to the Supreme Court.

"No law means no law—without any ifs, buts, or whereases."

—Justice Hugo Black

In addition, the Supreme Court held in *Barron v. Baltimore* (1833) that the word "Congress" as used in the First Amendment meant that the Bill of Rights restricted only the national government, not the states. The Court began to extend certain provisions of the Bill of Rights to the states in 1897 via the Fourteenth Amendment, a process known as **incorporation.**

Although the First Amendment says that Congress shall make "no law" regarding the freedoms it contains, the Supreme Court has ruled that almost all rights have limitations. Justice Hugo Black, however, believed that First Amendment rights were absolute. Yet the Court has held that the only unlimited right is the freedom to believe in abstract ideas—such as the Holy Trinity or communism. However, the government may regulate certain actions that embody those ideas.

…respecting an establishment of religion, or prohibiting the free exercise thereof;…

This portion of the First Amendment protects freedom of religion. It consists of two parts: the Establishment Clause and the Free Exercise Clause. The Establishment Clause prohibits the government from creating an official or established church, preferring one religion over another, or benefiting believers instead of nonbelievers. The Free Exercise Clause prohibits the government from interfering with the expression of religious beliefs. Sometimes these two clauses conflict, and it is difficult for the government to avoid an establishment of religion while at the same time protecting its free exercise.

Religious Liberty in Early America. In colonial America, established churches were the norm. Although many colonists had come to America to escape persecution from the established Church of England, they did not hesitate to create their own government-backed churches in the New World. The Puritan or Congregational Church became the official religion in the New England colonies, and the Church of England or Anglican Church was established in the southern colonies. The government compelled citizens of all faiths to support the established church through taxes. In addition, the established church punished sins as crimes. Colonists were forced to go to church on Sundays and could be whipped for failing to know religious doctrines.

In New England, Quakers—or the Society of Friends—were executed for their faith, and in southern colonies Baptists were required to be licensed in order to preach. Four colonies—Delaware, New Jersey, Pennsylvania, and Rhode Island—did not create established churches. Other colonies, such as Maryland, practiced "toleration" for differing beliefs, but they did not protect the full civil rights of all faiths. As George

Washington wrote to a Jewish synagogue in 1790, toleration implied the unacceptable premise that "it was by the indulgence of one class of people that another enjoyed the exercise of their natural rights."

After the Revolutionary War, more Americans clamored for freedom of religion. In 1786, Virginia passed a law to protect religious liberty—the most extensive at that time. Drafted by Thomas Jefferson, the Virginia Statute for Religious Freedom proclaimed that "all men shall be free to profess...their opinions in matters of religion, and that the same shall in nowise diminish, enlarge, or affect their civil capacities." No longer could Virginians be denied the right to vote or hold public office because of their religious beliefs.

This same principle would be included in the U.S. Constitution in 1787. Article VI forbade religious tests for federal offices, one of the few protections of individual liberties specified in the original Constitution. Nonetheless, several states believed that additional protections for religious liberty were needed, and they advocated such amendments during their ratification of the Constitution. James Madison drew on these proposals when he introduced his draft of the Bill of Rights after the First Congress convened in 1789.

This statue of Mary Dyer stands near the Massachusetts statehouse. She was hanged in Boston in 1660 for her Quaker beliefs. In her words, "My life not availeth me in comparison to the liberty of the Truth."

The Establishment Clause. The first part of the First Amendment's protection of freedom of religion is known as the Establishment Clause. It declares that Congress shall make no law "respecting an establishment of religion." Americans continue to disagree about what constitutes an establishment of religion. Accommodationists believe that the government must make allowances for the significant role that religion plays in American life. Separationists argue that the Constitution prohibits any mingling of church and state.

Baptists played a critical role in the early development of the separation of church and state in America. After Thomas Jefferson was elected president, the Danbury Baptist Association in Connecticut wrote him a letter protesting the fact that in their state "religion is considered as the first object of legislation." Jefferson replied in 1802 that the First Amendment prohibited the U.S. Congress from taking such action, "thus building a wall of separation between church and state."

The Supreme Court quoted Jefferson's metaphor in *Everson v. Board of Education* (1947). In that case, the Court for the first time incorporated the

> "It does me no injury for my neighbor to say there are twenty gods, or no god. It neither picks my pocket nor breaks my leg."
>
> —Thomas Jefferson

Establishment Clause to apply to the states—opening the door to a plethora of church-state cases. The Court outlined the prohibitions of the Establishment Clause as follows:

> Neither a state nor the federal government can set up a church. Neither can pass laws which aid one religion, aid all religions, or prefer one religion over another. Neither can force…a person to go to or to remain away from church against his will, or force him to profess a belief or disbelief in any religion.

Although the Supreme Court in *Everson* cited Jefferson's phrase of "a wall of separation between church and state," those words do not actually appear in the First Amendment. However, neither does the Constitution refer to the terms "God," "Creator," or "Divine Providence," unlike the Declaration of Independence. In addition to *Everson,* the Supreme Court has used a variety of legal tests regarding Establishment Clause issues. Chief Justice William Rehnquist has long objected to the "wall of separation" doctrine, and the Rehnquist Court has generally taken a more accommodationist view of church-state issues.

Brother Waller and the Parson *John Williams*

In his journal for May 1771, John Williams of Virginia described how a posse including an Anglican priest and a county sheriff beat an unlicensed Baptist preacher, Brother Waller, while he was leading worship.

Brother Waller informed us…[that] about two weeks ago on the Sabbath day down in Caroline County he introduced the worship of God by singing.… While he was singing, the parson of the parish would keep running the end of his horsewhip in [Waller's] mouth, laying his whip across the hymn book, etc. When done singing, [Waller] proceeded to prayer. In it he was violently jerked off of the stage, [they] caught him by the back part of the neck, beat his head against the ground, sometimes up, sometimes down. They carried him through a gate that stood some considerable distance, where [the sheriff] gave him…twenty lashes with his horse whip.… Then Brother Waller was released, went back singing praise to God, mounted the stage, and preached with a great deal of liberty.

Religion and Education. By far most Establishment Clause cases are about religion in the schools. Before taxes supported general public education, schools were largely run by churches. Many Americans became accustomed to sectarian values being part of the local curriculum—often to the disadvantage of religious minorities. But because public schools today are agents of the state, religious activity in them raises Establishment Clauses issues. So does public aid to private religious schools.

Vouchers. One form of government aid to religious schools is through vouchers, which allow parents to pay tuition at private schools using public funds. Supporters of vouchers charge that the public schools are failing low-income, minority students, and that vouchers are one way to improve student performance by increasing competition for tax dollars spent on education. Voucher advocates maintain that just as students may use government funds to attend religious colleges, parents should also have the choice of using tax dollars for tuition at private schools. Critics of vouchers believe that government funding of parochial schools violates the Establishment Clause, because such programs would directly fund religious instruction–a more crucial component of primary and secondary education at parochial schools than at religious colleges. Furthermore, critics charge, such programs would eviscerate the public schools, which must serve all students regardless of income or learning disabilities

In *Zelman v. Simmons-Harris* (2002), the Supreme Court ruled that a voucher system established in Cleveland, Ohio for poor children in failing schools did not violate the Establishment Clause. The Court held that a voucher program is constitutional if it is "neutral with respect to religion and provides assistance directly to a broad class of citizens," who then select religious schools out of a "genuine and independent private choice." The dissenting justices argued that using tax dollars to pay for religious indoctrination could never be "neutral" regarding religion.

Evolution. State laws governing how evolution is taught in the public schools also raises Establishment Clause questions. Some Americans believe the scientific theory of evolution conflicts with the biblical version of creation. In 1925, legendary lawyer Clarence Darrow unsuccessfully defended John Scopes against a charge of violating Tennessee law by teaching evolution. The state supreme court overturned Scopes's conviction, and the U.S. Supreme Court never ruled in his case. For the first time, the Supreme Court struck down a state law banning the teaching of evolution in *Epperson v. Arkansas* (1968). The Court also ruled in *Edwards v. Aguillard* (1987) that a Louisiana law mandating the teaching of biblical "creation science" along with the theory of evolution violated the Establishment Clause.

Equal Access. In 1984, Congress passed the Equal Access Act. It required that public high schools receiving government funds allow student groups to meet, regardless of their religious or political content–if the school allowed noncurricular clubs in general. The Supreme Court held that this law did not violate the Establishment Clause in *Westside Community Schools v. Mergens* (1990). Wrote Justice Sandra Day O'Connor: "There is a crucial difference between government speech endorsing religion, which the Establishment Clause forbids, and private speech endorsing religion, which the Free Speech and Free Exercise Clauses protect."

The Supreme Court extended this rationale regarding freedom of speech for religious groups in *Lamb's Chapel v. Center Moriches Union Free School District* (1993). In that case, the Court upheld the right of adult religious groups to use school facilities after hours, if other nonschool groups are allowed to meet. And in *Good News Club v. Milford Central School* (2001), the Court ruled that after-school religious groups involving young students must be allowed to meet on the same basis as nonreligious groups.

School Prayer. Perhaps the most controversial issue involving the Establishment Clause is prayer in the public schools. The Supreme Court ruled in *Engel v. Vitale* (1962) that official prayer in public schools violated the Establishment Clause, even if students were not forced to participate in such prayers. In that case, the New York State Board of Regents had composed a prayer to begin each school day: "Almighty God, we acknowledge our dependence upon Thee, and we beg Thy blessings upon us, our parents, our teachers, and our Country." But the Court held that "in this country it is no part of the business of government to compose official prayers for any group of the American people to recite as a part of a religious program carried on by government."

The next year, in *Abington School District v. Schempp* (1963), the Supreme Court also overturned a Pennsylvania law mandating that each school day open with the Lord's prayer and Bible readings. However, in *Wallace v. Jaffree* (1985), the Court indicated that an official "moment of silence" could pass constitutional muster if instituted with a secular purpose. Nonetheless, the Court struck down the Alabama law at issue in that case because its legislative history demonstrated that the state "intended to characterize prayer as a favored practice."

The Supreme Court also ruled in *Lee v. Weisman* (1992) that official prayers at graduation ceremonies in public schools were unconstitutional. Moreover, in *Santa Fe Independent School District v. Doe* (2000), the Court held that a high school's policy allowing students to vote on speakers before football games, and encouraging invocations, was public rather than private speech. In such cases, said the Court, the religious nature of the speech violated the Establishment Clause.

The Supreme Court has never outlawed voluntary prayer by individual students. But the Court has prohibited the public schools from sponsoring religious activity. The Court has even held that the study of religion or the Bible can be included in public school instruction, as long as it is carried out in a secular manner. Nonetheless, many Americans support a constitutional amendment that would allow official prayer in the public schools.

Religion in the Public Square. Besides education, the Establishment Clause also affects the role of religion in public life. In general, the Supreme

> "Too often, public school prayer is used by people to signal who is culturally in charge."
>
> — Fred Gedicks, Brigham Young University

William Murray: My Life Without God

Son of famed atheist Madalyn Murray O'Hair, William Murray was the plaintiff in a 1963 Supreme Court ruling that Bible readings in the Baltimore public schools were unconstitutional. In his autobiography, *My Life Without God,* Murray describes a troubled childhood during which his mother tried to defect to the Soviet Union with her two sons. As a middle-aged adult, struggling with divorce and alcoholism, Murray became a born-again Christian and

evangelist in 1980. He renounced his mother's atheism and advocated the return of official prayer to the public schools. In 1995, Madalyn Murray O'Hair disappeared, along with her son Jon and granddaughter Robin. Their murdered bodies were discovered in 2001.

Madalyn Murray O'Hair attended the hearing of her Supreme Court case in 1963 with sons William (left) and Jon (right).

Court has been more willing to allow religious expression in public settings when the impressionable nature of schoolchildren is not involved. Thus, the Court ruled in *Marsh v. Chambers* (1983) that prayers to open daily legislative sessions, even with government-funded chaplains, are constitutional. Noting the historical roots of such opening prayers, the Court argued that adult legislators were not subject to peer pressure or religious indoctrination.

State-sponsored holiday displays also raise Establishment Clause issues. During the winter, many local governments erect decorations celebrating Christmas, a Christian holiday, and Hanukkah, a Jewish holiday. The Supreme Court upheld such displays in *Lynch v. Donnelly* (1984), as long as they included secular symbols of the season as well as religious ones. This "two reindeer rule," as critics described it, led many municipalities to add Santa Claus and his sleigh to their holiday decorations. However, private groups have the right to place religious displays on public property, on a nondiscriminatory basis with other groups. In *Capitol Square Review v. Pinette* (1995), the Supreme Court allowed the Ku Klux Klan to display a cross on a public square near the state capitol of Ohio.

When Government Aids Religion. Another issue is at what point government regulations that benefit religion violate the Establishment Clause. Regarding tax exemption of religious property and contributions, the Supreme Court ruled in *Walz v. Tax Commission* (1970) that such exemptions were permissible because other nonreligious charitable and educational organizations also were tax exempt. The Supreme Court also upheld Sunday closing laws, or "blue laws," in *McGowan v. Maryland* (1961) because they served a secular purpose by establishing a uniform day of rest.

The Free Exercise Clause. The second part of the First Amendment's protection of freedom of religion is known as the Free Exercise Clause. It prevents Congress from "prohibiting the free exercise" of religion. The Establishment Clause limits government policies that help religion, whereas the Free Exercise Clause restricts government actions that hurt religion. In general, a person has an absolute right to freedom of religious belief; however, the government can regulate the actions a person takes to express those beliefs. Today, most Free Exercise cases do not involve laws that directly discriminate against a specific denomination, but rather general laws that have a negative impact upon a particular religious group.

Polygamy. The Supreme Court dealt with the Free Exercise Clause for the first time in *Reynolds v. United States* (1879). Federal law prohibited polygamy in the territory of Utah, but Reynolds claimed the law interfered with his right to exercise his Mormon faith. The Court upheld Reynolds's conviction, ruling that the Free Exercise Clause did not apply to acts that were "violations of social duties or subversive of good order." Some sects of Mormons still practice polygamy or "plural marriage."

Four of Tom Green's five wives testify at his 2001 trial in Utah. Green, an excommunicated Mormon, was convicted of bigamy.

Solicitation. The Court incorporated the Free Exercise Clause to apply to the states in *Cantwell v. Connecticut* (1940). In that case, the Supreme Court ruled that the Free Exercise Clause "embraces two concepts–freedom to believe and freedom to act. The first is absolute but, in the nature of things, the second cannot be." Still, the Court struck down a Connecticut law that mandated licenses for religious solicitors. A key tenet of Cantwell's faith as a Jehovah's Witness was zealous proselytizing. Jehovah's Witnesses were so active in civil liberties cases that from 1938 to 1946, their faith was the subject of twenty-three Supreme Court decisions.

Saluting the Flag. Jehovah's Witnesses also believed that pledging allegiance to the flag was a form of idolatry forbidden by the Ten Commandments. The U.S. flag salute during the 1930s involved an extended arm movement similar to the Nazi gesture of "Heil Hitler," as Jehovah's Witnesses pointed out. Many German Witnesses were executed by the Nazis for their beliefs, such as refusing to give the Hitler salute. Nonetheless, school districts in numerous American communities passed regulations that permanently suspended any students who failed to salute the flag, including Jehovah's Witness children. In *Minersville School District v. Gobitis* (1940), the Supreme Court upheld such flag-salute laws against the free exercise claims of Jehovah's Witnesses, ruling that religious liberty must give way to political authority.

After World War II, the flag salute changed from head salute followed by outstretched arm to hand over heart.

But several justices publicly changed their minds about the decision, particularly after it precipitated the worst religious violence in the United States in decades. In 1940 alone, more than 1,500 Witnesses were assaulted in 335 different attacks—including a castration in Nebraska. Only three years after *Gobitis,* while America was fighting World War II, the Supreme Court reversed itself in *West Virginia State Board of Education v. Barnette* (1943). That case also involved Jehovah's Witness schoolchildren.

Justice Robert H. Jackson's majority opinion in *Barnette* made clear that the compulsory flag salute laws violated not only free exercise of religion but also free speech: "If there is any fixed star in our constitutional constellation, it is that no official, high or petty, can prescribe what shall be orthodox in politics, nationalism, religion, or other matters of opinion or force citizens to confess by word or act their faith therein." Justice Jackson also emphasized that the Bill of Rights was designed to protect the rights of unpopular minorities:

> The very purpose of a Bill of Rights was to withdraw certain subjects from the vicissitudes of political controversy, to place them beyond the reach of majorities and officials, and to establish them as legal principles to be applied by the courts. One's right to life, liberty, and property, to free speech, a free press, freedom of worship and assembly, and

"I think the Jehovah's Witnesses ought to have an endowment in view of the aid which they give in solving the legal problems of civil liberties."

—Justice Harlan Fiske Stone

other fundamental rights may not be submitted to vote; they depend on the outcome of no elections.

A Compelling Interest. For many years, the Supreme Court ruled on free exercise claims using a particular legal test. First, the Court would decide if the religious beliefs at issue were sincere, although they did not need to be factually correct. "Men may believe what they cannot prove," said the Court in *United States v. Ballard* (1944). Next, the Court would normally require the government to show a "compelling interest"–a very high legal standard–for keeping a policy that burdened a religious practice.

Using this test, the Court struck down a variety of laws as unconstitutional under the Free Exercise Clause. In two cases involving Seventh-Day Adventists, the Supreme Court held that people who quit jobs that conflict with their religious beliefs are entitled to unemployment benefits. And in *Wisconsin v. Yoder* (1972), the Court ruled that the Amish did not have to comply with a compulsory school attendance law beyond the eighth grade. However, the Supreme Court did require the Amish to pay social security taxes, despite their belief in self-sufficiency, in *United States v. Lee* (1982). The Court also ruled in *Bob Jones University v. United States* (1983) that private religious schools may be denied tax-exempt status if they discriminate based on race. In *Goldman v. Weinberger* (1986), the Court upheld military rules prohibiting nonregulation headgear, despite a Jewish officer's request to wear a yarmulke on duty.

The Supreme Court significantly modified its "compelling interest" test for free exercise cases in *Employment Division v. Smith* (1990). In that case, Al Smith, a member of the Klamath tribe, was fired from his job as a substance abuse counselor for using peyote, a hallucinogenic cactus, as part of a religious ceremony. Smith argued that his taking peyote during a Native American ritual was no different than a Catholic alcoholism counselor receiving wine at communion. Smith was denied unemployment benefits because Oregon law prohibited the use of peyote. The Supreme Court ruled in *Smith* that when a criminal law was at issue, the government did not have to prove a compelling interest, unless the law specifically targeted certain religious groups.

A wide variety of religious organizations have criticized the *Smith* decision for unfairly penalizing minority religions. Congress enacted the Religious Freedom Restoration Act (RFRA) in 1993 to reinstate the compelling interest test in all free exercise cases. However, the Supreme Court declared RFRA unconstitutional in 1997, saying that Congress had exceeded its authority.

To the White Man's Altar *Garrett Epps*

In his book, To an Unknown God, *Garrett Epps describes a peyote ceremony held in Al Smith's honor after his Supreme Court case had been decided.*

The staff passed from hand to hand as old friends talked about Al Smith. First was June [Smith's wife].... She told his children yet again how their father had stood fast and how Stanley Smart [a medicine man] had been the one Indian elder to

counsel him to take the case to the white man's altar of justice and determine once and for all whether the Constitution was big enough to include peyote as well as bread and wine....

One speaker told of his vision of Al Smith as a culture hero. Such a hero is not a warrior who goes forth seeking enemies to kill. A real hero, said the speaker, is one who seeks only to make life—to nurture a family, to pass on knowledge to

those who will come after. But when the battle comes uninvited to his doorstep, the hero does not turn away. Others may warn him that he cannot win or that he should not win or that he is too unimportant to fight the giant with only his five smooth stones [the story of David and Goliath]. But the hero knows that no good comes from running away. He calls for water to wash his face, then stands to fight.

...or abridging the freedom of speech,...

Democracy is very difficult without freedom of speech. Unless there is a free exchange of opinions and ideas, the people do not have the information they need for effective self-government. Some legal scholars believe that the First Amendment only protects the political speech necessary to democratic government. Others argue that the right of self-expression–through art, literature, advertising, and even bad taste–makes a society truly free. Another free speech issue is whether the First Amendment safeguards spoken words alone, or also includes symbolic speech such as flag burning. Freedom of speech is not unlimited, and the Supreme Court has restricted expression such as obscenity and defamation.

Free Speech in American History. The first written protection of free speech in America was the Massachusetts Body of Liberties in 1641. This document was a great step forward from the English charters of liberty because neither the Magna Carta in 1215, nor later the English Bill of Rights in 1689, included freedom of speech or the press. After the American Revolution, the newly independent states formed constitutions, several of which mentioned freedom of speech. However, only three states added freedom of speech to their list of proposed amendments when ratifying the U.S. Constitution.

Only seven years after the First Amendment was approved in 1791, the nation erupted in a controversy over the extent of free speech. Under English law, the mere act of criticizing the government was a form of treason known as **sedition.** During a period of intense political rivalry, President John Adams and his Federalist allies in Congress enacted the Sedition Act of 1798, which essentially outlawed criticism of the U.S. government. The

> **"Jazz music is freedom of expression with a groove."**
>
> —Wynton Marsalis

sedition
the act of inciting people to change the government

law was enforced primarily against Adams's political opponents, Thomas Jefferson and his Democratic-Republican Party. The first person convicted under the act was Rep. Matthew Lyon of Vermont, who won reelection to Congress from his jail cell. Lyon had accused Adams of "an unbounded thirst for ridiculous pomp, foolish adulation, and selfish avarice." Another man was fined for making a derogatory comment about Adams's rear end.

Although truth was technically a defense against sedition in American law, colorful metaphors were difficult to prove factually before the Federalist-dominated judiciary. Consequently, the Democratic-Republicans never challenged the Sedition Act before the Supreme Court. Instead, Jefferson and James Madison wrote the Virginia and Kentucky Resolutions, which asserted that states had the power to declare laws like the Sedition Act unconstitutional. With the help of the unpopular Sedition Act, Jefferson and his party won both the presidency and Congress in the election of 1800. The Sedition Act expired in 1801, and not until 1917 was another national sedition law passed.

However, state and local governments limited free speech in several ways between 1800 and 1917. During this time, the First Amendment did not apply to the states. Southern states censored the mail throughout the antebellum period to keep out abolitionist materials. Proslavery legislators also prevented Congress from hearing petitions opposing slavery. After the

To Defend the Bill of Rights *Elizabeth Gurley Flynn*

Cities often banned public speaking on street corners during the early 1900s in order to stop union organizing. The Industrial Workers of the World, or Wobblies, led many free speech fights in the West to oppose these laws. Elizabeth Gurley Flynn helped organize such a protest in Missoula, Montana, in 1908.

We sent out a call to all "footloose rebels to come at once—to defend the Bill of Rights." A steady stream of I.W.W. members began to flock in by freight cars…. As soon as one speaker was arrested, another took his place….

There were some humorous aspects to our efforts. Not all

the I.W.W. workers were speakers. Some suffered from stage fright. We gave them copies of the Bill of Rights and the Declaration of Independence. They would read along slowly, with one eye hopefully on the cop, fearful that they would finish before he would arrest. One such was being escorted to jail, about two blocks away, when a couple of drunks got into a pitched battle. The cop dropped him to arrest them. When they arrived at the jail, the big strapping I.W.W. was tagging along behind. The cop said in surprise: "What are you doing here?" The prisoner retorted: "What do you want me to do—go back there and make another speech?"

Flynn was imprisoned for being a member of the Communist Party during the 1950s.

Civil War, the labor movement led the battle for free speech. Using permit systems, local governments closed streets and public parks to labor activists. Labor unions also claimed that picket lines for striking workers were protected speech, but businesses regarded them as coercive action. Courts often issued injunctions to prevent strikes.

During World War I, Congress passed another sedition law to restrict criticism of the war. The Espionage Act of 1917 prohibited any interference with the draft, as well as "any disloyal, profane, scurrilous, or abusive language about the form of government of the United States." The federal government convicted more than two thousand people of violating the Espionage Act. Many of them appealed their convictions to the Supreme Court, and for the first time in its history the Court ruled on free speech issues. In *Schenck v. United States* (1919), the Supreme Court held that the Espionage Act did not violate the First Amendment. With that case, the Court began a long process of answering two questions: what is free speech, and what are its limitations?

What Is Free Speech? The Supreme Court has repeatedly ruled that freedom of speech consists not only of spoken words but also other types of expression. The Court categorizes free speech activities as either **pure speech,** such as debates and public meetings that involve spoken words alone, or **speech-plus,** such as demonstrations and picketing that combine speech with action. Pure speech receives the highest form of First Amendment protection; government may regulate the action components of speech-plus. In *Thornhill v. Alabama* (1940), the Supreme Court ruled that nonviolent picketing is included in freedom of speech.

Symbolic Speech. Another type of speech is **symbolic speech.** Also known as "expressive conduct," symbolic speech consists of actions that are themselves a message, without spoken words. Some examples of symbolic speech are burning a draft card and burning an American flag. The Supreme Court has treated these two examples very differently.

In *United States v. O'Brien* (1968), the Court ruled that burning a draft card was not protected by the First Amendment, even though intended as a form of protest against the Vietnam War. The Court held that the government had a valid purpose in punishing the destruction of draft cards, which were necessary to raise and support an army. The goal of the government's action was to maintain the draft, not prevent dissent, said the Court.

But in *Texas v. Johnson* (1989), the Supreme Court ruled that burning the U.S. flag was protected by the First Amendment. The Court struck down a Texas law that prohibited the desecration of the American flag in a way "the actor knows will seriously offend" other people. Gregory Lee

pure speech

speech that involves only spoken words, without actions

speech-plus

speech that combines spoken words with action, such as demonstrations and picketing

symbolic speech

actions that are themselves a message, without spoken words; also known as "expressive conduct"

Protesters burn a flag at the Democratic National Convention in 2000.

"The flag is a special symbol for our country, but it is certainly no more than the Constitution itself."

—Rep. Jim Kolbe

"Joey" Johnson had burned a flag outside the 1984 Republican National Convention in Dallas as part of a political demonstration. The Court held that "government may not prohibit the expression of an idea simply because society finds the idea itself offensive or disagreeable."

To counteract the Court's decision, Congress passed the Flag Protection Act of 1989. That law prohibited flag desecration regardless of whether bystanders were offended. Nonetheless, in *United States v. Eichman* (1990), the Court held that the law violated the First Amendment because it punished any person "who knowingly mutilates, defaces, physically defiles,… or tramples upon any flag." Such terms, the Court said, outlawed disrespect for the flag, not the physical destruction of it. The Court noted that burning is the proper way to dispose of a tattered flag. Thus, argued the Court, the Flag Protection Act was punishing a person for the reason he burned the flag, which violated freedom of speech. Congress has repeatedly attempted to pass a constitutional amendment to outlaw flag desecration since the

Joey Johnson: An Exploiter's Vision of Freedom

Flag-burner Joey Johnson compared his Supreme Court case to a slam-dunk in basketball. Said Johnson: "It was a chance to really go up in the enemy's face and express enormous contempt for their system and their holy symbol— the American flag and the whole empire it presides over." A member of the Revolutionary Communist Youth Brigade, Johnson has referred to the Constitution as "an exploiter's vision of freedom." He argued that the First Amendment protects media conglomerates, not individual citizens. "My point was not to wrap myself in the First Amendment or the Constitution," he said. "The First Amendment is as much about the rights of property as it is the rights of individuals."

Eichman decision in 1990. As of 2002, all fifty states had passed resolutions saying they would ratify such an amendment if Congress passed it.

Public Forums. One of the concepts most fundamental to freedom of speech is the **public forum,** a venue such as a street or public park that is normally open to free speech activities. In such places, the government cannot ban the right to freedom of expression, although it can regulate the "time, place, and manner" of such speech. These regulations must be "content neutral" and cannot discriminate based on the nature of the message being expressed. For example, the government can prohibit amplified speech in public parks after dark, but it cannot make the rule apply only to antiabortion activists.

public forum
a place such as a public park or street that is normally open to First Amendment activities

The Right Not to Speak. The government cannot compel a person to speak. The Supreme Court upheld this principle in *West Virginia State Board of Education v. Barnette* (1943), ruling that Jehovah's Witness children could not be expelled from school for refusing to salute the flag. In another case involving a Jehovah's Witness, *Wooley v. Maynard* (1977), the Court held that citizens do not have to become "mobile billboards" for the state. Maynard was arrested for repeatedly covering up the words "Live Free or Die" on his automobile's license plate. Maynard argued that the New Hampshire motto violated his religious beliefs about salvation.

"Purging money from politics is like trying to stop water rushing downhill. Dam one stream and another quickly forms."
—Paul Gigot,
Wall Street Journal

Campaign Finance Laws. The Supreme Court ruled in *Buckley v. Valeo* (1976) that in political campaigns "money is speech" protected by the First Amendment. In that case, the Court struck down campaign finance laws that restricted how much an individual could spend on behalf of a candidate through independent expenditures. However, the Court upheld limits on direct contributions to the candidate's campaign, ruling that large donations could give the appearance of corruption.

Greater Power for Wealthy Candidates Senator Mitch McConnell

A vigorous opponent of restrictions on "soft money," or campaign contributions to political parties, Senator Mitch McConnell (R-Ky.) argues that such laws violate the First Amendment and undermine democracy.

The parties are vital institutions in our democracy, smoothing ideological edges and promoting citizen participation.... If special interests cannot give to parties as they have, they will use their money to influence elections in other ways: placing unlimited, unregulated, and undisclosed issue advertisements; mounting their own get-out-the-vote efforts; forming their own action groups....

The power of special interests will not be deterred or diminished. Their speech, political activity, and right to "petition the government for a redress of grievances" (that is, to lobby) are protected by the First Amendment. Political spending will not be reduced; it will just not flow through the parties.

Do we really want the two-party system, which has served us so well, to be weakened in favor of greater power for wealthy candidates and single-issue groups? [Soft money limits] will not take any money out of politics. It just takes the parties out of politics.

No True Free Speech *Doris "Granny D" Haddock*

A retired shoe-factory worker and great-grandmother, ninety-year-old Doris "Granny D" Haddock walked 3,200 miles to advocate campaign finance reform. Her fourteen-month trek from Los Angeles to the nation's capital concluded on February 29, 2000.

In my long walk, I am trying to get some new laws passed that will make it easier for people to be responsible for their own communities and their own government. I worry that the influence of very rich companies and very rich people make it difficult for regular people to feel they are in charge of their own affairs. We need to get the big, special interest contributions out of our elections. Those contributions shout down you and me, and there is no true free speech nor true political equality so long as this condition persists....

A flood of special interest money has carried away our own representatives, and all that is left of them—at least for those of us who do not write $100,000 checks—are the shadows of their cardboard cutouts. If you doubt it, write a letter to them and see what rubber stamp drivel you get back. For all we know, they might all have died ten years ago and the same letters continue to be sent out.

Haddock supported the campaign finance bill Congress passed in 2002.

> **"As long as we live in a democracy, there is one basic truth that gives me hope: the chairman of Exxon has the same number of votes as you or I—one."**
>
> —Michael Moore, author

Some critics of the Court's decision argue that campaign expenditures are property, not speech, and can be regulated by the government. Others believe that the First Amendment fully protects both contributions and expenditures–and a candidate should be punished only for actual corruption, not implied corruption. During the 1999–2000 election cycle, congressional candidates spent more than one billion dollars, according to the Federal Election Commission–the largest amount in its twenty-five-year history. Advocates of campaign finance reform want to curtail the unlimited "soft money" that can now be donated to political parties, which they say evades the purpose of the restrictions on "hard money" contributions directly to political candidates. Opponents of campaign finance laws argue that the very purpose of the First Amendment is to protect political speech as fully as possible. And, they add, limits on individual contributions merely give incumbents and wealthy candidates an unfair advantage in elections.

What Are the Limits of Free Speech? Certain categories of speech are not protected at all by the First Amendment. These include obscenity, defamation, fighting words, and speech that incites illegal action. Other categories of speech–such as speech in schools–are covered by the First Amendment, but in a limited manner.

Obscenity. The Supreme Court has had difficulty developing a legal definition for **obscenity,** which in general is speech or action that portrays sex or nudity in a manner contrary to societal standards of decency. In *Miller v. California* (1973), the Court held that speech or conduct was obscene if it met all three of the following guidelines:

1. "whether the average person, applying contemporary community standards, would find that the work, taken as a whole, appeals to the prurient [obsessively sexual] interest;"
2. "whether the work depicts or describes, in a patently offensive way, sexual conduct specifically defined by the applicable state law;" and
3. "whether the work, taken as a whole, lacks serious artistic, political, or scientific value."

The standards for obscenity are the only criteria regarding the First Amendment that vary from community to community, rather than a uniform national standard. For instance, under the First Amendment, flag burning must be allowed in every state. However, Chief Justice Warren Burger wrote in his majority opinion in Miller: "It is neither realistic nor constitutionally sound to read the First Amendment as requiring that the people of Maine or Mississippi accept public depiction of conduct found tolerable in Las Vegas, or New York City."

Speech can be "indecent" without being legally obscene. The Supreme Court has struck down several laws that attempt to regulate indecent but not obscene speech. In *Reno v. American Civil Liberties Union* (1997), the Court held that the federal Communications Decency Act violated the First Amendment. Congress had passed the law in 1996 in order to keep children from accessing indecent material via the Internet. But the Court ruled that the law was vague and overbroad, thereby unconstitutionally limiting adults' free speech. And in *Ashcroft v. Free Speech Coalition* (2002), the Supreme Court also struck down the

obscenity

speech or action that portrays sex or nudity contrary to societal standards of decency

"I know it when I see it." —Justice Potter Stewart, on hard-core pornography

Attorney General John Ashcroft appears in front of The Spirit of Justice, *a statue at the Justice Department auditorium. In 2002, the department erected a screen in front of the statue to avoid pictures such as this one.*

defamation

hurting a person's reputation by spreading falsehoods

slander

defamation using spoken words

libel

defamation using written words

fighting words

abusive and insulting comments delivered face-to-face to a specific individual

"**Governments that begin by burning books end up by burning people.**"

—Alan Dershowitz

Child Pornography Prevention Act of 1996, which made it illegal to produce or possess "virtual" child pornography that is created by computer images but does not involve actual children.

Defamation. The First Amendment does not protect **defamation,** or hurting another person's reputation by spreading falsehoods. Defamation using spoken words is **slander;** defamation using written words is **libel.** A person cannot prove defamation if the statements at issue are true. Lawsuits alleging defamation can exercise a chilling effect on free speech. Therefore, in cases involving public officials and public figures, the Supreme Court has erected very high thresholds for defamation. Such cases are usually brought against the print or broadcast media, so they are discussed in greater depth under freedom of the press.

Fighting Words. Another type of speech that is not protected by the First Amendment is known as **fighting words,** abusive and insulting comments delivered face-to-face to a specific individual. In *Chaplinsky v. New Hampshire* (1942), the Supreme Court upheld the conviction of Chaplinsky, a Jehovah's Witness, for calling a police officer "a damn Fascist and a racketeer." Such "fighting words," the Court said, "have a direct tendency to cause acts of violence."

Hate speech. Some legal scholars maintain that racial and ethnic slurs are a type of "fighting words" that should be included among limitations on free speech, just like slander and libel. Certain colleges and cities have enacted "hate speech" codes that prohibit derogatory remarks on the basis of religion, gender, sexual orientation, or race. Critics of the codes charge that enforcing "politically correct" speech does not end bigotry. They argue that such codes punish any speech that hurts someone's feelings.

In *R.A.V. v. St. Paul* (1992), the Supreme Court struck down a city ordinance in St. Paul, Minnesota, that prohibited the use of certain symbols "that arouse anger, alarm, or resentment in others on the basis of race, color, creed, religion, or gender." The statute applied to both public and private property. A white juvenile, R.A.V., was convicted under the statute for burning a cross in the yard of a black family. The Supreme Court overturned the conviction because the St. Paul law punished speech based on its content, but the Court noted that R.A.V. could be prosecuted for arson instead. However, in *Wisconsin v. Mitchell* (1993), the Supreme Court upheld a law that increased the penalties for "hate crimes" committed due to such factors as the victim's race, religion, or sexual orientation. An assault was not expressive conduct under the First Amendment, said the Court, and different motives often lead to increased punishment in the criminal law.

Speech That Incites Illegal Action. Through a long line of cases, the Supreme Court has developed a standard for when speech that advocates unlawful action is not protected by the First Amendment. Originally, in *Schenck v. United States* (1919), the Court ruled that speech that creates a "clear and present danger" of illegal acts was not covered by the First Amendment. In that case, the Court upheld the conviction of Schenck under the Espionage Act for distributing pamphlets that encouraged young men to resist the draft during World War I.

In the 1950s, the Court ruled on several laws designed to prohibit membership in the Communist Party. Congress passed the Smith Act in 1940, which outlawed advocating the violent overthrow of the U.S. government. The Supreme Court upheld the Smith Act under the First Amendment in *Dennis v. United States* (1951), but in *Yates v. United States* (1957) the Court ruled that the law did not prohibit advocacy of violent revolution as an abstract idea, rather than as a specific action.

Finally, in *Brandenburg v. Ohio* (1969), the Court articulated its current standard for punishing speech that incites illegal action. Such action must be "imminent," said the Court, and probable. Thus, the Supreme Court ruled that a Ku Klux Klan leader's cry at a rally for members to violently oppose civil rights laws was protected speech. However, a specific call to bomb churches at a designated place and time would not be.

Speech in Schools. Students do not have the same free speech rights as adults. However, the Supreme Court ruled in *Tinker v. Des Moines School District* (1969) that neither students nor teachers "shed their constitutional rights to freedom of speech or expression at the schoolhouse gate." In that case, thirteen-year-old Mary Beth Tinker and her older brother John wore

> **"Free speech is intended to protect the controversial and even outrageous word; and not just comforting platitudes too mundane to need protection."**
>
> —General Colin Powell

The Nastiest Word in the English Language *Randall Kennedy*

Harvard Law professor Randall Kennedy, an African American, examines the history of a hateful epithet in his book Nigger: The Strange Career of a Troublesome Word. *Kennedy concludes that censorship is not the appropriate response.*

Why does *nigger* generate such powerful reactions? Is it a more hurtful racial epithet than insults such as *kike, wop, wetback, mick, chink,* and *gook*? Am I wrongfully offending the sensibilities of readers right now by spelling out *nigger* instead of using a euphemism such as *N-word*? Should blacks be able to use *nigger* in ways forbidden to others?…

Protecting foul, disgusting, hateful, unpopular speech against government censorship is a great achievement of American political culture…. There is much to be gained by allowing people of all backgrounds to yank *nigger* away from white supremacists, to subvert its ugliest denotation, and to convert the N-word from a negative into a positive appellation. This process is already well under way, led in the main by African American innovators who are taming, civilizing, and transmuting "the filthiest, dirtiest, nastiest word in the English language" [according to O. J. Simpson prosecutor Christopher Darden]. For bad and good, *nigger* is thus destined to remain with us for many years to come—a reminder of the ironies and dilemmas, the tragedies and glories, of the American experience.

censorship

government control of free expression

seditious libel

printing criticism of the government

black armbands to school as a protest of the Vietnam War. They were both suspended, but the Supreme Court ruled that their actions were symbolic speech protected by the First Amendment. However, the Court excluded any student speech that would "materially and substantially disrupt" the classroom.

Similarly, in *Bethel School District v. Fraser* (1986), the Supreme Court ruled that school officials could discipline a student for making a sexually suggestive speech, even though it was not technically obscene. And in *Hazelwood School District v. Kuhlmeier* (1988), the Court distinguished between "school-sponsored expressive activities" and speech by individual students. The Court held that in activities such as student newspapers and class plays, school officials could exercise a legitimate editorial function that was consistent with their educational mission.

...or of the press;...

Originally, freedom of the press referred to the printed word alone, such as books and newspapers. But today broadcast media are also included, although they receive less protection under the First Amendment than printed matter. Yet despite the changing nature of the media, freedom of the press has involved a constant struggle between the government and the people over access to information.

American Roots of a Free Press. Governments have always exercised **censorship,** the official control of free expression. But with the invention of movable type by Johann Gutenberg in the fifteenth century came a rapid increase in printed materials. Now, kings and churches devised lists of banned books and pamphlets. In England, Henry VIII required that books be licensed before they could be published, and his daughter Elizabeth I ordered that all written works must be submitted to official censors for prior approval. The press was also licensed in England's colonies in North America. One of the most contentious doctrines was **seditious libel,** under which a printer could be punished for publishing criticism of the government. Such criticism, said the crown, led to revolution and social unrest. Truth was no defense, because accurate criticism would provoke the greatest upheaval.

But in 1735, the trial of John Peter Zenger for seditious libel planted the first roots of a free press in America. Zenger was a German immigrant whose English was limited. The printer of the *New York Weekly Journal,* Zenger served as the front for several wealthy lawyers who wrote anonymous articles criticizing the royal governor. When Zenger was jailed for seditious libel, his wife, Anna, kept the newspaper going. Although threatened with a death sentence, Zenger refused to reveal the names of his writers. Zenger's attorney argued that truth should be a defense for seditious libel, and an American jury refused to convict Zenger.

Zenger's acquittal brought an end to most prosecutions for seditious libel in America. However, licensing continued under the colonial legislatures. After the Revolutionary War, Virginia was the first state to include freedom of the press in its constitution. During the ratification debates on the Constitution, more states recommended including freedom of the press than free speech in a proposed Bill of Rights. Indeed, Thomas Jefferson wrote: "Were it left to me to decide whether we should have a government without newspapers, or newspapers without a government, I should not hesitate a moment to prefer the latter."

Prior Restraint. The bedrock principle of a free press is that, absent great exigencies, the government may not censor a work before it is published—a practice known as **prior restraint.** However, the government can punish authors or editors after publication. In *Near v. Minnesota* (1931), the Supreme Court incorporated freedom of the press to apply to the states, holding that a Minnesota law authorizing prior restraints violated the First Amendment. The Court held that merely because "miscreant purveyors of scandal" could abuse freedom of the press did not lessen the prohibitions on prior restraint. The Court did say that prior restraint might be justified in cases of national security, such as preventing the publication of troop movements during wartime.

That standard was at issue in *New York Times v. United States* (1971), which involved the publication of the Pentagon Papers, a secret analysis of the causes of the Vietnam War. A former Pentagon employee, Daniel Ellsberg, illegally leaked the documents to the *New York Times* and the *Washington Post,* which both published excerpts. A federal court issued an injunction prohibiting further publication, the first time in American history that the U.S. government had obtained a prior restraint. But the Supreme Court ruled that the government had not proven that the Pentagon Papers would endanger national security.

The burden against prior restraint is so great that the Supreme Court has held that it is not overcome even by a defendant's right to a fair trial. In *Nebraska Press Association v. Stuart* (1976), the Court struck down a judge's gag order barring the media from covering certain details of a murder trial. Instead, the Court held that judges must take other steps to guarantee a fair trial despite pretrial publicity, such as sequestering the jury or changing the venue of the trial.

"Censorship... remains the strongest drive in human nature, with sex a weak second."
—Nat Hentoff

"The press was to serve the governed, not the governors."
—Justice Hugo Black

prior restraint
censoring a work before it is published

"I thought I would probably go to prison for the rest of my life."
—Daniel Ellsberg

To Destroy a Newspaper *Katharine Graham*

In her autobiography Personal History, *Katharine Graham describes how she made the fateful decision to publish the Pentagon Papers, which endangered the first public offering of Washington Post Company stock.*

At this point, Ben [Bradlee, the executive editor] and the editors got on various extensions at Ben's house. I asked them what the big rush was, suggesting we at least think about this for a day. No, Ben said, it was important to keep up the momentum of publication and not to let a day intervene after getting the story. He also stressed that by this time the grapevine knew we had the Pentagon Papers. Journalists inside and outside were watching us.

I could tell from the passion of the editors' views that we were in for big trouble on the editorial floor if we didn't publish. I well remember Phil Geyelin's [editorial page editor] response when I said that deciding to publish could destroy the paper. "Yes," he agreed, "but there's more than one way to destroy a newspaper."

Graham celebrates her victory in the Pentagon Papers case.

Libel. Another way that freedom of the press can be limited is through laws that make libel easy to prove. Fearing lawsuits, the press censors itself. In *New York Times v. Sullivan* (1964), the Supreme Court set a new standard that made libel very difficult to prove for public officials. Civil rights leaders had purchased an advertisement in the *New York Times* charging that the police in Montgomery, Alabama, abused African Americans. Police commissioner L. B. Sullivan sued the *Times* for libel because several details in the ad were incorrect, and he won the largest libel judgment ever awarded in Alabama.

The Supreme Court unanimously overturned the Alabama jury's verdict. The Court said that in order to protect robust public debate, criticism of public officials deserved a wide berth. Therefore, mere errors of fact, or even carelessness in publishing the errors, was not enough to justify a libel suit by a public official. Instead, said the Court, the official must prove that a newspaper printed the error with **actual malice,** meaning "with knowledge that it was false or with reckless disregard of whether it was false or not." The Supreme Court later applied this standard for libel to public figures as well as public officials.

In his book about the *Sullivan* case, *New York Times* columnist Anthony Lewis noted that by 1964 public officials in the South had filed libel lawsuits of almost $300 million against the media. "The aim was to discourage not false but true accounts of life under a system of white supremacy," wrote Lewis. He added: "Commissioner Sullivan's real target was the role of the American press as an agent of democratic change."

> **"The First Amendment rocks."**
>
> —Oprah Winfrey, on winning a libel lawsuit

actual malice

knowledge that a statement is false or reckless disregard of whether it is false

Nonprint Media. Although freedom of the press is not limited to the printed word, other forms of media do not receive as much protection under the First Amendment. The Supreme Court has ruled that broadcast media, which use the public airwaves, can be regulated by the federal government in ways that newspapers cannot be. But improved technology and expanded channels decreased the government's regulatory role. Cable television, which uses private wires instead of public airwaves, is a hybrid under the first Amendment; it receives more protection than broadcast media but less than print media. In 1997, the Supreme Court upheld a "must-carry" law requiring cable companies to reserve certain channels for network broadcast stations at no cost.

…or the right of the people peaceably to assemble, and to petition the Government for a redress of grievances.

The freedoms of assembly and petition have been linked both in history and in Supreme Court decisions. During the first century after the Bill of Rights was ratified, the right to petition overshadowed the right to assembly, but later on they reversed roles. In fact, fewer court decisions deal with freedom of petition than any other part of the First Amendment.

Historical Background. In England, the Magna Carta of 1215 was the work of noblemen who forced King John to address their petitions for changes in his practices. Later, the English Parliament would not appropriate funds for the king unless he answered its petitions. The English Bill of Rights gave all subjects the right to petition in 1689. One of the reasons listed in the Declaration of Independence for the American Revolution is that King George III failed to hear petitions from the colonies. After the war, several of the states protected assembly and petition in their new constitutions. When the U.S. Bill of Rights was being drafted, some members of Congress argued that freedom of assembly should be deleted because it was too trivial. However, another representative maintained that without freedom of assembly, every other right in the Bill of Rights could be taken away.

Peaceable Assembly. The Supreme Court incorporated freedom of assembly to apply to the states in *DeJonge v. Oregon* (1937). However, the assembly must be peaceful; citizens may not riot or block public streets. The Court held in *Cox v. New Hampshire* (1941) that governments may restrict the time, place, and manner of assemblies, just as with free speech, but such regulations cannot be used as a pretext to prevent free assemblies. In *Hague v. CIO* (1939), the Court ruled that the mayor of Jersey City, New Jersey, was using a permit system to prevent union organizing by the

> **"Only people with the world's most free and open press and the greatest cornucopia of media outlets in the history of the planet could feel so comfortable trashing the entire enterprise."**
>
> —Anna Quindlen

Committee for Industrial Organization (CIO). However, in *Lloyd Corporation v. Tanner* (1972), the Supreme Court held that freedom of assembly does not apply in shopping malls because they are privately owned.

Sometimes a disruptive bystander tries to stop a peaceful assembly by exercising a **heckler's veto.** By provoking violence, such onlookers encourage police to end the demonstration. In *Feiner v. New York* (1951), the Supreme Court upheld the actions of police to end an inflammatory speech by Feiner, which the Court regarded as an incitement to riot. But in *Gregory v. Chicago* (1969), the Court set aside the conviction of comedian Dick Gregory for disorderly conduct during a civil rights march in an all-white neighborhood. The Court ruled that the police should have done more to protect the marchers.

Freedom of Association. Although it is not specifically listed in the First Amendment, freedom of association is nonetheless protected by the Supreme Court. Some legal scholars argue that it is implied by other rights in the First Amendment such as the freedoms of assembly and petition. In *NAACP v. Alabama* (1958), the Court first recognized freedom of association, overturning a law that required civil rights organizations to turn over their membership lists. The Court also ruled in 1967 that state loyalty oaths forcing teachers to declare they were not members of the Communist Party violated the First Amendment.

Groups that exclude members based on their gender or sexual orientation also claim protection by the First Amendment. In 1995, the Supreme Court held that a privately sponsored St. Patrick's Day parade can exclude homosexual groups whose viewpoint they oppose. And in *Boy Scouts v. Dale* (2000), the Court upheld the First Amendment right of the Boy Scouts to prevent gay men from becoming scoutmasters.

heckler's veto

ability of a hostile bystander to end a peaceful assembly

"Every time I hear those words I say to myself, 'That man is a Red, that man is a Communist.' You never hear a real American talk like that."

—Frank Hague, on free speech

AMENDMENT II

A well regulated Militia, being necessary to the security of a free State, the right of the people to keep and bear Arms, shall not be infringed.

THE SECOND AMENDMENT: THE RIGHT TO BEAR ARMS

The American Revolution was fought by minutemen, ready with their guns at a moment's notice. Early Americans believed that a militia, composed of citizen-soldiers, was a better safeguard of their liberties than a standing or permanent army. Today the militia consists of the National Guard, drilling in state units. Does the Second Amendment protect only the right of the states to have militias, or does it give individuals a right to bear arms for self-defense as well as national defense? That question is at the heart of the debate over the Second Amendment and gun control.

A well regulated Militia, being necessary to the security of a free State,...

The Second Amendment is the only part of the Bill of Rights that has a introductory clause defining its purpose. Because a **militia** is "necessary to the security of a free state," the amendment says, "the right of the people to keep and bear arms shall not be infringed." Some legal scholars interpret the first clause of the Second Amendment as giving the people the right to bear arms only as part of a "well regulated militia." To these scholars, such a militia would be today's National Guard, which is the modern-day successor to the minutemen of the colonial period. Other scholars emphasize that a militia, at the time of the adoption of the Bill of Rights, consisted of "the body of the people," as affirmed in several of the state resolutions proposing that a bill of rights be added to the Constitution.

During the colonial period, Americans came to despise the British use of a **standing army,** a permanent force of professional soldiers. Americans preferred the part-time citizen soldiers of a militia, whose roots in the

"The framers recognized that self-government requires the people's access to bullets as well as ballots."
—Akhil Reed Amar

militia
part-time citizen soldiers who defend their communities in emergencies

standing army
a permanent army of professional soldiers

A minuteman was an elite militia member trained to have his gun ready at a moment's notice.

"We the People or We the Sheeple?... 'Baaaaa' or 'Freedom!'"

—Ted Nugent, on gun rights

community would make them less likely to oppress their neighbors. Under the militia system, all free adult males were required to own arms and ammunition and to "muster" or assemble periodically for training.

...the right of the people to keep and bear Arms, shall not be infringed. This second part of the Second Amendment says that the right to bear arms belongs to "the people." Supporters of an individual right to bear arms, rather than the collective right of a state to have a militia, point out that the phrase "the people" also appears in the First, Fourth, and Ninth Amendments. These rights apply to individuals not states, they argue, and so does the Second Amendment. Since law professor Sanford Levinson's article in 1989, "The Embarrassing Second Amendment," more and more constitutional scholars have been affirming some sort of an individual right to bear arms.

As of 2002, the Supreme Court had not yet ruled definitively on whether the Second Amendment protects an individual or collective right to bear arms. In *United States v. Miller* (1939), the Court upheld the

Our First Freedom *Charlton Heston*

Longtime president of the National Rifle Association, actor and activist Charlton Heston believes that the right to bear arms makes all other rights possible.

As the Roman orator Cicero put it two thousand years ago, "There exists a law, not written down anywhere but inborn in our hearts; a law that comes to us not by training or custom or reading but from nature itself.... That, if our lives are endangered, any and every method of protecting ourselves is morally right."

It's no coincidence that the American Revolution was sparked by British troops attempting to seize the colonists' arms at Lexington and Concord. No less than the urban single mother of today, who lives behind barred windows where the police fear

At a National Rifle Association convention, Charlton Heston proclaims that his gun would have to be pried "from my cold dead hands."

to tread, the colonists understood the awesome power and protection of the right to keep and bear arms.

When all else fails, it is the one right that prevails. It alone offers the absolute capacity to

live free from fear. It is the one right that allows "rights" to exist at all. This is why the Second Amendment—the right to keep and bear arms—is our first freedom as Americans.

The Right to Blow People Away *Pete Hamill*

Journalist Pete Hamill believes that the framers of the Second Amendment did not intend for individuals to have a right to bear arms independent of serving in the organized militia.

By all definitions, and aided by common sense, the right to bear and keep arms is connected to service in a part-time military organization, regulated by an elected government. It is not about having the personal ability to blow people away....

The framers of the Bill of Rights were intelligent men and in attempting to establish their contract with the people...they were careful about what they wrote. So they said that citizens could keep arms in order to serve as part of a militia. That militia must be "well-regulated." Our evolving modern version of the 18th century militia is the National Guard, controlled by individual states, but subject to service when the nation itself decides that a call-up is "necessary to the security of a free state." In the National Guard today, citizen soldiers are trained in the use of weapons, usually in armories. They go off during the summers for additional training in the field. They do not bring their machine guns home with them. Those weapons remain in the armories. That is, they are regulated.

National Firearms Act of 1934 against a Second Amendment challenge. The act required sawed-off shotguns, a favorite weapon of gangsters, to be registered. However, in 2001 a federal appellate court did rule that the Second Amendment protected an individual right to bear arms outside the militia, a position endorsed by Attorney General John Ashcroft.

The Supreme Court has held that the Second Amendment does not apply to the states, so it does not bar gun control measures by local or state governments. In 1982, a federal appellate court upheld an ordinance by Morton Grove, Illinois, that banned the possession of handguns in the home. In *Printz v. United States* (1997), the Supreme Court did declare the Brady Handgun Violence Prevention Act to be unconstitutional, but not based on the Second Amendment. The Brady Act required local law enforcement officers to run background checks before authorizing handgun purchases. The law was named in honor of press secretary James Brady, who was paralyzed during an assassination attempt on President Ronald Reagan.

Legal scholars point out that, even if the Second Amendment does protect an individual right to bear arms, no right is absolute. Therefore, gun control measures would not always violate the Second Amendment. Just as free speech does not protect obscenity, they say, the Second Amendment does not include an unlimited right to own guns. In the words of journalist Wendy Kaminer: "The irony of the Second Amendment debate is that acknowledging an individual right to bear arms might facilitate gun control more than denying it ever could."

In *Federalist* 46, James Madison emphasized "the advantage of being armed, which the Americans possess over the people of almost every other nation." But contemporary Americans disagree over whether Madison is still right.

"An 18th-century right to bear arms is as out of place as silk knee britches and tricornered hats."

—Daniel Lazare

AMENDMENT III

No Soldier shall, in time of peace be quartered in any house, without the consent of the Owner, nor in time of war, but in a manner to be prescribed by law.

THE THIRD AMENDMENT: QUARTERING OF TROOPS

Contemporary Americans pay little heed to the Third Amendment, yet it was near and dear to the hearts of their ancestors. Colonial Americans had chafed at being forced to provide room and board for British soldiers, and they made sure the new Constitution protected them from such a practice. In fact, more states included this provision in proposed amendments to the Constitution than freedom of speech. But the Supreme Court has never specifically ruled on the meaning of the Third Amendment, although the Court has cited it as support for a constitutional right of privacy.

No Soldier shall, in time of peace be quartered in any house, without the consent of the Owner,...
This part of the Third Amendment contains an outright ban on quartering soldiers during peacetime in "any house" without the owner's permission. The term "any house" includes both public houses, such as hotels and inns, and private homes. New York was the first American colony to ban the quartering of troops in private homes without the owner's consent, as part of its Charter of Liberties and Privileges in 1683. But ironically, the only major incident during the colonial period in which the British used force to quarter troops in private homes was also in New York. It happened during the French and Indian War (1754–1763), in which the British defended the disputed western territories of their American colonies from the French and their allied Native American tribes. In 1756, the citizens of Albany refused to quarter British troops in their homes while a barracks was being built, and the commander of the British army took the homes by force.

After the war was over, the British soldiers did not leave America. England thought the Americans should rightfully bear the costs of their own defense, and Parliament passed the first Quartering Act in 1765. It required colonial legislatures to pay for the room and board of British soldiers stationed in America, and rent quarters when the regular barracks overflowed. The colonists opposed the Quartering Act as a tax forcing them to pay for a permanent or standing army they did not want. Tensions over the Quartering Act led to the Boston Massacre in 1770. The Massachusetts legislature refused to house thousands of British troops who had come to Boston to enforce taxes on imports. Friction with townspeople led to a confrontation outside the Customs House, in which British soldiers killed five Americans. Parliament passed a second Quartering Act in 1774, as part of a series of laws the Americans called Intolerable Acts. The new law authorized British troops to be quartered in private homes, as well as public houses.

When the colonies separated from England two years later, they specifically included in the Declaration of Independence as one of their grievances that the king had agreed to laws "for quartering large bodies of armed troops among us." After the Revolutionary War, several states prohibited peacetime quartering of troops as part of their constitutions. And during the ratification debates on the U.S. Constitution, Patrick Henry objected to its lack of a ban on peacetime quartering of troops. His arguments carried great weight, and the Third Amendment was ratified as part of the Bill of Rights in 1791.

This engraving of the Boston Massacre by Paul Revere demonstrates the violence that resulted from the Quartering Act of 1765.

...nor in time of war, but in a manner to be prescribed by law.
The Third Amendment does allow troops to be quartered in houses without the owners' consent during wartime. However, adequate procedures for reimbursing the owners must be enacted. Some legal scholars argue that during the Civil War, the quartering of Union troops in privates homes violated the Third Amendment, because Congress never authorized such action.

But the Supreme Court has never heard a case specifically about the Third Amendment, nor has it ruled that the Third Amendment applies to the states as well as the national government. The only court case that did address the issue of quartering troops was *Engblom v. Carey* (1982), decided by the U.S. Court of Appeals for the Second Circuit—one level below the Supreme Court. In that case, the circuit court ruled that the state of New York violated the Third Amendment when it took over the rented, on-site dorm rooms of striking prison guards and housed National Guard troops there instead. However, Marianne E. Engblom, one of the striking guards, lost her case on other grounds.

The Third Amendment has long been understood to reinforce a citizen's right to privacy. In 1833, Justice Joseph Story wrote in his famous treatise on the Constitution that the Third Amendment protects "that great right of the common law, that a man's house shall be his own castle, privileged against all civil and military intrusion." Later Supreme Court rulings would extend this principle to support a generalized right to privacy not specifically mentioned in the Constitution. Justice William Douglas wrote in *Poe v. Ullman* (1961): "Can there be any doubt that a Bill of Rights that in time of peace bars soldiers from being quartered in a home 'without the consent of the owner' should also bar the police from investigating the intimacies of the marriage relation?" The Supreme Court later ruled in *Griswold v. Connecticut* (1965) that the Third Amendment—along with the First, Fourth, Fifth, and Ninth Amendments—established "zones of privacy" that gave married couples the right to use contraceptives.

Many Americans believe that the right to privacy is one of the most important constitutional freedoms. Although today the Third Amendment is seldom used to protect private homes from soldiers, it does continue to help keep those homes private from the government.

AMENDMENT IV

The right of the people to be secure in their persons, houses, papers, and effects, against unreasonable searches and seizures, shall not be violated, and no Warrants shall issue, but upon probable cause, supported by Oath or affirmation, and particularly describing the place to be searched, and the persons or things to be seized.

THE FOURTH AMENDMENT: UNREASONABLE SEARCHES AND SEIZURES

Colonial Americans were intimately familiar with the invasive power of government. British officials ransacked their homes and arrested them without warrants. The purpose of the Fourth Amendment is to prevent such arbitrary actions and protect Americans' privacy against the government. In the words of Justice Louis Brandeis, the Fourth Amendment secures "the right to be let alone—the most comprehensive of rights and the right most valued by civilized men." Therefore, the Fourth Amendment requires that searches and seizures must be reasonable, and that warrants for searches and arrests must be specific. One of the most controversial Fourth Amendment questions is whether evidence from an illegal search should be excluded at a criminal trial. The Supreme Court is constantly trying to find the right balance under the Fourth Amendment between catching criminals and protecting privacy.

The right of the people to be secure in their persons, houses, papers, and effects, against unreasonable searches and seizures, shall not be violated,...
The first part of the Fourth Amendment prohibits unreasonable searches and seizures, but it does not define what they are. In colonial times, unreasonable searches were carried out with open-ended warrants that did not specify who was to be searched and what was to be seized. However, the Supreme Court has ruled that not all searches require warrants under the Fourth Amendment to be "reasonable." Nonetheless, the Fourth Amendment prevents police from conducting all-purpose dragnets merely to sweep for crime.

general warrants

orders allowing government agents to search anywhere and anyone they wanted

writ of assistance

a type of general warrant used by British customs officials to search colonial homes and businesses for smuggled goods on which import taxes had not been paid

James Otis defended Boston merchants against general warrants.

"A man's house is his castle; and whilst he is quiet he is as well guarded as a prince in his castle."

—James Otis

Historical Background. A common English practice was the use of **general warrants,** which allowed the crown's agents to search anywhere they wanted and seize anything they pleased. American colonists resisted general warrants mightily. British customs officials used a type of general warrant known as a **writ of assistance** to search colonial homes and businesses for smuggled goods on which import taxes had not been paid.

In 1761, James Otis, a prominent Boston lawyer, resigned a post with the crown in order to oppose the writs of assistance in court. Arguing on behalf of Boston merchants, Otis lost his court case. But as John Adams—who witnessed Otis's argument—later wrote: "Then and there the child Independence was born." After the Revolutionary War, eight states prohibited general warrants in their new constitutions.

A Reasonable Expectation of Privacy. The Fourth Amendment specifically protects the people "in their persons, houses, papers, and effects." Therefore, the Supreme Court originally interpreted this phrase to limit the Fourth Amendment to actual invasions of certain defined locations, such as the home or the physical body. Under this theory, for example, the Court held in *Olmstead v. United States* (1928) that the Fourth Amendment did not require a warrant for wiretapping, if the listening devices were located outside the home.

But the Supreme Court later overturned the *Olmstead* decision in *Katz v. United States* (1967). The Court ruled that "the Fourth Amendment protects people, not places." Thus, the Court held that the amendment applied not just in homes, but wherever a person had "a reasonable expectation of privacy." Thus, said the Court, the Fourth Amendment protected Katz from a wiretap placed on the outside of a public phone booth, because he had a reasonable expectation that his conversation would be private. Conversely, the Court held, "what a person knowingly exposes to the public, even in his own home" is not covered by the Fourth Amendment.

Applying this "reasonable expectation of privacy" test, the Supreme Court has still given a high level of Fourth Amendment protection to the home and its surrounding area. But the Court ruled in *California v. Greenwood* (1988) that garbage bags placed on the curb outside a home for pickup had been exposed to the public sufficiently to remove a reasonable expectation of privacy. Even though the garbage bags were opaque and sealed, said the Court, narcotics officers could open them and use the evidence found inside.

In *Kyllo v. United States* (2001), however, the Court declined to treat heat waves escaping from a home like garbage bags discarded on the sidewalk. Suspecting Kyllo of growing marijuana, agents used a thermal imaging device to scan his home for evidence of high-intensity lamps. The police then used the results of that test to obtain a search warrant for Kyllo's home, where they discovered a closet full of marijuana plants. The Supreme Court held that Kyllo did have a reasonable expectation of privacy from police surveillance of his home, if the search was carried out by high-tech equipment not in general use.

Reasonable Searches and Seizures. Once it has decided that a reasonable expectation of privacy exists for a certain area, the Supreme Court must then determine if the search in question is "reasonable" under the Fourth Amendment. To meet this test, most searches and seizures require probable cause—that is, a reasonable belief that a particular person has committed a particular crime—even if they do not require a warrant. Probable cause is discussed in greater detail in the section on warrants that follows. However, the Court has recognized certain exceptions in which a warrantless search or seizure does not need probable cause in order to be reasonable. Some of these exceptions include:

Stop and Frisk. The Supreme Court held in *Terry v. Ohio* (1968) that police officers, based on their street experience but not necessarily probable cause, may stop suspects and pat them down to look for weapons. The Court expanded this category of warrantless searches and seizures in *Minnesota v. Dickerson* (1993), ruling that a police officer may also seize contraband, not just weapons, during a "pat down." However, such contraband must be obvious through the defendant's clothing.

Airport Searches. The courts have ruled that, due to the danger of airplane hijacking, searches of all passengers without probable cause are reasonable, at least using metal detectors. After the hijackings on September 11, 2001, airports are increasing their searches of passengers without probable cause.

U.S. soldiers conducted intensified searches of airline passengers after the September 11, 2001 attacks.

Sobriety Checkpoints. Law enforcement officers may stop all drivers at roadblocks to check for drunk driving, as long as individual motorists are not singled out in "spot checks." The officer may then require further testing, such as a Breathalyzer, if she has probable cause that an individual motorist has been drinking. But in *Indianapolis v. Edmond* (2000), the Supreme Court ruled that police could not conduct roadblocks looking for evidence of drug use, because the program did not have a specific purpose of promoting highway safety.

> "In many cases, invading privacy is not the only way to ensure our safety; it's just the easiest."
>
> —Caroline Kennedy and Ellen Alderman

Consent Searches. Probable cause is not required if a person consents to a search. Consent must be obtained from the appropriate person, however. A landlord is not authorized to grant a search of a tenant's home, but the tenant's roommate is.

Drug Testing. Without probable cause, the government may test certain employees for drugs, such as those involved in public safety or law enforcement. But in *Chandler v. Miller* (1997), the Supreme Court struck down a Georgia law requiring state candidates to pass a drug test before being listed on the ballot, because there were no "special needs" such as public safety involved.

Student Searches. Public school officials do not need probable cause in order to search students, held the Supreme Court in *New Jersey v. T.L.O.* (1985). However, police officers do need probable cause before conducting a search on school premises. Although the Fourth Amendment does apply to public school students, their rights are not the same as adults in similar circumstances. For example, the Court upheld drug testing of student athletes without individual suspicion of wrongdoing in *Vernonia School District 47J v. Acton* (1995). And in *Board of Education v. Earls* (2002), the Court also held that schools may require students participating in any extracurricular activity to submit to random drug tests.

What Do You Have to Hide? *William Safire*

New York Times columnist William Safire believes that a national identification card would compromise privacy, not combat terrorism.

Fear of terrorism has placed Americans in danger of trading our "right to be let alone" for the false sense of security of a national identification card. All of us are willing to give up some of our personal privacy in return for greater safety. That's why we gladly suffer the pat-downs and "wanding" at airports, and show a local ID before boarding. Such precautions contribute to our peace of mind….

But in the dreams of Big Brother and his cousin, Big Marketing, nothing can compare to forcing every person in the United States—under penalty of law—to carry what the totalitarians used to call "papers." The plastic card would not merely show a photograph, signature, and address, as drivers' licenses do. That's only the beginning. In time,…the card would contain not only a fingerprint, description of DNA and the details of your eye's iris, but a host of other information about you….

The universal use and likely abuse of the national ID—a discredit card—will trigger questions like: When did you begin subscribing to these publications and why were you visiting that spicy or seditious Web site? Why are you afraid to show us your papers on demand? Why are you paying cash? What do you have to hide?

…and no Warrants shall issue, but upon probable cause, supported by Oath or affirmation, and particularly describing the place to be searched, and the persons or things to be seized.

Known as the Warrant Clause, the second half of the Fourth Amendment requires that all **warrants,** or court orders, for searches and seizures must be based on **probable cause,** a reasonable belief that a particular person has committed a particular crime. Probable cause is more than just the arbitrary whim of a law enforcement officer, although it is less proof than required to convict a person of a crime. To demonstrate probable cause, a police officer must go before a neutral magistrate, who makes an independent determination of whether a warrant is justified. Furthermore, the warrant must specify where the search will occur and what or whom is being seized.

The Warrant Clause does not say under what circumstances a warrant is necessary; it merely sets forth the conditions required to get a warrant. The Supreme Court has ruled that, although warrants are a preference under the Fourth Amendment, they are not required in all cases due to the practical demands of police work.

Arrests. Police do not need to get a warrant if they see a person in the process of committing a crime. But police always need a warrant if arresting an alleged criminal in his home. If an officer makes an arrest without a warrant, he must still go before a magistrate to demonstrate probable cause for the arrest within forty-eight hours. The Supreme Court ruled in *Wilson v. Layne* (1999) that police are not allowed to bring the media on "ride-alongs" while they make arrests in a person's home, even if the police have a warrant. But in *Atwater v. Lago Vista* (2001), the Court held that police officers have the discretion to arrest a person even for a minor traffic offense that normally would be punishable only by a fine. Such warrantless arrests are justified, said the Court, because sentences can vary depending on factors of which officers are not always aware.

Searches. Most police searches are made without a warrant. Some of the principal exceptions to the warrant requirement are listed below. However, in contrast to "reasonable" searches discussed in the previous section, probable cause is always necessary in these examples, even if warrants are not.

Search Incident to a Lawful Arrest. This is the most common type of warrantless search. In *Chimel v. California* (1969), the Supreme Court ruled that police may search an arrested suspect and the surrounding area for weapons or evidence that may be destroyed—even once the suspect has been handcuffed and taken away from the scene.

Plain View. An officer does not need a warrant to seize evidence that is in plain view, if the officer is where he or she legally has a right to be. When an officer stops someone for speeding, for example, he does not need a warrant to seize marijuana that is visible on the dashboard.

Exigent Circumstances. A warrant is not required for a search during an emergency. If a home is burning, or someone is screaming inside, police do not need a warrant to enter.

warrants
court orders allowing certain actions, such as arrests or searches

probable cause
a reasonable belief that a particular person has committed a particular crime

Dollree Mapp: The Criminal Who Went Free

Cleveland police went to the home of Dollree Mapp in 1957, looking for a suspect in a bombing. A few days earlier, an explosion had rocked the house of Don King, then an alleged gambling racketeer and later a prominent boxing promoter. Mapp, the ex-wife of a boxing champion, refused to let police in without a search warrant. The police officers waited three hours, then broke into the house and presented Mapp with a piece of paper they said was a warrant. Mapp grabbed the paper from the officers and stuffed it down the bosom of her blouse. The police handcuffed her and retrieved the alleged warrant, but later claimed it had been lost. While searching Mapp's home, the police discovered several nude drawings and some erotic books. She was convicted of possessing obscene materials, a felony under Ohio law. The Supreme Court overturned Mapp's conviction, holding that the evidence against her should be excluded because it was the fruit of an illegal search. More than twenty years later, one of the arresting officers admitted that he did not have a properly executed search warrant.

Hot Pursuit. Police may follow a suspect into a building without a warrant, if they are in hot pursuit of the alleged criminal. Any evidence discovered during the pursuit may also be seized.

Automobiles. Searches of automobiles do not require warrants because courts have held that there is a decreased expectation of privacy in cars. Also, suspects can easily move cars before police can get warrants.

exclusionary rule

legal doctrine that excludes from a trial any evidence seized illegally by police

The Exclusionary Rule. If the police conduct an illegal search, the Supreme Court has held that any evidence seized during that search must be excluded in court. This remedy, known as the **exclusionary rule,** is designed to give police an incentive not to violate the Fourth Amendment. However, sometimes when evidence is excluded, a suspect cannot be convicted. Some legal experts believe that a better method of enforcing the Fourth Amendment would be to allow police officers to be sued for damages by the persons they searched illegally. Yet other scholars point out that such lawsuits are impractical for those already serving jail sentences. They argue that the law-abiding public has an interest in police officers doing their jobs properly, even if that means some criminals at times go free.

"The criminal is to go free because the constable has blundered."

—Judge Benjamin Cardozo

The Supreme Court applied the exclusionary rule to federal cases in *Weeks v. United States* (1914). But the Court did not extend the exclusionary rule to state cases until *Mapp v. Ohio* (1961). In his opinion for the majority, Justice Tom Clark pointed out that it was illogical to require the exclusionary rule of the federal government but not the states:

> Moreover, our holding that the exclusionary rule is an essential part of both the Fourth and Fourteenth Amendments is not only the logical dictate of prior cases, but it also makes very good sense. There is no war between the Constitution and

common sense. Presently, a federal prosecutor may make no use of evidence illegally seized, but a state's attorney across the street may.... Thus, the state by admitting evidence unlawfully seized, serves to encourage disobedience to the federal Constitution which it is bound to uphold.

"The criminal goes free, if he must, but it is the law that sets him free."

—Justice Tom Clark

Exceptions to the Rule. The exclusionary rule continues to be controversial in American society. Consequently, the Supreme Court has recognized several exceptions to the exclusionary rule. In *United States v. Leon* (1984), the Court ruled that if police officers believe that the search warrant they are executing is legal, if they are acting in "good faith," then the evidence may be admitted in court even if the warrant is later discovered to be invalid on technical grounds. And in *Nix v. Williams* (1984), the Court announced the "inevitable discovery" exception, holding that evidence will not be excluded if police can prove that they would have found it independently of the illegal search.

Because They Can *Alan Dershowitz*

Harvard Law professor Alan Dershowitz believes that one result of the exclusionary rule has been a rise in police perjury to avoid the rule's consequences.

I once asked a policeman, "Why do cops lie so brazenly in search-and-seizure cases?" He responded with a rude macho joke: "Why do dogs lick their balls?" To which the answer is "Because they can." Police know they can get away with certain kinds of common lies.... Even a

judge who is courageous enough to blow the whistle on the pervasiveness of police perjury in general is not willing—or able—to do anything about it in a particular case....

Everyone is happy with this result. The cop gets credit for a good drug bust. His supervisor's arrest statistics look good. The prosecutor racks up another win. The judge gets to give his little lecture on "rectitude" without

endangering his reelection prospects by actually freeing a guilty criminal. The defense lawyer collects his fee in dirty drug money, knowing that there is nothing more he can do. The public is thrilled that another drug dealer is off the street. It is this benign attitude toward police perjury in the context of search and seizure that makes it so acceptable—indeed so essential—a part of our criminal justice system.

AMENDMENT V

No person shall be held to answer for a capital, or otherwise infamous crime, unless on a presentment or indictment of a Grand Jury, except in cases arising in the land or naval forces, or in the Militia, when in actual service in time of War or public danger; nor shall any person be subject for the same offence to be twice put in jeopardy of life or limb, nor shall be compelled in any criminal case to be a witness against himself, nor be deprived of life, liberty, or property, without due process of law; nor shall private property be taken for public use, without just compensation.

THE FIFTH AMENDMENT: DUE PROCESS OF LAW

grand jury

a large jury, normally of twenty-three citizens, that determines if there is enough evidence to charge a defendant with a crime

petit jury

a trial jury, usually of six to twelve citizens, that decides the facts in a civil or criminal case

indictment

formal criminal charge issued by a grand jury when a prosecutor has enough evidence for trial

The Fifth Amendment guarantees five rights of a very diverse nature. The most popularly known right in the Fifth Amendment, the right against self-incrimination in criminal cases, is commonly referred to as "taking the Fifth." Other rights in the Fifth Amendment include the right to have serious criminal charges screened by a grand jury; to avoid being tried twice for the same offense; to have due process of law; and to receive just compensation when private property is taken for public use. The longest amendment in the Bill of Rights, the Fifth Amendment is a hodgepodge of provisions affecting both criminal law and civil law. But all of them limit the power of the government to take action against the individual.

No person shall be held to answer for a capital, or otherwise infamous crime, unless on a presentment or indictment of a Grand Jury, except in cases arising in the land or naval forces, or in the Militia, when in actual service in time of War or public danger;...
This provision in the Fifth Amendment gives civilians who are accused of serious crimes the right to a **grand jury,** which determines if enough evidence exists to prosecute. A grand jury (from the French for "large") normally consists of twenty-three persons, whereas a **petit jury** (from the French for "small") has six to twelve members. Petit juries determine the actual guilt of a defendant at trial. If the grand jury believes the prosecutor has sufficient evidence, it will issue an **indictment** formally charging the

accused with a crime, known as a "true bill." If not, the grand jury will return a "no true bill." The grand jury also has the power to return a **presentment,** in which it charges a person with a crime independently of the prosecutor.

The grand jury originated in England in the twelfth century to limit the government's power to charge defendants with a crime, unless justified by the evidence. Grand juries were the earliest type of jury used in England, originating in the twelfth century. In America, the grand jury took on added importance as a protection against the crown's arbitrary power. Nonetheless, the Supreme Court has never incorporated the Fifth Amendment's grand jury provision to apply to the states, so it limits only the federal government. Instead of a grand jury, most states allow the prosecutor to file an **information,** a sworn statement that she has enough evidence for a trial. Still, a judge must hold a preliminary hearing to evaluate the evidence before an information can be filed. The preliminary hearing is open to the public, and both the defendant and the prosecutor present their cases before a judge.

In contrast to the information system, a grand jury meets in secret and only the prosecutor can present evidence. Secrecy is critical to protect the reputations of people who are not actually indicted, say proponents of the grand jury. But critics charge that grand juries return indictments in the vast majority of cases, and that they no longer serve as an independent check on prosecutions. According to one prominent New York judge, prosecutors could get a grand jury to "indict a ham sandwich." At times, however, the grand jury can exercise considerable discretion and refuse to bring charges on humanitarian grounds, such as when a distraught father turns off life support for his brain-dead son.

presentment

formal criminal charge issued by a grand jury independent of a prosecutor

information

a sworn statement by a prosecutor that he has enough evidence for a trial

Special counsel Kenneth Starr convened a grand jury in 1998 to investigate charges that President Bill Clinton had committed perjury about his affair with White House intern Monica Lewinsky. Grand juries can be used to investigate as well as prosecute crimes.

No One Ever Asked Me to Lie *Monica Lewinsky*

Monica Lewinsky testified before a grand jury in August 1998 that President Bill Clinton never asked her to lie about their relationship. Her testimony, later released by the House of Representatives, illustrates the broad discretion that grand juries have.

A JUROR: Monica, none of us in this room are perfect. We all fall and we fall several times a day. The only difference between my age and when I was your age is now I get up faster. If I make a mistake and fall, I get up and brush myself off. I used to stay there a while after a mistake. That's all I have to say.

A: Thank you....

A JUROR: Could I ask one? Monica, is there anything that you would like to add to your prior testimony, either today or the last time you were here, or anything that you think needs to be amplified on or clarified? I just want to give you the fullest opportunity.

A: I would. I think because of the public nature of how this investigation has been and what the charges aired, that I would just like to say that no one ever asked me to lie and I was never promised a job for my silence. And that I'm sorry. I'm really sorry for everything that's happened. (The witness begins to cry.)...

A JUROR: Can I just say—I mean, I think I should seize this opportunity now, that we've all fallen short. We sin every day. I don't care whether it's murder, whether it's affairs or whatever. And we get over that. You ask forgiveness and you go on.

There's some that are going to say that they don't forgive you, but he whose sin—you know—that's how I feel about that. So to let you know from here, you have my forgiveness. Because we all fall short....

A: Thank you....

...nor shall any person be subject for the same offence to be twice put in jeopardy of life or limb,...

One of the most ancient rights in the Bill of Rights is the protection against **double jeopardy,** which began in Greek and Roman law. Once the defendant has been acquitted, the Fifth Amendment forbids him from being tried again. Otherwise, the government could use its enormous resources to keep charging the defendant until it got a conviction, whether he was innocent or not. The Double Jeopardy Clause specifically addresses endangering "life or limb," which refers to an early American practice of punishing crimes by cutting off ears or damaging other limbs. However, the Supreme Court has broadened this language to include prison sentences.

Double jeopardy does not apply when the accused is retried because of a previous mistrial, in which the jury was unable to reach a verdict. Nor is it a violation of double jeopardy for the defendant to be granted a new trial on appeal, or for the prosecution to appeal for a harsher sentence. And a single episode of crime can lead to several different charges. For example, a rapist might be charged with kidnapping, sexual assault, and attempted murder. Both the state and federal governments may prosecute a defendant for the same crime, such as murder, without violating double jeopardy.

Only in capital cases does double jeopardy apply to sentencing proceedings, according to the Supreme Court. The state has just one chance to sentence a person to death for a crime. And double jeopardy

double jeopardy

trying a defendant more than once for the same offense

does not apply to civil cases that arise from a criminal act—such as when the family of a murder victim sues the alleged killer for money damages, even if he was acquitted of the crime (as in the O. J. Simpson case).

...nor shall be compelled in any criminal case to be a witness against himself,...

This provision in the Fifth Amendment is known as the right against **self-incrimination.** A defendant cannot be forced to testify against himself or herself. In popular culture, this right is commonly referred to as "taking the Fifth." It became especially prominent during the congressional hearings held by Senator Joseph McCarthy to investigate alleged communists during the 1950s. McCarthy derisively used the term "Fifth Amendment communists" to refer to people who refused to answer his questions based on their right against self-incrimination.

Confessions or Evidence. In America, many people see pleading the Fifth Amendment as tantamount to admitting guilt. But in England the right against self-incrimination grew out of the abuse of a system of **inquisition,** or questioning accused persons under oath to determine their guilt. The Star Chamber, a notorious royal court that met in secret, would require religious dissenters to answer questions about their faith under oath. If defendants told the truth, they risked their lives; if they lied, they risked their souls. Puritan printer John Lilburne refused to take the Star Chamber's oath in 1637. He argued that, lacking evidence against him, the Chamber was trying to entrap him through its crafty questions. As a result of Lilburne's protest, Parliament later abolished the Star Chamber.

In America, the criminal law works according to a system of **accusation,** in which the government must present evidence proving a defendant committed a crime. The defendant is presumed to be innocent until proven guilty, and the state may not demand that the accused testify against himself. Coerced confessions are also a violation of the Fifth Amendment right against self-incrimination, even though they can make a police officer's job easier. Moreover, torture produces inherently unreliable confessions, because defendants will say anything to make the pain stop.

Voluntariness. The Supreme Court has ruled that in order for a confession to be admitted in court as evidence, it must be truly voluntary. In a series of cases, the Court overturned convictions based on confessions obtained through physical coercion and other "third degree" tactics. But in *Miranda v. Arizona* (1966), the Supreme Court held that coercion is inherent to some degree in any custodial questioning by police. Chief Justice Earl Warren, himself a former prosecutor, quoted from police manuals in his

---

self-incrimination
compelling a defendant to testify against himself

inquisition
questioning accused persons under oath to determine their guilt

accusation
forcing the government to prove its case through evidence

> "I am deeply troubled about asserting these rights, because it may be perceived by some that I have something to hide."
>
> —Kenneth Lay

majority decision for the Court. Chief Justice Warren wrote that "such an interrogation environment is created for no purpose other than to subjugate the individual to the will of his examiner."

In *Miranda,* the Court held that a defendant must know his rights before he can voluntarily waive them. The Court announced a new rule, holding that state and local police officers must follow the practice of the Federal Bureau of Investigation (**FBI**) and give suspects the following warnings before any questioning begins:

> You have the right to remain silent.
> If you give up the right to remain silent, anything you say can be used against you.
> You have the right to have an attorney present during questioning.
> If you cannot afford an attorney, one will be appointed for you before any questioning begins.

Ken Lay, former chairman of Enron, took the Fifth Amendment when testifying before Congress in 2002 about his company's bankruptcy, one of the largest in U.S. history.

Any statements that the defendant makes prior to being given these "Miranda warnings" are excluded from evidence at trial. And, under the "fruit of the poisonous tree" doctrine, any evidence that police discover as a result of such statements is also excluded– unless they can prove that it would have been inevitably discovered. Police also must entirely stop questioning whenever the defendant invokes his right to remain silent, and they may not repeatedly persist in trying to get him to talk.

The *Miranda* decision caused considerable outcry. Critics charged that the Court was not interpreting the Constitution, but rather creating its own rules of law enforcement. Congress passed a law in 1968 seeking to overturn *Miranda* and reinstate any confessions that were otherwise voluntary. However, that law was seldom enforced until the case of *Dickerson v. United States* (2000). In an opinion by Chief Justice William Rehnquist, the Court struck down the 1968 law, noting that *Miranda* had become "part of national culture." The Court said that "*Miranda* announced a constitutional rule that Congress may not supersede legislatively."

But the Supreme Court has limited the effects of *Miranda* at times by narrowly construing when it applies. For example, in *Illinois v. Perkins*

(1990), the Court ruled that Miranda warnings were not required when a jailed suspect confessed to a police officer posing as an inmate. The *Miranda* decision protected suspects from coercion, not deception, said the Court. And in *New York v. Quarles* (1984), the Court created a "public safety" exception to *Miranda.* The Court said that an armed suspect's weapon was admissible even without Miranda warnings, when the police had asked a suspect where he had hidden his gun during his arrest—so that others would not find it and get hurt.

Immunity. A person is protected by the Fifth Amendment whenever she is forced to give answers in any government proceeding, civil or criminal. But if government grants a witness immunity from prosecution, it can force her to testify. There are two types of such immunity: total immunity, in which the witness cannot be prosecuted at all; or "use" immunity, in which the government may prosecute the witness based on evidence discovered independently of the testimony. For example, Lt. Col. Oliver North's conviction based on the Iran-Contra affair was overturned because it relied on his immunized testimony before Congress in 1987. Yale law professor Akhil Reed Amar argues that the Fifth Amendment should apply only in a limited way to congressional hearings, in order to allow Congress to do an effective job of legislating.

> "If the government becomes a lawbreaker, it breeds contempt for law."
>
> —Justice Louis Brandeis

> "When Congress needs facts to determine whether existing laws are working and how they might be fixed, it often meets a Fifth Amendment stone wall."
>
> —Akhil Reed Amar

Ernesto Miranda: You Have the Right to Remain Silent

After working all night long at his produce job, Ernesto Miranda had barely fallen asleep when Phoenix police officers came to his home on March 13, 1963. They were investigating a kidnapping and rape. An ex-con, Miranda had served time both as an adult and a juvenile, and had been charged with sexual offenses. The police brought Miranda back to the station house for questioning, where after two hours of interrogation he confessed. Said Miranda years later, "they get you in a little room and they start badgering you one way or the other, 'you better tell us…or we're going to throw the book at you.'… And I haven't had any sleep since the day before." Even after his confession was thrown out by the Supreme Court, Miranda was convicted in a second trial of rape and kidnapping in 1967. After being released on parole, he made extra money autographing Miranda warning cards used by the police. In 1976, Ernesto Miranda was killed in a barroom knife fight. Police used a warning card from Miranda's pocket to advise one of the suspected killers of his rights.

Ernesto Miranda spent much of his life in and out of jails.

Nontestimonial Evidence. The Fifth Amendment applies only to testimonial evidence. It does not prevent the defendant from having to produce physical evidence—such as blood samples, fingerprints, or handwriting exemplars. The defendant can also be compelled to stand in a police lineup and repeat certain phrases at the victim's request. However, a lie-detector test is considered to be testimonial evidence, so the government cannot force the accused to submit to one.

…nor be deprived of life, liberty, or property, without due process of law;…

The Constitution protects "due process of law" in two places: the Fifth Amendment, which restricts only the national government; and the Fourteenth Amendment, which restricts only the states. Due process of law has never been precisely defined. Its roots come from the Magna Carta of 1215, which limited King John's power over his nobles. That document prevented punishment except according to the "law of the land," which evolved into due process of law. The underlying concept is that government may not behave arbitrarily and capriciously, but must act fairly according to established rules. Due process has two categories: substantive and procedural. Under substantive due process, the content of a law must itself be fair; under procedural due process, the rules by which a law is implemented must be fair.

Substantive Due Process. Under substantive due process, the Supreme Court will examine the content of a law to determine whether it violates fundamental rights not specifically mentioned in the Constitution. Some legal scholars believe that, by definition, due process refers to procedures, so that substantive due process is a contradiction in terms. Most cases involving substantive due process are based on the Fourteenth Amendment, so that chapter discusses the issue in more depth. But in *Bolling v. Sharpe* (1954), the Supreme Court used substantive due process under the Fifth Amendment to strike down a federal law that segregated schools in the District of Columbia. The Court could not base its decision on the Equal Protection Clause of the Fourteenth Amendment, which prohibits unreasonable discrimination, because it applies only to the states.

Procedural Due Process. The government must follow fair procedures in both criminal and civil cases, in order to safeguard the individual against the power of the state. The Supreme Court has ruled that the Due Process Clause requires the government to comply with certain standards in criminal cases beyond the rights specifically mentioned in the Bill of Rights, such as trial by jury. These due process rights include the right to a presumption of innocence and to have the government prove its case "beyond a reasonable doubt." The Court also ruled in the case of *In re Gault* (1967) that juveniles were entitled to some of the same procedural rights as adults, although not all, when being tried in juvenile court.

In civil cases, the Supreme Court has ruled that the government cannot deprive a citizen of certain liberty or property interests without due process of law. The issue then becomes what process is due, or what procedures are necessary to protect such interests. Usually, the government may not deny a citizen a benefit–such as a job or social security payments–without notice and a hearing. For example, in *Goldberg v. Kelly* (1970), the Court held that the government cannot take away welfare benefits with notifying the persons affected and giving them a chance to be heard. And the Court ruled in *Goss v. Lopez* (1975) that public school students were entitled to a certain level of due process before they were suspended.

...nor shall private property be taken for public use, without just compensation.

The Just Compensation Clause limits the power of the government to take private property for public use, known as **eminent domain.** This right to just compensation traces its roots to England's Magna Carta. The very first Supreme Court case based on the Bill of Rights, *Barron v. Baltimore* (1833), involved the Just Compensation Clause. The city of Baltimore had damaged John Barron's wharf during street construction, and he sued to have the city pay for repairs. But the Court ruled that the Bill of Rights did not apply to the states, and that principle did not change until after the Fourteenth Amendment was ratified in 1868.

Much of America's infrastructure–highways, railroads, and dams–was built through the power of eminent domain. Today, a common question under the Fifth Amendment is how much the government can regulate the use of private property without constituting a "taking" that requires just compensation. The Supreme Court has upheld zoning laws and historic preservation statutes that regulate property without compensation. But in the 1990s, the Court placed more limits on such regulation. In *Lucas v. South Carolina Coastal Council* (1992), the Court ruled that a local government could not rezone beachfront property to absolutely forbid development without paying just compensation to its owner. And in *Dolan v. City of Tigard* (1994), the Court held that a city cannot compel a property owner to donate land for public use in order to obtain a development permit, unless the city proves that such a condition is connected to the nature of the development.

Under the Fifth Amendment, any takings of private property must be for "public use." However, the courts generally defer to legislative definitions of a valid public purpose. In Michigan, state courts upheld the

---

"While the Constitution protects against invasions of individual rights, it is not a suicide pact."
—Justice Arthur Goldberg

eminent domain
the government's power to take private property for public use

city of Detroit's condemnation of a Polish neighborhood to make way for a General Motors plant, even though title to the property was given to the company and not retained by the city. And in *Hawaii Housing Authority v. Midkiff* (1984), the Supreme Court upheld a law that conveyed the title of land from one set of private individuals to another, in order to prevent a concentration of land ownership. When a taking is justified, the government only has to pay an owner the fair market value of the property, not moving expenses or replacement costs in another neighborhood.

AMENDMENT VI

In all criminal prosecutions, the accused shall enjoy the right to a speedy and public trial, by an impartial jury of the State and district wherein the crime shall have been committed, which district shall have been previously ascertained by law, and to be informed of the nature and cause of the accusation; to be confronted with the witnesses against him; to have compulsory process for obtaining witnesses in his favor, and to have the Assistance of Counsel for his defence.

> **"Rights come from wrongs."**
> —Alan Dershowitz

THE SIXTH AMENDMENT: THE RIGHT TO A FAIR TRIAL

Colonial Americans had frequently experienced the disadvantages faced by those accused of crimes under English law. Therefore, as early as the Massachusetts Body of Liberties in 1641, they protected the right to a speedy trial, by a jury, and with counsel. After independence, many states also protected such rights in their constitutions. The Sixth Amendment was added to the U.S. Constitution to ensure that criminal defendants received a fair trial–although it does not use those exact words. The amendment repeats Article III's guarantee of a trial by jury in criminal cases, but it adds other important rights as well–such as the right to subpoena witnesses and to have a lawyer. The Sixth Amendment attempts to balance the enormous power of the state, which pays for both police and prosecutors to prove guilt, against the power of the individual to prove innocence.

In all criminal prosecutions, the accused shall enjoy the right to a speedy and public trial,...
Although the Sixth Amendment refers to "all criminal prosecutions," its protections do not always apply to every minor offense, such as jaywalking or speeding. Under the Sixth Amendment, the defendants must receive speedy and public trials, although defendants may waive those rights if they choose.

Speedy Trial. The defendant must be brought to trial quickly, because, as legal scholars say, "justice delayed is justice denied." A person is assumed by the law to be innocent until proven guilty, but a long delay before the trial can damage that person's reputation in the community. Sometimes a defendant is denied bail and therefore remains in jail until the case is tried; the Sixth Amendment ensures that the defendant does not languish in jail. Also, witnesses' memories can fade over time; a speedy trial often guarantees a more accurate verdict. Defendants can move to delay their trials if they need more time to prepare their defense, or if they think the passage of time and dimming of memories will hurt the prosecution's case.

If the prosecution does not bring the case to trial in a speedy manner, then it must drop the charges against the defendant. The Supreme Court has rejected a specific time frame for when a defendant must be tried in order to receive a speedy trial, but in *Barker v. Wingo* (1972) the Court did establish general guidelines that apply both to state and federal cases. Congress enacted fixed time limits for the federal government to bring criminal charges in the Speedy Trial Act of 1974. Currently, federal prosecutors must start their trials no more than one hundred days after making an arrest. In addition, some states have passed laws limiting the time before a defendant is tried.

Public Trial. Besides a speedy trial, the defendant is also entitled to a public trial. The purpose of this right, said the Supreme Court, is to serve as "a safeguard against any attempt to employ our courts as instruments of persecution." In England, Charles I used the Star Chamber, a special court that met in secret, to suppress dissent in the 1630s. The Star Chamber thus became a potent symbol in America of a tyrannical court.

However, the Supreme Court has ruled that a trial can become too public. In *Sheppard v. Maxwell* (1966), the Court held that excessive pretrial publicity can prejudice the jury and deny the defendant a fair trial. The case involved Dr. Sam Sheppard, who was accused of murdering his wife in Cleveland. According to the Supreme Court, Sheppard's case became "a Roman holiday for the news media." In high-profile cases, said the Court, the judge must take active steps to guarantee an impartial jury, such as moving the **venue** or location of the trial and **sequestering** the jury.

Sometimes the defendant's Sixth Amendment right to a fair trial conflicts with the public's First Amendment right to attend and speak about criminal trials. The Supreme Court has ruled that the right to a public trial under the Sixth Amendment is for the benefit of the defendant, not the general public or the media. However, the Court held in *Richmond Newspapers v. Virginia* (1980) that the First Amendment gives the public a right to attend criminal trials in most cases. In addition, judges may not ban the media or issue gag orders limiting trial coverage, although they may take other steps to isolate the jury from prejudicial publicity if necessary.

venue

the location of a trial

sequestering

isolating the jury from the community and the news media during a trial

...by an impartial jury of the State and district wherein the crime shall have been committed, which district shall have been previously ascertained by law,...

Trial by jury was one of the most precious rights to early Americans. That's why the Constitution protects it three times: for criminal trials in Article III and the Sixth Amendment, and for civil trials in the Seventh Amendment. Trial by jury began in civil cases, so much of its history is discussed in the chapter on the Seventh Amendment. By the thirteenth century, trial by jury had been established in England for criminal cases, although it was not used in all trials.

The American colonists depended on juries for justice independent of the crown. Americans were outraged when Parliament allowed the colonists to be tried in courts without juries for violations of the Stamp Act of 1765. Furthermore, Americans could be transported back to England for trial. The Declaration of Independence cited both these practices as offenses by the king, and after the Revolution many states included defendants' rights in their new constitutions.

But a jury trial is becoming a rarer commodity in criminal cases. As of 2000, only 4.3 percent of federal criminal charges culminated in jury verdicts, compared to 10.4 percent in 1988. By far most criminal cases are resolved through **plea bargains,** in which the defendant pleads guilty in exchange for a reduced sentence, thus saving the government the costs of a trial.

plea bargains

process in which the defendant pleads guilty to criminal charges in exchange for a reduced sentence

Standards for Jury Trials. The Supreme Court ruled in *Duncan v. Louisiana* (1968) that trial by jury in criminal cases applied to the states. However, the Court has established different federal and state standards for this right, unlike any other right it has nationalized within the Bill of Rights. The federal government must have twelve-person juries that issue unanimous verdicts in criminal trials. States can have smaller juries that render verdicts that are not unanimous–except in death penalty cases. A state jury must have at least six members in a noncapital criminal trial, and that small a jury must issue a unanimous verdict. Only serious charges, those in which the maximum sentence is at least six months in jail, mandate a jury trial. The Supreme Court held in *Lewis v. United States* (1996) that sentences for multiple charges cannot be added together; only the sentence for the most serious offense counts toward the six-month test.

Impartial Jury. The Sixth Amendment also requires that the jury be impartial. The prosecuting and defense attorneys question potential jurors, in a process known as **voir dire,** about their knowledge of the case and possible biases. Either attorney may challenge a prospective juror for cause if evidence indicates the juror is biased. The attorneys may also exclude a

voir dire

questioning potential jurors to reveal their biases and knowledge of the case

peremptory challenge

excluding a potential juror without cause

"Life is full of close calls, but the question of O. J. Simpson's guilt was not one of them."

—George Will

certain number of jurors without giving any reason, through a **peremptory challenge.** The Sixth Amendment does not prohibit the use of peremptory challenges in a discriminatory manner. But the Supreme Court has ruled that such discrimination against racial groups and women does violate the Equal Protection Clause of the Fourteenth Amendment.

To secure an impartial jury, it must be chosen from a "representative cross-section of the community." Thus, the Supreme Court has ruled that particular groups—such as African Americans or women—must not be systematically excluded from the pool of potential jurors. In capital trials the state may exclude jurors who categorically refuse to impose the death penalty under any circumstances, although not those with moral reservations about capital punishment. Only the jury pool, not the final jury, has to be representative of the community in order to meet Sixth Amendment standards.

Local Jury. In addition to being impartial, a jury must also be local—from "the state and district wherein the crime shall have been committed." This provision is designed to prevent the British practice of carrying Americans across the seas to be tried by unsympathetic English juries. However, the defendant can waive the right to a local jury and request the judge to change the venue of the trial, if the community is biased due to pretrial publicity.

The Simpson Verdict. Perhaps the most controversial example of the jury system in action was the murder trial of former football star O. J. Simpson in 1995. A jury acquitted Simpson of the murders of his ex-wife, Nicole Brown, and her friend Ronald Goldman. Critics of the verdict charged that the jury had ignored the evidence and rendered a racially biased decision. Supporters

argued that the jury had properly done its job, because the prosecution—due to evidence of significant police misconduct—had not proven its case "beyond a reasonable doubt," as required by law. Simpson was later convicted in a civil trial and forced to pay damages to the victims' families. In the words of journalist Betsy Streisand: "For many Americans, the O. J. Simpson trial has become the criminal justice system's Vietnam—an event of sickening revelation."

O. J. Simpson celebrates his acquittal with attorneys F. Lee Bailey and Johnnie Cochran. Simpson was denied bail and served sixteen months in jail before he was ultimately acquitted of two murders.

...and to be informed of the nature and cause of the accusation;...
The Sixth Amendment gives defendants the right to know the charges against them. This information is necessary to prepare a proper defense. Normally, the judge informs the defendant of the charges against him at the **arraignment,** a court hearing where the defendant enters a plea of guilty or not guilty. A grand jury usually must return an indictment before the defendant is arraigned for a **felony,** a serious crime with a sentence of more than a year in prison. But nothing more than the arraignment is required for a **misdemeanor,** a minor offense with a sentence of a brief jail term or a small fine.

The charges against the defendant must be sufficiently detailed for him to offer an adequate defense. The government cannot accuse a person of a crime, for example, without stating the alleged time and place it occurred. Otherwise, the defendant would be unable to offer an alibi. Although the Supreme Court has not officially extended to the states the defendant's Sixth Amendment right to know the charges, that right is considered to be an element of due process of law, which applies to the states through the Fourteenth Amendment.

...to be confronted with the witnesses against him;...
This provision, known as the Confrontation Clause, prevents a witness from testifying in secret against the accused. It enables a defendant to challenge a witness's truthfulness in open court. Through the process of **cross-examination,** the defendant can ask questions to dispute the witness's testimony. Unless the defendant is unruly, he has the right to be in the courtroom at all times. But the judge may remove a disruptive defendant from the courtroom.

In most cases, the Confrontation Clause also prohibits **hearsay,** in which a witness testifies about the statement of a third party rather than something he or she directly observed. For example, Mary testifies that John said Jacob robbed a bank. But Mary herself did not witness Jacob committing a crime, and John is unavailable to be cross-examined. Normally, Mary's testimony would not be allowed. However, there are many exceptions to the hearsay rule, such as if John were dead or a codefendant in the crime.

Besides hearsay, the Supreme Court will also allow other exceptions to the defendant's right to cross-examine witnesses. A witness can refuse to answer certain questions because of a privilege, such as the confidentiality of the confessional. The Supreme Court has ruled that, under the Sixth Amendment, a witness must merely be available for cross-examination by the defendant, not compelled to answer all questions.

An especially controversial issue is whether the Sixth Amendment

---

"If we made a mistake, I would rather it be a mistake on the side of a person's innocence."

—Anise Aschenbach, Simpson juror

arraignment
a court hearing where the defendant pleads guilt or innocence

felony
a serious crime with a sentence of more than a year in prison

misdemeanor
a minor offense with a sentence of a brief jail term or a small fine.

cross-examination
the process of asking questions to challenge a witness's testimony

hearsay
testimony about the statement of a third party, rather than something directly observed

> "In this country, if someone dislikes you, or accuses you, he must come up in front.... The phrase still persists, 'Look me in the eye and say that.'"
>
> —Justice Antonin Scalia

requires face-to-face confrontation between a witness and the defendant. In general, such a confrontation is believed to increase the likelihood that the witness is telling the truth, because often witnesses find it easier to lie about a defendant behind his back rather than to his face. However, many states have laws that permit alleged victims in child abuse cases to testify without directly seeing the accused. The Supreme Court struck down such a law in *Coy v. Iowa* (1988), where the defendant was hidden behind a screen while the child testified. But in *Maryland v. Craig* (1990), the Court upheld a law that allowed a child abuse victim to testify on close-circuit television. Wrote Justice Sandra Day O'Connor for the Court: "the Confrontation Clause reflects a preference...for face-to-face confrontation at trial...a preference that must occasionally give way to considerations of public policy."

...to have compulsory process for obtaining witnesses in his favor,...

subpoena

a court order forcing a witness to testify or produce relevant evidence

The state can compel witnesses to testify in criminal cases, and the Sixth Amendment gives the defendant the same power. Using a **subpoena,** a court order forcing a witness to testify or produce relevant materials, the defendant can gather the evidence necessary to present a valid defense. In *United States v. Nixon* (1974), the Supreme Court ruled unanimously that even the president must comply with a subpoena in a criminal case, unless military or diplomatic secrets are involved. President Richard Nixon had been

To this cartoonist, President Nixon was caught in his own web by the release of the White House tapes on the Watergate affair.

subpoenaed during the Watergate trials to produce tape recordings of conversations in the White House. He refused, on the grounds that such communications were protected by executive privilege under Article II. Although the Court recognized executive privilege for the first time, it still held that the Sixth Amendment right of compulsory process overcame a general claim of privilege not based on national security.

...and to have the Assistance of Counsel for his defence.

The right to counsel is the most important in the Sixth Amendment, because without it the defendant is unable to assert any other rights he has. It is almost impossible for a layperson to navigate the complicated legal system alone. The Sixth Amendment originally protected only the right to have a lawyer present, but now it also includes the right to a court-appointed lawyer in most criminal cases if the defendant cannot pay for one. Under English law, a defendant had no right to counsel in felony cases, because the judge was presumed to be protecting the defendant's rights.

Capital Cases. In a series of cases, the Supreme Court expanded the right to have a court-appointed attorney. The Court required legal representation for indigent defendants charged with federal felonies in *Johnson v. Zerbst* (1938), but it moved more incrementally for the right to such counsel in state cases. In *Powell v. Alabama* (1932), the Court ruled that in death penalty cases the states must provide counsel for poor people. The Court overturned the convictions of the "Scottsboro Boys," nine African American teenagers accused of raping two white women on a freight train outside Scottsboro, Alabama. Without the right to counsel, said the Court, a defendant "though he be not guilty, faces the danger of conviction because he does not know how to establish his innocence." Although one of the alleged victims later recanted her testimony, several of the Scottsboro defendants were sentenced to death on retrials. None was ever executed, but they spent many years in prison, always declaring their innocence.

Noncapital Cases. The *Powell* case was the first step by which the Supreme Court applied the right to counsel to the states. But in *Betts v. Brady* (1942), the Court held that states only had to appoint counsel in noncapital cases under "special circumstances," such as when the defendant was mentally handicapped or otherwise incapacitated from presenting a defense. The Court overturned *Betts* in *Gideon v. Wainwright* (1963), requiring counsel for indigent defendants in all felony trials. In that case, Clarence Earl Gideon had sent a handwritten petition on prison stationery asking the Court to overturn his conviction for burglary because he was denied a lawyer. Gideon, an ex-con, had been accused of breaking into a poolroom and stealing about sixty-five dollars in change, which offenses combined to make a felony under Florida law. After the Gideon decision, the Court also extended the right to counsel in state cases to

Clarence Earl Gideon filed handwritten petitions from prison until the Supreme Court appointed a lawyer to represent him in his appeal.

misdemeanors, if the defendant could be imprisoned when convicted.
Quality of Defense. Although the Supreme Court has ruled that an indigent defendant is entitled to court-appointed counsel, that lawyer does not necessarily have to be experienced in criminal defense. In *Strickland v. Washington* (1984), the Court held that a defendant must receive "effective assistance of counsel," but not an error-free defense. According to *Strickland,* a lawyer's inexperience alone will not justify a new trial unless his specific errors deprived the defendant of adequate representation.

Present During Questioning. The Court has also held in *Escobedo v. Illinois* (1964) that a defendant's right to counsel applies during police questioning, not just at trial. Such interrogations often resulted in confessions, if a lawyer was not present to advise the defendant of his right to remain silent. Said the Court: "If the exercise of constitutional rights will thwart the effectiveness of a system of law enforcement, then there is something very wrong with that system."

Clarence Earl Gideon: The Bottom of Society's Barrel

An uneducated drifter, Clarence Earl Gideon had already served multiple prison terms for burglary before his handwritten appeal on prison stationery reached the Supreme Court. Gideon also spent three years in a juvenile reformatory. "Of all the prisons I have been in," he said, "that was the worst." Viewed as a hard-core recidivist, Gideon nonetheless fought from prison for his right to a lawyer. "I suppose," he wrote, "I am what is called [an] individualist, a person who will not conform." But when Gideon won his Supreme Court case, and was retried in Florida, he fired the ACLU attorneys who represented him. Wrote one of the ACLU lawyers later: "It has become almost axiomatic that the great rights which are secured for all of us by the Bill of Rights are constantly tested and retested in the courts by the people who live in the bottom of society's barrel.... It is probably a good thing that it is immaterial and unimportant that Gideon is something of a 'nut.'" But Gideon's stubbornness paid off. The local lawyer Gideon demanded later won his acquittal.

AMENDMENT VII

In suits at common law, where the value in controversy shall exceed twenty dollars, the right of trial by jury shall be preserved, and no fact tried by a jury shall be otherwise re-examined in any Court of the United States, than according to the rules of the common law.

THE SEVENTH AMENDMENT: TRIAL BY JURY IN CIVIL CASES

The Constitution includes trial by jury for the third time in the Seventh Amendment. It protects the right to a jury trial in **civil cases,** those deciding disputes between private parties over noncriminal matters, such as personal injuries or contracts. **Criminal cases** are those in which the government punishes individuals for committing crimes. The Seventh Amendment also limits a judge's power to overturn factual decisions by a jury, which could otherwise render a jury's power meaningless. Some Americans believe that, in an age of increasingly complex litigation, a civil jury is an incompetent artifact that actually endangers due process of law. Others argue that trial by jury, in both civil and criminal cases, ensures that the American people participate directly in self-government.

civil cases

those lawsuits deciding disputes between private parties over noncriminal matters, such as personal injuries or contracts

criminal cases

those in which the government punishes individuals for committing crimes

In suits at common law, where the value in controversy shall exceed twenty dollars, the right of trial by jury shall be preserved,…
This provision in the Seventh Amendment protects the right to trial by jury in civil cases. When the Seventh Amendment was drafted, the amount in controversy had to exceed twenty dollars before the right to a jury would apply. Today, that amount seems minuscule.

Juries were first used in civil cases, not for criminal trials. During the Middle Ages, the English used trial by jury to resolve disputes, instead of religious practices believed to reveal the will of God. Among these practices was trial by ordeal, in which a person had to pass a physical test proving that he or she was telling the truth, such as holding hot metal. Another method was trial by battle, in which whoever won an armed contest would prevail. In trial by oath giving, the party won who could get the most neighbors to swear oaths to God on his behalf, thus risking damnation for their immortal souls.

> "The jury system puts a ban upon intelligence and honesty, and a premium upon ignorance, stupidity, and perjury. It is a shame that we must continue to use a worthless system because it *was* good a thousand years ago."
>
> —Mark Twain

But after the Norman Conquest in 1066, the English used trial by jury as the dominant practice of deciding the truth. In the beginning, jurors were those citizens from the local community who had probably witnessed the disputed events. Conversely, today's juries are specifically selected from people who have no personal knowledge of the case or its history. Although the Magna Carta of 1215 did not explicitly protect the right to trial by jury, it did prevent English nobles from being punished "except by lawful judgment of his peers," meaning his aristocratic equals. This provision led to the assumption that a "jury of one's peers," or fellow citizens, would issue a judgment in a trial by jury. However, in the nineteenth century England eliminated trial by jury in civil cases to increase the efficiency of the courts.

In America, trial by jury became increasingly important to the colonists as protection against the power of royal officials. In fact, by 1776 all thirteen colonies protected trial by jury in civil cases. Nonetheless, the right was not included in the original text of the Constitution, and seven states included it in their proposed amendments for a Bill of Rights.

Some legal scholars have proposed that, like English courts, Americans abolish trial by jury in civil cases. Particularly in complex civil litigation, they believe, juries are not the most efficient and competent dispensers of justice. They maintain that juries in some complicated trials–which can involve hundreds of plaintiffs and last more than a year–produce such erratic verdicts that they violate due process of law. But other legal experts maintain that trial by jury, both in civil and criminal cases, is essential to democratic self-government. Only in juries, they point out, do the people directly participate in decision making. In both the executive and legislative branches, the people elect representatives who exercise power on their behalf. Furthermore, these scholars say, judges can be ignorant and incompetent, too.

The Solemn Task of Self-Government Akhil Reed Amar

Yale Law professor Akhil Reed Amar sees the jury as the crucible of democracy, in which citizens grapple with the difficult issues of self-government face-to-face.

The jury box provides a unique forum for interaction among citizens who might otherwise never engage each other, people who live in different neighborhoods, attend different schools, worship in different congregations.... In the jury box, we meet citizen to citizen, face to face, not just to exchange greetings or currency, but to listen to, learn from, and work with one another in the solemn task of self-government. Nowhere else, not even in the voting booth, must Americans come together in person to deliberate collectively about fundamental matters in our shared public life. Democracy is well served by the dialogue that takes place in the jury room.

Thus far, the Supreme Court has not recognized a complexity exception to the Seventh Amendment. The Supreme Court has also never incorporated the right to trial by jury in civil cases to apply to the states. Moreover, the Court uses different standards for jury trials in civil and criminal cases. Although federal criminal trials must have a twelve-person jury, the Court ruled in *Colgrove v. Battin* (1973) that civil trials only need a minimum of six jurors. But in general civil cases require unanimous verdicts, just as do federal criminal cases, unless the litigants stipulate otherwise.

...and no fact tried by a jury, shall be otherwise re-examined in any Court of the United States, than according to the rules of the common law.

What if a judge could ignore a jury's verdict, or instruct the jury to make a particular finding on the evidence? The framers of the Constitution were well aware of *Bushell's Case* (1670), an appeal of an English judge's punishment of jurors who refused to find William Penn, a Quaker and later founder of Pennsylvania, guilty of unlawful assembly. To avoid such injustice, the framers included a provision in the Seventh Amendment prohibiting a judge from disregarding a jury's determination of the facts, except under circumstances determined by law.

In *Baltimore and Carolina Line v. Redman* (1935), the Supreme Court upheld the general principle that a jury decides the facts of a case, and the judge determines what law is relevant to those facts. The judge's job is to advise the jury of what verdict, under the law, is required if the jury finds certain facts to be true. The judge gives these legal instructions to the jury before it deliberates. However, the distinction between the law and the facts in a case is not always clear. In addition, the Supreme Court ruled in 1996 that in certain types of federal cases involving citizens from different states, the federal judge can apply a state law restricting jury awards for "excessive" damages without violating the Seventh Amendment.

"Where do they dig up some of these jurors anyway? Last time I served, I sat with the flotsam of the universe."
—Whoopi Goldberg

These jurors listen to the judge's instructions in a lawsuit about smoking.

AMENDMENT VIII

Excessive bail shall not be required, nor excessive fines imposed, nor cruel and unusual punishments inflicted.

THE EIGHTH AMENDMENT: CRUEL AND UNUSUAL PUNISHMENT

bail

money or property posted as security to obtain release from jail pending trial

The Eighth Amendment protects the rights of prisoners before they are tried and after they are convicted. It prohibits excessive **bail,** money or property posted as security to obtain release from jail pending trial. The amendment also bars excessive fines and "cruel and unusual" punishments if the accused is found guilty. An example of constitutional plagiarism, the Eighth Amendment comes almost word for word from the English Bill of Rights of 1689. However, in 1641 the Massachusetts Body of Liberties had also provided for bail and forbade cruel and unusual punishments. Nonetheless, the Puritans allowed the death penalty for blasphemy and used physical punishments such as cutting off ears and branding with a hot iron. According to the Supreme Court, cruel and unusual punishment is defined by "evolving standards of decency." But Americans continue to debate whether such standards should include the death penalty.

Excessive bail shall not be required, nor excessive fines imposed,...
This provision in the Eighth Amendment does not give an unconditional right to bail. Instead, it specifies that bail, when allowed, shall not be "excessive." Federal and state laws establish the conditions whereby bail is granted. For example, bail may be denied in capital cases or if the defendant has threatened witnesses. Bail allows the defendant to remain free pending trial, because a person is assumed to be innocent until proven guilty.

The purpose of bail is generally to guarantee that the defendant will appear in court. The Supreme Court ruled in *Stack v. Boyle* (1951) that any bail beyond that necessary to ensure the defendant's presence at trial is "excessive." But Congress passed the Bail Reform Act in 1984, allowing federal courts for the first time to deny bail based on predictions of the future dangerousness of the defendant. This practice, known as preventive detention, was upheld by the Supreme Court in *United States v. Salerno* (1987).

The Eighth Amendment also prohibits excessive fines. The Supreme Court has ruled that the amendment only limits fines levied by the government, not punitive damages in private lawsuits. The Eighth Amendment's restrictions on excessive bail and fines have not been incorporated by the Supreme Court to apply to the states.

...nor cruel and unusual punishments inflicted.

Although this provision bans punishments that are "cruel and unusual," it does not specify what they are. In *Trop v. Dulles* (1958), the Supreme Court ruled that the prohibition on cruel and unusual punishments "must draw its meaning from evolving standards of decency that mark the progress of a maturing society." Therefore, certain punishments that were acceptable when the Eighth Amendment was ratified, such as whippings and cutting off ears, are no longer permissible today. The most controversial question about the Eighth Amendment is whether American society can "evolve" to the point that the death penalty becomes unconstitutional.

Capital Punishment. In early America, death was the automatic sentence for murder. State laws began to distinguish between types of murder, and jurors were given more discretion in issuing death sentences. However, these laws gave jurors no guidance in choosing life or death for a defendant. Social scientists noted that jurors did not treat like cases alike, and that if they followed a pattern it was based on race. African Americans were sentenced to death far more often than whites, and defendants executed for rape were virtually always black men charged with attacking white women.

In *Furman v. Georgia* (1972), the Supreme Court held that the death penalty, as then carried out in the United States, was "wantonly" and "freakishly" imposed and therefore violated the Eighth Amendment. The Court did not declare that capital punishment was unconstitutional per se, but that the states had to give judges and juries more guidance in imposing the death penalty. A moratorium on executions ensued, until approximately three-fourths of the states had enacted new statutes.

The Court ruled in *Gregg v. Georgia* (1976) that "the punishment of death does not invariably violate the Constitution." The death penalty was not "unusual" punishment, said the Court, because so many states had passed laws restoring capital punishment after Furman. Moreover, in addition to deterrence of future murderers, Justice Potter Stewart maintained that retribution was a sufficient justification for the death penalty "in an ordered society that asks its citizens to rely on legal processes rather than self-help to vindicate their wrongs." However, Justice William Brennan's dissent argued that "the law has progressed to the point...that

"Without the Eighth Amendment, the U.S. would be just another police state, governed by fear."
—Coretta Scott King

the punishment of death, like punishments on the rack, the screw, and the wheel, is no longer morally tolerable in our civilized society."

In *Gregg,* the Court upheld a Georgia law that limited jury discretion by dividing a capital trial into a guilt phase and a sentencing phase. First, the jury must determine if the defendant was guilty of the crime. Then, in the sentencing phase, the jury had to consider both aggravating and mitigating circumstances to decide if the defendant deserved to die for his crime. **Aggravating circumstances,** such as the inhuman manner in which the crime was committed, increased the gravity of the crime. **Mitigating circumstances,** such as the character and life history of the defendant, lessened the severity of the crime. However, the Supreme Court ruled in *Woodson v. North Carolina* (1976) that a state law totally removing discretion by making a death sentence mandatory violated the Eighth Amendment.

In general, the Supreme Court has held that the death penalty should be used only for the crime of murder. The Court struck down laws that allowed capital punishment for rape convictions in *Coker v. Georgia* (1977). The Court has also limited death sentences under the **felony-murder rule,** in which accomplices are convicted of murder—even if another person actually killed the victim—when it was committed as part of a felony such as kidnapping or robbery. In *Enmund v. Florida* (1982), the Supreme Court ruled that minor accomplices could not be sentenced to death under the felony-murder rule. However, in *Tison v. Arizona* (1987), the Court upheld the death penalty for a major participant in a felony murder who was reckless to human life.

The Supreme Court has also considered whether the death penalty is unconstitutional when applied to certain types of defendants. The Court has allowed capital punishment for juveniles sixteen and older. In 1989, the Supreme Court ruled that a national consensus did not exist against executing the mentally retarded. However, in *Atkins v. Virginia* (2002), the Court noted the increasing number of states that barred capital punishment for the mentally retarded and concluded that such punishment would now be "unusual" and violate the "evolving standards of decency" of the Eighth Amendment.

Because death is different, the ultimate penalty that society can impose, the Supreme Court has ruled that capital punishment cases require extraordinary procedures. Like other defendants, death row inmates can appeal their sentences directly through state courts—where most murder trials occur—or indirectly through federal courts if their constitutional rights have been violated. These indirect appeals are known as petitions for **habeas corpus,** which can last many years in capital cases. The Supreme Court upheld limits on habeas corpus petitions under the Antiterrorism and Effective Death Penalty Act in *Felker v. Turpin* (1996), ruling that the law

aggravating circumstances

factors that increase the severity of a crime

mitigating circumstances

factors that decrease the severity of a crime

felony-murder rule

legal doctrine by which accomplices are convicted of murder—even if another person actually killed the victim—when it was committed as part of a felony such as kidnapping or robbery

habeas corpus

a court order directing that an officer who has custody of a prisoner show cause why the prisoner is being held did not violate Article I's protection of habeas corpus. Congress passed the law to reduce delays in executions, which it said were undermining the impact of the death penalty.

However, Americans are also concerned about the increasing number of death row inmates who have been released after evidence of their innocence has been discovered. Some defendants have come within days of being executed before they were exonerated. As of 2002, more than one hundred death row inmates have been released due to evidence of their innocence since 1973. Such cases prove that the risk of executing innocent defendants is too high, say critics of the death penalty. But supporters of capital punishment argue that these cases demonstrate that the legal system can correct its mistakes.

Many states have adopted lethal injection instead of the electric chair, which legal experts argue is a cruel method of execution. Justice William Brennan called electrocution "the contemporary technological equivalent of burning people at the stake."

In *Callins v. Collins* (1994), Justice Harry Blackmun stated that, after twenty years of trying to "tinker with the machinery of death," he had concluded that it was impossible to fairly and accurately administer the death penalty. But Justice Antonin Scalia pointed out that the Fifth Amendment of the Constitution contained specific references to the death penalty, so it clearly did not violate "cruel and unusual punishment." According to Justice Scalia, the proper recourse for innocent death row inmates who had exhausted their court appeals was a clemency petition to the executive branch.

Punishments Other Than Death. Under the Eighth Amendment, punishments must generally be proportional to the crime committed. Therefore, in *Trop v. Dulles* the Supreme Court ruled that depriving an army deserter of citizenship was cruel and unusual punishment. However, the Court has rarely struck down sentences for noncapital crimes as disproportionate, instead deferring to the judgment of legislators. In *Harmelin v. Michigan* (1991), for example, the Court refused to overturn a mandatory life sentence without parole for a first-time offender who used cocaine.

The Supreme Court has also ruled that the Eighth Amendment prohibits inhumane prison conditions. But the Court will not intervene unless prisons are deplorable, not merely uncomfortable. Prisons are also responsible for inmates' health care, held the Court in *Estelle v. Gamble* (1976). In addition, prison officials must not disregard the physical safety of

"We punish criminals mostly to pay them back, and we execute the worst of them out of moral necessity."

—Walter Berns, *Wall Street Journal*

"Speaking as a person who is supposed to be dead, I believe the death penalty should be abolished, period. Because you can't be sure."

—Kirk Bloodsworth, exonerated defendant

"Capital
punishment...
is a government
program, so
skepticism is
in order."

—George Will

inmates. Some prisoner advocates argue that rape among inmates has become so common that prison officials are allowing it in violation of the Eighth Amendment. They say that rape and the possibility of death by AIDS definitely constitute cruel and unusual punishment.

One area where the Supreme Court has not extended Eighth Amendment protection is the public schools. In *Ingraham v. Wright* (1977), the Court ruled that schools are not constitutionally forbidden to use corporal punishment, even if the student needs medical attention as a result. Unlike prisoners, said the Court, schoolchildren had recourse for excessive punishment through the community's supervision of the schools.

Timothy McVeigh: American Terrorist

A decorated veteran of the Persian Gulf War, Timothy McVeigh became increasingly disillusioned with the U.S. government when he returned home. As a survivalist and weapons enthusiast, McVeigh opposed the actions of the Alcohol, Tobacco, and Firearms (ATF) agency to enforce gun control laws. He regarded the ATF's raid on the Branch Davidian compound in Waco, Texas, as a sign that the federal government was out of control and violating the spirit of the U.S. Constitution. On the one-year anniversary of that raid—April 19, 1995—McVeigh detonated a truck bomb outside a federal office building in Oklahoma City, killing 168 people. Of those, nineteen were children enrolled in a day-care center. McVeigh later referred to them as "collateral damage," a phrase he borrowed from military statements during the Gulf War. McVeigh wore a T-shirt during the Oklahoma City bombing that quoted Thomas Jefferson: "The tree of liberty must be refreshed from time to

McVeigh's truck bomb destroyed the Alfred E. Murrah Federal Building and murdered 168 Americans.

time with the blood of patriots and tyrants." After a postponement of his execution due to FBI errors, Timothy McVeigh was put to death by lethal injection on June 11, 2001—the first federal prisoner to be executed in thirty-eight years. He died unrepentant of his crimes.

One White Banker Per Week *George Carlin*

With his typically biting satire, comedian George Carlin proposes that, in order to stop drug dealing, Americans should execute the bankers who launder drug money.

Many people in this country want to expand the death penalty to include drug dealers. This is really stupid. Drug dealers aren't afraid to die. They're already killin' each other by the hundreds every day. Drive-bys, turf wars, gang killings. They're not afraid to die. The death penalty means very little unless you use it on people who are afraid to die. Like the bankers who launder the drug money. Forget dealers. If you want to slow down the drug traffic, you have to start executing some of these white, middle-class Republican bankers. And I don't mean soft American executions like lethal injections. I'm talkin' about crucifixion, folks. I say bring back crucifixion! A form of capital punishment the Christians and Jews of America can really appreciate....

And I'll guarantee you one thing: you start nailin' one white banker per week to a big wooden cross on national television, and you're gonna see that drug traffic begin to slow down mighty fuckin' quick. Why you won't even be able to buy drugs in schools and prisons anymore.

AMENDMENT IX

The enumeration in the Constitution, of certain rights, shall not be construed to deny or disparage others retained by the people.

THE NINTH AMENDMENT: UNENUMERATED RIGHTS

unenumerated rights

those rights not specifically listed in the Constitution

One of the arguments against adding a bill of rights to the Constitution was that such a list might imply those were the only rights the people had. Therefore, when James Madison introduced the Bill of Rights in Congress, he included a provision protecting rights "retained by the people," but not written down in the Constitution. These **unenumerated rights** referred to in the Ninth Amendment have proven to be very controversial. Libertarians believe that the Ninth Amendment includes certain fundamental rights, such as privacy, that are so important they must be protected by judges, whether or not they are specifically listed in the Constitution. Advocates of judicial restraint argue that such interpretations of the Ninth Amendment give judges too much discretion, and that it is the job of state legislatures and the people themselves to protect unenumerated rights.

The enumeration in the Constitution, of certain rights,…

The rights that are specifically listed in the Constitution receive the highest form of judicial protection. These rights–such as freedom of religion, freedom of speech, and the right to a trial by jury–are considered to be among the most important that Americans have, and judges clearly have the power to compel government officials to enforce them. The Supreme Court has also recognized certain unenumerated rights not listed in the Constitution. Included among these unenumerated rights are the right to travel, the right to vote, and the right to privacy.

Although the Ninth Amendment ostensibly protects unenumerated rights, it has never been the basis for a majority decision of the Supreme Court. Instead, the Court has relied on other provisions in the Constitution. For instance, the Court ruled that freedom of association is implied by other First Amendment rights. Also, the Court has held that some aspects of the right to privacy are derived from the Third, Fourth, and Fifth Amendments.

But the most common way that the Supreme Court recognizes unenumerated rights is through the Due Process Clause of the Fourteenth Amendment. That amendment says that no state shall deprive any person "of life, liberty, or property without due process of law." If the Supreme Court determines that a right not listed in the Constitution is "fundamental," then it becomes a "liberty" interest covered by the Due Process Clause. This method of protecting unenumerated rights is known as substantive due process, which is explained in greater detail in the Fourteenth Amendment chapter.

The Right to Privacy. Perhaps the most controversial right not specifically listed in the Bill of Rights is the right to privacy. The Supreme Court has recognized many aspects of the right to privacy—among them the right to marry, to have children, and to have an abortion. In *Griswold v. Connecticut* (1965), the Court struck down an 1879 state law that prohibited the use of contraceptives, at least as applied to married couples. The Court's opinion by Justice William O. Douglas declared that "specific guarantees in the Bill of Rights have penumbras, formed by emanations from those guarantees that help give them life and substance." A penumbra is a type of astronomical shadow. Douglas added that "zones of privacy" created by the First, Third, Fourth, Fifth, and Ninth Amendments protected marital privacy. In a concurring opinion by Justice Arthur Goldberg, three justices argued that the Ninth Amendment itself protected the right to marital privacy.

After the *Griswold* decision, the Supreme Court ruled in several cases that sexual privacy applied outside marriage as well. Such privacy included a woman's right to have an abortion, held the Court in *Roe v. Wade* (1973):

> This right of privacy, whether it be founded in the Fourteenth Amendment's concept of personal liberty and restrictions upon state action, as we feel it is, or, as the district court determined, in the Ninth Amendment's reservation of rights to the people, is broad enough to encompass a women's decision whether or not to terminate her pregnancy.

Because the Supreme Court's abortion cases are based on the Fourteenth Amendment, they are discussed in greater detail in that chapter.

Until *Bowers v. Hardwick* (1986), a case involving a gay man, the Court consistently upheld the right to sexual privacy. Michael Hardwick contested a Georgia law prohibiting sodomy—defined as oral or anal sex—as a violation of his sexual privacy under the Ninth and Fourteenth Amendments. An Atlanta police officer with an expired warrant for a misdemeanor offense had witnessed Hardwick, in his own bedroom,

"There's no way the Supreme Court can say that I can't have sex with a consenting adult in the privacy of my own bedroom."

—Michael Hardwick

> **"I view the Framers as teachers, not wardens."**
>
> —Randy Barnett

engaging in oral sex with another adult male and arrested him for sodomy. The Supreme Court upheld Georgia's sodomy law, saying that the Court refused to recognize "a fundamental right to engage in homosexual sodomy." However, Justice Harry Blackmun's dissent emphasized that the law applied to both heterosexuals and homosexuals: "Unlike the Court, the Georgia legislature has not proceeded on the assumption that homosexuals are so different from other citizens that their lives may be controlled in a way that would not be tolerated if it limited the choices of those other citizens."

...shall not be construed to deny or disparage others retained by the people.

Perhaps the biggest debate over the Ninth Amendment is who should protect the rights it includes. Do rights that are "retained by the people" receive protection by the courts, or by state legislatures, or by the people themselves? Some legal scholars believe that the Ninth Amendment's vague language could give unelected judges an unlimited license to create constitutional rights and overturn the decisions of democratic majorities. As Judge Robert Bork testified at his confirmation hearings for a Supreme Court appointment in 1987:

> I do not think you can use the Ninth Amendment unless you know something of what it means. For example, if you had an amendment that says "Congress shall make no" and then there was an inkblot, and you cannot read the rest of it, and that is the only copy you have, I do not think the court can make up what might be under the inkblot.

President Gerald Ford and Senator Robert Dole supported the Supreme Court nomination of Judge Robert Bork (center).

Other legal experts see the Ninth Amendment as something more than an inkblot, although they disagree over exactly how its protections should be implemented. Constitutional scholar John Hart Ely, for example, argues that judges should only recognize Ninth Amendment rights that strengthen participation in the democratic process, not that reflect choices among substantive values.

But other scholars maintain that the language of the Ninth Amendment is no more vague than other constitutional phrases, such as "due process of law," that judges frequently interpret. According to law professor Randy Barnett, refusing to allow judges to recognize Ninth Amendment rights would be to "disparage" them in relation to the rights protected by the first eight amendments. The Ninth Amendment, Barnett says, must be implemented as fully as any other part of the Bill of Rights.

In James Madison's original version of the Bill of Rights, one proposed amendment both retained unenumerated rights for the people and reserved undelegated powers to the states. These provisions were later split into the Ninth and Tenth Amendments. Consequently, some commentators believe that the Ninth and Tenth Amendments have virtually the same meaning, and that unenumerated rights should be protected by the states, not the federal courts. Others argue that the Ninth Amendment secures implied rights for individuals, just as the Article I's Necessary and Proper Clause secures implied powers for Congress.

But thus far a majority of the Supreme Court has not agreed with either interpretation, preferring to ignore the Ninth Amendment altogether. That's why many scholars refer to it as the forgotten amendment.

> **"In sophisticated legal circles, mentioning the Ninth Amendment is a surefire way to get a laugh."**
>
> —John Hart Ely

Where Do Rights Come From?

The Ninth Amendment raises the question of what a "right" is, and where it comes from. A right is a power or privilege that belongs to a person by law, nature, or tradition. Natural rights are based on the belief that all people have certain rights simply by being human. Therefore, the government cannot create or destroy natural rights, but it doesn't necessarily protect them, either. Legal or positive rights are those recognized by the statutes and court decisions of a society's government. Since legal rights are created by the government, the government can also take them away. The Ninth Amendment says that just because certain rights are not listed in the Constitution doesn't mean they don't exist. But does the Ninth Amendment refer to legal rights, that should be enforced by courts, or natural rights?

AMENDMENT X

The powers not delegated to the United States by the Constitution, nor prohibited by it to the States, are reserved to the States respectively, or to the people.

THE TENTH AMENDMENT: STATES' RIGHTS

The other nine amendments in the Bill of Rights all refer, in some way, to the rights of individuals. But the Tenth Amendment protects powers, not rights—and of the states, not individuals. Although the states had to give up many powers in order to create the new Constitution, they insisted an amendment be added that affirmed their ongoing role in the governmental design. In fact, the Tenth Amendment was the only part of the Bill of Rights that was recommended by all the state conventions that submitted proposed amendments. From the beginning of the nation, the proper balance between the powers of the federal government and the powers of the states caused major dissension, culminating in the Civil War. And in the words of Chief Justice John Marshall, this issue "will probably continue to arise, as long as our system shall exist."

The powers not delegated to the United States by the Constitution, nor prohibited by it to the States,...

The Articles of Confederation had limited the national government to the powers *expressly* listed—and some members of Congress wanted James Madison's version of the Tenth Amendment to say so as well. But Madison resisted, arguing that implied powers were necessary to the proper functioning of the national government. This debate over **federalism,** the system of shared power between national and state governments, continued throughout American history. Some argued in favor of **states' rights,** saying that the states had sovereign powers equal to the federal government. Others defended **nationalism,** the supremacy of the federal government over the states.

Chief Justice John Marshall led the Supreme Court to issue many rulings during the early 1800s that supported national supremacy. In *McCulloch v. Maryland* (1819), the Court construed the Tenth Amendment

federalism

the system of shared power between national and state governments

states' rights

doctrine that the states have sovereign powers equal to the national government

nationalism

the supremacy of the federal government over the states

narrowly, and the implied powers of the national government broadly. Marshall's opinion for a unanimous Court noted that the word "expressly" had been omitted from the Tenth Amendment, unlike the Articles of Confederation. This indicated, said the Court, that the framers of the Constitution intended the Necessary and Proper Clause, or Elastic Clause, in Article I to give Congress implied powers. Therefore, the Court declared that Congress had the power to establish a national bank, although it was not specifically listed in the Constitution, and Maryland did not have the power to tax a bank created by the federal government.

When Marshall died in 1835, Roger Taney became chief justice of the United States. Appointed by Andrew Jackson, Taney supported a states' rights philosophy. He promoted a doctrine of "dual sovereignty," in which both the states and the national government were supreme within their spheres of action. Even after the Civil War, this doctrine dominated Supreme Court interpretations of the Tenth Amendment. In *Hammer v. Dagenhart* (1918), the Court ruled that Congress did not have the power under Article I's Commerce Clause to prohibit goods produced by child labor from interstate commerce. Such regulation of social policy, said the Court, was a local power reserved to the states under the Tenth Amendment.

But during the Great Depression and World War II, the Supreme Court began to recognize a more expansive view of national power. In *United States v. Darby Lumber Company* (1941), the Court held that the Tenth Amendment was merely a "truism that all is retained which has not been surrendered" to the national government, not an independent source of states' rights. In *Darby,* the Court overruled the *Hammer* decision and upheld the power of Congress to set wage and hour regulations for employees of companies engaged in interstate commerce.

Roger B. Taney served as the nation's fifth chief justice (1836–64) and vigorously supported states' rights.

The Supreme Court vacillated on the proper balance between state and federal power during the 1970s and 1980s. But under Chief Justice William Rehnquist, the Court has issued a wide range of decisions reaffirming the role of the states and limiting the powers of Congress. In *Printz v. United States* (1997), for example, the Court struck down the Brady Handgun Violence Prevention Act, which required state and local law enforcement officers to conduct background checks before a person could purchase a handgun. The Court ruled that the law exceeded Congress's power under the Commerce Clause, because it infringed on the system of "dual sovereignty" created by the Constitution, including the Tenth Amendment.

> "The future smiles upon the states.... As the dimly understood trends of the global order descend upon us, our need for smaller, more accessible governance will only increase."
>
> —Judge J. Harvie Wilkinson, III

From 1995 to 2002, the Court has consistently curtailed federal authority, striking down more than twenty-five laws enacted by Congress. From 1937 until 1995, conversely, the Supreme Court overturned just one federal law as exceeding the commerce power.

...are reserved to the States respectively, or to the people.

The debate over the proper meaning of the Tenth Amendment has not taken place only in the courts. Battles over federalism fueled American politics for centuries and led to the greatest threat to the U.S. Constitution– the Civil War. Sectional strife characterized the American nation from the beginning, and was pushed to the breaking point by disputes over slavery. The modern-day civil rights movement also resurrected struggles between the federal government and the states.

The doctrine of states' rights was promoted by two of the nation's founders, Thomas Jefferson and James Madison. During disputes over the Alien and Sedition Acts of 1798, which they regarded as unconstitutional, Jefferson and Madison advocated the idea that states could declare acts of Congress unconstitutional. During this time, the Federalists, the political party that had drafted the laws, also dominated the federal courts. Jefferson's Kentucky Resolution and Madison's Virginia Resolution, passed by the legislatures of those states, declared that when the federal government exceeded its powers, the states could refuse to obey. In Madison's words, the states are "duty bound to interpose for arresting the progress of the evil." Jefferson's election to the presidency in 1800 resolved the crisis, because he allowed the Alien and Sedition Acts to expire.

nullification

doctrine that states can declare an act of the federal government to be null and void; also known as interposition

Madison's language of interposition, or **nullification,** came back to haunt him. During the War of 1812, known as "Mr. Madison's War," New England states threatened to secede at the Hartford Convention in 1814. But the war ended soon thereafter, and New England's vital trade with Great Britain resumed. Less than twenty years later, South Carolina also threatened to secede over trade problems due to high federal tariffs. Vice President John Calhoun of South Carolina quoted Madison in a famous address supporting nullification. Calhoun resigned his office to oppose President Andrew Jackson over the nullification issue. Only when Congress authorized Jackson to use force to collect the tariff, and a compromise tariff was also passed, did South Carolina back down. But in 1860 South Carolina finally did secede, followed by ten other southern states. The ensuing Civil War cost more than half a million American lives. Only after the war was over did the Supreme Court declare in *Texas v. White* (1869) that the Constitution "in all its provisions, looks to an indestructible Union, composed of indestructible states."

During the 1950s, Southern states renewed their claim of states' rights after the Supreme Court ruled in *Brown v. Board of Education* (1954) that public schools must be desegregated. In early 1956, both Alabama and Virginia passed nullification resolutions. In March, one hundred members of the U.S. Congress issued the Southern Manifesto, protesting "the Supreme Court's encroachments on rights reserved to the states and to the people." These legislators argued that education had long been the province solely of state and local governments, and the federal government had no right to intervene. Several southern states established "sovereignty commissions" to fight integration.

Two presidents called in U.S. troops to enforce desegregation orders of the federal courts. In 1957, Dwight Eisenhower ordered the 101st Airborne Division to protect the "Little Rock Nine," the first black students to attend Central High School in Little Rock, Arkansas. In 1962, John F. Kennedy sent federal troops to end rioting at the University of Mississippi when James Meredith became the first African American to enroll there.

"It ought to be possible...for American students of any color to attend any public institution they select without having to be backed up by troops."
—John F. Kennedy

President John F. Kennedy sent in federal troops to quell a riot of more than two thousand people, in which two persons were killed, when James Meredith integrated the University of Mississippi in October 1962.

During the civil rights movement, the federal government established its supremacy over the states, at least regarding equal opportunity in education. But the debate over the proper balance between state and federal power continued. President Ronald Reagan promoted a "New Federalism" in the 1980s to reduce the size and cost of the federal government. And President Bill Clinton declared during his second term that "the era of big government is over."

Deprived of the Power of Self-Government *William Simmons*

States' rights became a rallying cry in the South after the Brown *decision in 1954. William Simmons, a leader of the segregationist Citizens' Council, describes his reaction when black student James Meredith integrated the University of Mississippi in 1962.*

When Meredith was brought in to Ole Miss by the U.S. marshals and the riots broke out, I was in the Citizens' Council office in Jackson.... There was a lot of excitement because rumors were flying that Governor Barnett would be arrested by United States marshals. Many people, probably several thousand, surrounded the governor's mansion...as a sort of human barrier, to protect the governor.... We thought the use of marshals was pretty bad. We viewed the whole episode as an attack on the authority of the state....

After it was all over, the next day was a beautiful fall day.... We were on the third floor, and my wife was standing there beside me. We looked at the people walking down the street, normally going about their everyday affairs, and I turned to her and I said, "These people have just been deprived of the power of self-government, and they don't know it." That's the shock. The realization came to me that the enormous usurpation of power by the federal government had succeeded and from then on things would never be the same.

AMENDMENT XI

The Judicial power of the United States shall not be construed to extend to any suit in law or equity, commenced or prosecuted against one of the United States by Citizens of another State, or by Citizens or Subjects of any Foreign State.

THE ELEVENTH AMENDMENT: LAWSUITS AGAINST STATES

Added to the Constitution just a few years after the Bill of Rights, the Eleventh Amendment protects the states against lawsuits in federal courts by citizens of other states or a foreign nation. The Eleventh Amendment is the first constitutional amendment to specifically overturn a Supreme Court decision. Although the Eleventh Amendment was not very significant for many years, the Supreme Court has lately used the amendment in several cases to strike down federal laws that it believes overstep state power.

The Judicial power of the United States shall not be construed to extend to any suit in law or equity, commenced or prosecuted against one of the United States by Citizens of another State, or by Citizens or Subjects of any Foreign State.
Many states believed that if they ratified the Constitution, Article III would explicitly allow lawsuits against them in federal courts by citizens of another state or of a foreign country. Federalists urged the states not to worry, because they would be protected by the doctrine of **sovereign immunity,** in which a sovereign government (such as a state or nation) cannot be sued without its consent.

> **sovereign immunity**
> doctrine that a sovereign government cannot be sued without its consent

Yet an early Supreme Court case fulfilled the states' worst fears. In *Chisholm v. Georgia* (1793), the Court upheld a default judgment against Georgia for failing to pay a Revolutionary War debt to a merchant for clothing supplied. The Court ruled that sovereignty applied only to the national government, not the states, for the purposes of such lawsuits. In 1794, Congress passed a constitutional amendment to reverse the Court's ruling, and it was ratified in 1795.

The Supreme Court broadened the reach of the Eleventh Amendment in *Hans v. Louisiana* (1890), when it ruled that citizens of a state could not sue that state in federal court. The Court argued that, beyond its literal words, the Eleventh Amendment reasserted the traditional doctrine of broad sovereign immunity for the states. However, there are certain exceptions to sovereign immunity. The state may waive its privilege and consent to be sued. Also, the Eleventh Amendment does not prevent the U.S. government or another state from suing a state in federal court. Moreover, Congress has the power under the Fourteenth and Fifteenth Amendments to hold states accountable for violating particular rights.

But the Supreme Court has recently begun to curtail this power as applied to "private causes of action," in which Congress allows individuals to sue states directly for damages. For example, the Court has struck down laws that allow individuals to sue states for patent infringement, age discrimination, and violating fair labor standards. Supporters of these decisions argue that they preserve the role of the states in the federal system. Critics charge that states are now free to discriminate because the federal government does not have the resources to bring lawsuits on behalf of individuals.

AMENDMENT XII

The Electors shall meet in their respective states and vote by ballot for President and Vice President, one of whom, at least, shall not be an inhabitant of the same state with themselves; they shall name in their ballots the person voted for as President, and in distinct ballots the person voted for as Vice President, and they shall make distinct lists of all persons voted for as President, and of all persons voted for as Vice President, and of the number of votes for each, which lists they shall sign and certify, and transmit sealed to the seat of the government of the United States, directed to the President of the Senate;—The President of the Senate shall, in the presence of the Senate and House of Representatives, open all the certificates and the votes shall then be counted;—The person having the greatest number of votes for President, shall be the President, if such number be a majority of the whole number of Electors appointed; and if no person have such majority, then from the persons having the highest numbers not exceeding three on the list of those voted for as President, the House of Representatives shall choose immediately, by ballot, the President. But in choosing the President, the votes shall be taken by states, the representation from each state having one vote; a quorum for this purpose shall consist of a member or members from two-thirds of the states, and a majority of all the states shall be necessary to a choice. *And if the House of Representatives shall not choose a President whenever the right of choice shall devolve upon them, before the fourth day of March next following, then the Vice President shall act as President, as in case of the death or other constitutional disability of the President.*—The person having the greatest number of votes as Vice President, shall be the Vice President, if such number be a majority of the whole number of Electors appointed, and if no person have a majority, then from the two highest numbers on the list, the Senate shall choose the Vice President; a quorum for the purpose shall consist of two-thirds of the whole number of Senators, and a majority of the whole number shall be necessary to a choice. But no person constitutionally ineligible to the office of President shall be eligible to that of Vice President of the United States.

THE TWELFTH AMENDMENT: CHOOSING THE EXECUTIVE

The Twelfth Amendment changed the way the president and vice president were chosen under Article II. Originally, the electoral college voted for two people on the same ballot, without distinguishing between offices. The person who received the most electoral votes became president; the runner-up was vice president. But the advent of political parties, and a tie in the electoral college, prompted Americans to adopt the Twelfth Amendment in 1804 to create separate balloting for the president and the vice president.

The Electors shall meet in their respective states and vote by ballot for President and Vice President, one of whom, at least, shall not be an inhabitant of the same state with themselves; they shall name in their ballots the person voted for as President, and in distinct ballots the person voted for as Vice President, and they shall make distinct lists of all persons voted for as President, and of all persons voted for as Vice President, and of the number of votes for each, which lists they shall sign and certify, and transmit sealed to the seat of the government of the United States, directed to the President of the Senate;—...

As political parties emerged, the pitfalls of electing the president and vice president on the same ballot became clear. John Adams, a Federalist, was elected president in 1796, but his vice president was his rival Thomas Jefferson, a Democratic-Republican. In 1800, Jefferson tied in the electoral college with Aaron Burr, who was supposed to be Jefferson's running mate. But Burr refused to withdraw from the race, and the election went to the House of Representatives—which chose Jefferson after thirty-six ballots. As a result, the Twelfth Amendment was proposed and ratified before the next presidential election, and thereafter electors voted for president and vice president on separate ballots.

Yet there were some objections to separate balloting during the debate over the Twelfth Amendment. Opponents of the amendment argued that under such a system, in which the two candidates ran for office as part of one ticket, little care would be given to the qualifications of the vice president. "They will seek a man of moderate talents," said one senator, "whose ambition is bounded by that office, and whose influence will aid them in electing the President."

Some of the provisions in the Twelfth Amendment are the same as in the original version of Article II. For instance, electors are not allowed to vote for both presidential and vice presidential candidates from their own state. This restriction was an issue in the 2000 election, because vice presidential candidate Dick Cheney had been registered to vote in Texas only days before Texas governor George W. Bush chose him as a running mate. But Cheney quickly moved his voter registration to Wyoming, where he had longtime ties, and a federal appellate court ruled that as a result Texas electors could vote for both Bush and Cheney. Electors cast their votes in their state capitals on the first Monday after the second Wednesday in December, a date set by federal law.

…The President of the Senate shall, in the presence of the Senate and House of Representatives, open all the certificates and the votes shall then be counted;—The person having the greatest number of votes for President, shall be the President, if such number be a majority of the whole number of Electors appointed; and if no person have such majority, then from the persons having the highest numbers not exceeding three on the list of those voted for as President, the House of Representatives shall choose immediately, by ballot, the President. But in choosing the President, the votes shall be taken by states, the representation from each state having one vote; a quorum for this purpose shall consist of a member or members from two-thirds of the states, and a majority of all the states shall be necessary to a choice.…
Federal law sets January 6 as the date upon which the president of the Senate, who is the sitting vice president of the United States, counts the electoral votes before a joint session of Congress. If no presidential candidate has a majority of the electoral votes, then the House of Representatives chooses among the top three vote getters (Article II had allowed five finalists). To choose a president at that point, the House votes by state delegations, with each state having one vote. Therefore, small states are disproportionately represented in the House's decision, just as in the electoral college. Only twice in American history has the House of Representatives chosen the president: Thomas Jefferson in 1800 and John Quincy Adams in 1824.

In 1800, for the only time in U.S. history, the sitting vice president, Thomas Jefferson (bottom), opposed the president, John Adams (top), for reelection.

...And if the House of Representatives shall not choose a President whenever the right of choice shall devolve upon them, before the fourth day of March next following, then the Vice President shall act as President, as in case of the death or other constitutional disability of the President.—...
Section 3 of the Twentieth Amendment changed this portion of the Twelfth Amendment. The Twentieth Amendment establishes January 20 as the new Inauguration Day for the president. It also states that, if a president has not been chosen by the beginning of the new term, then the vice president elect—not the sitting vice president—shall serve as acting president until a president is chosen.

...The person having the greatest number of votes as Vice President, shall be the Vice President, if such number be a majority of the whole number of Electors appointed, and if no person have a majority, then from the two highest numbers on the list, the Senate shall choose the Vice President; a quorum for the purpose shall consist of two-thirds of the whole number of Senators, and a majority of the whole number shall be necessary to a choice....
If no vice-presidential candidate has a majority of electoral votes, then the Senate chooses from among the top two candidates. However, when the Senate selects the vice president, it votes as an entire body, not by state delegations as does the House. But small states are also disproportionately represented in the Senate.

...But no person constitutionally ineligible to the office of President shall be eligible to that of Vice President of the United States.
Any vice-presidential candidate must be at least thirty-five years old, a natural born citizen, and fourteen years a resident of the United States. Therefore, if the president dies or is disabled in office, the vice president will meet the constitutional qualifications for office set forth in Article II.

AMENDMENT XIII

SECTION 1. Neither slavery nor involuntary servitude, except as a punishment for crime whereof the party shall have been duly convicted, shall exist within the United States, or any place subject to their jurisdiction.

SECTION 2. Congress shall have power to enforce this article by appropriate legislation.

> **"What, to the American slave, is your Fourth of July?"**
> —Frederick Douglass

THE THIRTEENTH AMENDMENT: ABOLISHING SLAVERY

From the beginning of the American republic, slaves argued that they, too, were included in the Declaration of Independence's self-evident truth that "all men are created equal." Sectional division over the "peculiar institution" of American slavery would plague the nation until at last it culminated in a civil war that cost more than six hundred thousand lives. But out of that war came a constitutional amendment resolving, once and for all, that slavery could not exist in a government created by "we the people."

SECTION 1. Neither slavery nor involuntary servitude, except as a punishment for crime whereof the party shall have been duly convicted, shall exist within the United States, or any place subject to their jurisdiction.

The Thirteenth Amendment, ratified in 1865, resulted from more than two hundred years of failed compromises over slavery in America. Congress, acting under the Articles of Confederation, had banned slavery in federal territory in 1787, but the new Constitution written later that year did not outlaw slavery. The arrival of the cotton gin in 1795 drastically expanded the profitability of slave labor in the South, and with westward expansion came intense pressure to keep the balance between the free states of the North and the slave states of the South. Trying to resolve this conflict, the Supreme Court made a controversial ruling in 1857 about the status of slaves, and instead precipitated civil war.

Roots of American Slavery. Approximately eleven million African slaves arrived in the New World–transported principally by Portuguese, British, Spanish, and French slave traders. By far most of these slaves were delivered to the sugar plantations of Brazil and the West Indies (today's Caribbean nations), where they quickly died of disease and maltreatment. About five hundred thousand of the African slaves arrived in British North America. Slavery had existed thoughout human history, but in America slavery was established as a permanent and inheritable legal condition defined by the color of a person's skin. The first Africans to settle in British North America arrived on a Dutch ship in Jamestown, Virginia, in 1619– one year before the Mayflower landed at Plymouth, Massachusetts. At first, such Africans may have been treated like indentured servants, who were free to work for pay and own land after their term of service was over. But Massachusetts legalized slavery in 1641, the first English North American colony to do so; Connecticut acted similarly in 1650; and Virginia followed in 1661. In 1663, Virginia courts declared that a child born to a slave mother automatically became a slave. Slavery was legal in all thirteen states when the Declaration of Independence was written in 1776.

Westward Expansion. Abolitionist forces grew after the Revolutionary War, and Congress in 1787 outlawed slavery in the Northwest Territory, created by the cession of western lands from the original states. The new Constitution in 1787 both recognized and limited slavery in certain ways– and the framers generally believed that only the states, not the federal government, had the power to abolish slavery. Additionally, Eli Whitney's invention of the cotton gin made slavery much more profitable in the South. When Congress outlawed the international slave trade in 1808, as permitted by the Constitution, the market for domestic slaves increased dramatically. Slaves from Maryland and Virginia were sold to new owners raising cotton farther south and west.

After the Louisiana Purchase in 1803, the creation of new states from these western territories strained the uneasy balance between slave and free states in the Union. Under the Missouri Compromise in 1820, Maine was admitted as a free state and Missouri was admitted as a slave state, with slavery forbidden elsewhere in the Louisiana Territory above Missouri's southern border. After the Mexican-American War in 1848, the United States acquired more western lands, leading to more sectional crisis over slavery. Finally, in the Compromise of 1850, California was admitted as a free state while the residents of the Utah and New Mexico territories decided for themselves about slavery. Perhaps the most controversial provision in this compromise was the Fugitive Slave Act, which for the first time authorized federal agents to detain and return fugitive slaves.

Article IV of the Constitution had required states to relinquish fugitive slaves, but juries in free states were reluctant to find in favor of slaveholders. Now slave catchers could bypass state courts entirely, and they were often accused of kidnapping free blacks.

"I looked at my hands to see if I was the same person."
—Harriet Tubman, on escaping to freedom

Dred Scott and His Family. In 1846, a slave named Dred Scott sued for his freedom in Missouri, along with his wife and two daughters. Scott's lawsuit charged that he was free because his owner had taken him and his family into free territory for a time. Indeed, that was the usual outcome of such cases under Missouri law. But with increased tensions over slavery, Dred Scott lost and his case eventually became embroiled in a national controversy.

The Supreme Court first heard Dred Scott's case in early 1856, but then ordered that it be reargued after the presidential election of 1856. In an action that would today be regarded as clearly unethical, president-elect James Buchanan secretly lobbied certain justices to overturn the Missouri Compromise in the *Dred Scott* case. He hoped thereby to resolve the political controversy over slavery with a legal ruling based on the Constitution. Buchanan was inaugurated on March 4, 1857, and on March 6 Chief Justice Roger Taney issued the decision Buchanan wanted.

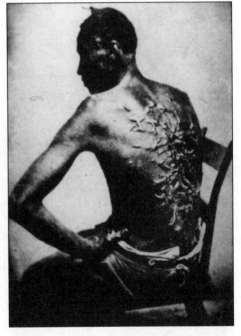

In *Dred Scott v. Sandford* (a spelling error on the Court's part; Scott's owner was named Sanford), the Court made several controversial rulings. First, Taney's opinion stated that African Americans, free or slave, could never be citizens of the United States. He maintained that blacks were "beings of an inferior order" who "had no rights which the white man was bound to respect." Since Dred Scott was not a citizen, he could not bring suit in federal court and the Court lacked jurisdiction to hear the case.

The whipping scars on the back of this slave, photographed in 1863, demonstrate the brutality of slavery.

Chief Justice Taney could have ended his opinion there. However, he went on to hold that, based on the Due Process Clause, Congress could not deprive slaveholders of their property anywhere in the United States, including federal territories. Therefore, the Missouri Compromise was unconstitutional. Under the *Dred Scott* ruling, federal territories could not outlaw slavery until they became states—at which point slaveholders could have formed a majority in the territory. Critics charged that the *Dred Scott* decision in effect nationalized slavery, by allowing slaveholders to bring slaves into any part of the Union.

Secession and War. The nation was in an uproar after the *Dred Scott* ruling. In Illinois, the Supreme Court's decision became the focal point of the legendary 1858 debates between Stephen Douglas and Abraham Lincoln for a seat in the U. S. Senate. During his campaign, Lincoln declared: "A house divided against itself cannot stand. I believe that this government cannot endure permanently half slave and half free." Lincoln lost the Senate, but he won the presidency in 1860. However, he did so without any votes from the South, and in December South Carolina seceded from the Union. By the time Lincoln was inaugurated on March 4, 1861, the Confederate States of America had been formed. The Civil War began on April 12, 1861, when Confederate forces fired on Fort Sumter.

At first, Lincoln tried to ameliorate the slaveholding states, hoping to

restore the Union quickly. Lincoln even supported the Corwin Amendment, passed by Congress in 1861, which if ratified would have added an unamendable provision to the Constitution forbidding Congress to outlaw slavery. But the slaves themselves began to flee to Union lines, prompting a crisis of what to do with such "contraband." In 1862, Congress authorized the confiscation of all rebel property–including slaves.

In late 1862, Lincoln issued his Emancipation Proclamation, which took effect on January 1, 1863. It freed all slaves in Confederate states not under

In his second inaugural address, Abraham Lincoln referred to the Civil War as the punishment of a just God for slavery.

Union control. According to historian James McPherson: "The old cliché that the proclamation did not free a single slave because it applied only to the Confederate states where Lincoln had no power, completely misses the point. The proclamation announced a revolutionary new war aim–the overthrow of slavery by force of arms if and when Union armies conquered the South."

The Second American Revolution. Lincoln and others became convinced that only a constitutional amendment would finally end slavery. After Lincoln won reelection in 1864, and Union hopes of victory improved, Congress passed the Thirteenth Amendment in January 1865.

Although Lincoln lived to see the Confederates defeated, he was assassinated in April before the Thirteenth Amendment was ratified at the end of that year. The Thirteenth Amendment freed almost four million slaves. Many historians refer to the Civil War as the second American Revolution, because by abolishing slavery the United States at long last began to fulfill the Declaration of Independence's promise that "all men are created equal."

An Unalienable Right to Freedom

Petition by Massachusetts Slaves

Echoing the words of the Declaration of Independence, the slaves of Massachusetts petitioned the state legislature for freedom in 1777.

The petition of a great number of blacks detained in a state of slavery in the bowels of a free and Christian country humbly show that your petitioners apprehend that they have in common with all other men a natural and unalienable right to that freedom which the Great Parent of the Universe has bestowed equally on all mankind and which they have never forfeited by any compact or agreement whatever. They were unjustly dragged by the hand of cruel power from their dearest friends and some of them even torn from the embraces of their tender parents—from a populous, pleasant, and plentiful country, and in violation of the laws of nature and of nations and in defiance of all the tender feelings of humanity brought here to be sold like beasts of burden and like them condemned to slavery for life, among a people professing the mild religion of Jesus....

Your petitioners...cannot but express their astonishment that it has never been considered that every principle from which America has acted in the course of their unhappy difficulties with Great Britain pleads stronger than a thousand arguments in favor of your petitioners.

Not We, the White People *Frederick Douglass*

Frederick Douglass, an abolitionist orator and runaway slave, criticized the Dred Scott case's holding that African Americans—free or slave— could never be citizens under the Constitution.

We, the people—not we, the white people—not we, the citizens, or the legal voters—not we, the privileged class, and excluding all other classes but we, the people; not we, the horses and cattle, but we the people—the men and women, the human inhabitants of the United States, do ordain and establish this Constitution.

Douglass escaped from slavery in Maryland and became a prominent abolitionist.

Who Freed the Slaves? *Barbara J. Fields*

In this excerpt from her well-known essay, historian Barbara Fields emphasizes that Abraham Lincoln was slow to the cause of emancipation, and it was the slaves themselves who won their own freedom.

A black soldier in Louisiana, born a slave, dismissed with contempt those northerners, including Abraham Lincoln, who proposed to save the Union without disturbing slavery: "Our union friends says the[y] are not fighting to free the Negroes; we are fighting for the union.... Very well, let the white fight for what the[y] want and we Negroes fight for what we want.... Liberty must take the day, nothing shorter."...

The slaves decided at the time of Lincoln's election that their hour had come. By the time Lincoln issued his Emancipation Proclamation, no human being alive could have held back the tide that swept toward freedom.... The government discovered that it could not accomplish its narrow goal—union—without adopting the slaves' nobler one—universal emancipation.

"The black holocaust is far and away the most heinous human rights crime visited upon any group of people in the world over the last 500 years."

—Randall Robinson

SECTION 2. Congress shall have power to enforce this article by appropriate legislation.

The Thirteenth Amendment is the first constitutional amendment to give Congress specific power to enforce it. After the end of the Civil War, some Radical Republicans argued that the Thirteenth Amendment gave Congress the power to give freed slaves equal rights, not just end the legal relationship of slavery. But Congress decided that the Fourteenth Amendment, ratified in 1868, was necessary to grant freed slaves citizenship and "equal protection of the laws."

In the *Civil Rights Cases* (1883), the Supreme Court ruled that under Section 2 of the Thirteenth Amendment Congress had the power to remove the "badges and incidents" of slavery. However, the Court defined that phrase narrowly, and held that Section 2 did not apply to private discrimination. But in 1968, the Court reversed itself and ruled that Section 2 did allow Congress to prevent discrimination in private real estate transactions. The Court has also held that the Thirteenth Amendment's ban on "involuntary servitude" included peonage laws—which forced laborers to work to pay off debts that were often fraudulent and prevented them from quitting their jobs.

Reparations. At his second inauguration in March 1865, President Abraham Lincoln saw the Civil War as a just God's retribution for slavery—which might continue "until all the wealth piled by the bondsman's 250 years of unrequited toil shall be sunk, and until every drop of blood drawn with the lash shall be paid by another drawn with the sword." But some Americans believe that the "badges and incidents" of slavery have continued long past the Civil War, and that the nation owes a financial and moral debt to African Americans that should be paid. These scholars argue that just as the United States compensated the heirs of survivors of the Japanese American internment camps, it should find a way to establish a fund to repay African Americans for the negative effects of slavery. Such scholars point to high rates of poverty and incarceration among the black community as evidence of the ongoing impact of both slavery and more than one hundred years of state-sponsored racial discrimination afterward.

Opponents of reparations charge that many Americans came to the country long after slavery ended, and that they should not be held accountable for its effects. They also believe that government programs should focus on all those who need help to overcome poverty and discrimination, not African Americans who are already successful. In addition, these critics argue that reparations have in the past gone only to direct victims of government abuse and their immediate heirs, not those who suffered from generations of injustice.

As of 2001, more than one hundred thousand federal tax returns have claimed a "reparations credit" for slavery. Scam artists convinced many African Americans that they were due such reparations on their taxes, and the Internal Revenue Service erroneously paid out more than $30 million in refunds in 2000 and 2001. However, Congress has not passed any authorization for slavery reparations.

> **"Slavery is embedded in American prosperity."**
> —Henry Louis Gates, Jr.

Reparations Would Divide Americans *Linda Chavez*

Syndicated columnist Linda Chavez argues against reparations lawsuits being pursued by a team of lawyers— including Johnnie Cochran, O. J. Simpson's defense attorney.

Reparations would divide Americans into oppressors and oppressed. In order to justify reparations for crimes committed some 135 years earlier, it is necessary not only to identify present-day victims but current victimizers, as well. Are all blacks victims? Is Oprah Winfrey a victim, despite her millions and her undeniable success and fame? What about Tiger Woods—is he only a partial victim because he is part Asian and white as well as black? Or Hakeem Olajuwon, whose ancestors remained free in Africa?

And what about the victimizers? Are the descendants of the men who gave their lives in the Civil War to end slavery guilty, too? Are the grandsons and granddaughters of Italian and Polish immigrants, who came to America long after slavery was abolished, culpable nonetheless? What about the Mexican and Chinese immigrants who just arrived within the last decade? Will everyone be taxed to pay out reparations—including blacks? And who will determine how much each victim is owed?

But most importantly, do Johnnie Cochran and his fellow trial lawyers really believe that the problems that still plague the black community will in any way be solved by reparations?… Or will the talk of reparations simply pump up more business for a group of already successful and wealthy black lawyers like Cochran?

AMENDMENT XIV

SECTION 1. All persons born or naturalized in the United States, and subject to the jurisdiction thereof, are citizens of the United States and of the State wherein they reside. No State shall make or enforce any law which shall abridge the privileges or immunities of citizens of the United States; nor shall any State deprive any person of life, liberty, or property, without due process of law; nor deny to any person within its jurisdiction the equal protection of the laws.

SECTION 2. Representatives shall be apportioned among the several States according to their respective numbers, counting the whole number of persons in each State, excluding Indians not taxed. But when the right to vote at any election for the choice of electors for President and Vice President of the United States, Representatives in Congress, the Executive and Judicial officers of a State, or the members of the Legislature thereof, is denied to any of the *male* inhabitants of such State, *being twenty-one years of age,* and citizens of the United States, or in any way abridged, except for participation in rebellion, or other crime, the basis of representation therein shall be reduced in the proportion which the number of such *male* citizens shall bear to the whole number of male citizens *twenty-one years of age* in such State.

SECTION 3. No person shall be a Senator or Representative in Congress, or elector of President and Vice-President, or hold any office, civil or military, under the United States, or under any State, who, having previously taken an oath, as a member of Congress, or as an officer of the United States, or as a member of any State legislature, or as an executive or judicial officer of any State, to support the Constitution of the United States, shall have engaged in insurrection or rebellion against the same, or given aid or comfort to the enemies thereof. But Congress may by a vote of two-thirds of each House, remove such disability.

SECTION 4. The validity of the public debt of the United States, authorized by law, including debts incurred for payment of pensions and bounties for services in suppressing insurrection or rebellion, shall not be questioned. But neither the United States nor any State shall assume or pay any debt or obligation incurred in aid of insurrection or rebellion against the United States, or any claim for the loss or emancipation of any slave; but all such debts, obligations and claims shall be held illegal and void.

SECTION 5. The Congress shall have the power to enforce, by appropriate legislation, the provisions of this article.

THE FOURTEENTH AMENDMENT: EQUAL PROTECTION OF THE LAWS

A lthough the Thirteenth Amendment abolished slavery, it did not resolve the legal status of former slaves under federal and state law. After the Civil War, many southern states passed "Black Codes" designed to severely restrict the lives of newly freed slaves and keep them in virtual slavery. Through the Fourteenth Amendment, former slaves were granted citizenship and promised "equal protection of the laws." This protection from unreasonable discrimination eventually extended to other groups as well. The Fourteenth Amendment became the basis for claims of legal equality.

Because the Fourteenth Amendment specifically addressed the states, it drastically expanded the reach of the U.S. Constitution. The Supreme Court used the amendment to apply most provisions in the Bill of Rights to state governments. As a result, the Fourteenth Amendment is cited more often in modern litigation than any other. In fact, many constitutional scholars believe that, through its wide scope and promise of equality, the Fourteenth Amendment created a new Constitution.

SECTION 1. All persons born or naturalized in the United States and subject to the jurisdiction thereof, are citizens of the United States and of the State wherein they reside....

This section of the Fourteenth Amendment defines both national and state citizenship, which had previously been left up to the states to decide. In *Dred Scott v. Sandford* (1857), the Supreme Court had ruled that African Americans, free or slave, could never be citizens of the United States. The Fourteenth Amendment overturned this decision by defining citizenship in the Constitution for the first time.

> "I cannot consider the Bill of Rights to be an outworn 18th-century 'straightjacket.'"
> —Justice Hugo Black

After the Civil War, Congress sought to protect the rights of newly freed slaves. Southern legislatures, dominated by former Confederates, had enacted "Black Codes" to regulate every aspect of the lives of freedmen—forbidding them to vote, own firearms, or travel freely. Congress passed the Fourteenth Amendment in 1866 as the cornerstone to its plan for Reconstruction. Southern states were required to ratify the amendment in order to be readmitted to the Union.

When the amendment was ratified in 1868, "all persons born or naturalized in the United States" automatically became citizens of both the American nation and the state in which they resided. No longer could states keep people, especially African Americans, in a legal no-man's land by denying them citizenship. However, the Fourteenth Amendment only applied to those persons "subject to the jurisdiction" of the United States—not American Indians. Native Americans were not granted U.S. citizenship until 1924.

…No State shall make or enforce any law which shall abridge the privileges or immunities of citizens of the United States;…
This clause of the Fourteenth Amendment echoes the language in Article IV, which also protects the "privileges and immunities" of citizens. The question of exactly what rights are covered under "privileges and immunities"—both in Article IV and the Fourteenth Amendment—remains unclear. Some constitutional scholars believe that the principal author of the Fourteenth Amendment, Representative John Bingham of Ohio, intended for the Privileges or Immunities Clause to apply the provisions in the Bill of Rights to state governments.

But the Supreme Court disagreed with this interpretation in the *Slaughterhouse Cases* (1873). Of course, the Supreme Court eventually did apply most provisions in the Bill of Rights to the states, bit by bit, through the Due Process Clause of the Fourteenth Amendment. Yet in the *Slaughterhouse Cases,* the Court interpreted the Privileges or Immunities Clause very narrowly, holding that it protected only the rights of national citizenship—such as access to the courts and the right to travel to the government's capital. This limited interpretation resulted in few Supreme Court cases being decided on the Privileges or Immunities Clause. However, in *Saenz v. Roe* (1999), the Supreme Court resurrected this part of the Fourteenth Amendment, holding that it forbade states to reduce welfare benefits for newly arrived residents because that restricted the right to travel.

…nor shall any State deprive any person of life, liberty, or property, without due process of law;…
The Due Process Clause in the Fourteenth Amendment is identical to that

in the Fifth Amendment, except that the former applies directly to the states, whereas the latter restricts the federal government. The Fourteenth Amendment's Due Process Clause has had two major effects: applying the Bill of Rights to the states through the doctrine of **incorporation,** and protecting rights that are not specifically listed in the Constitution through **substantive due process.** Although generally due process means that legal procedures must be fair, substantive due process requires that the content of the law itself be fair.

Incorporation of the Bill of Rights. Originally, James Madison had intended for some provisions in the Bill of Rights to apply to the states. He included among his proposed amendments one that prohibited the states from violating the "equal rights of conscience, or the freedom of the press, or the trial by jury in criminal cases." Congress rejected this amendment, although Madison considered it "the most valuable amendment on the whole list." Therefore, as the Supreme Court ruled in *Barron v. Baltimore* (1833), the Bill of Rights restricted only the federal government, not the states. But after the Fourteenth Amendment was ratified, the Court held that certain fundamental rights in the Bill of Rights were "incorporated," or included, in the amendment's Due Process Clause. Thus, the Court began the process of nationalizing, one by one, most of the major provisions of the Bill of Rights.

Selective Incorporation. Rather than applying the entire Bill of Rights to the states at once, the Supreme Court used a process of **selective incorporation.** Under the test outlined by Justice Benjamin Cardozo in *Palko v. Connecticut* (1937), the Supreme Court would determine whether a right was "fundamental" and necessary to "a scheme of ordered liberty." If so, that right was incorporated into the Due Process Clause. Advocates of selective incorporation argued that the states should be free to develop new criminal and civil procedures, rather than be limited by the Bill of Rights.

Total Incorporation. Justice Hugo Black, along with others on the Supreme Court, believed that selective incorporation allowed judges too much discretion to choose among rights. Instead, Justice Black supported **total incorporation,** in which the Bill of Rights would be applied all at once to the states. Black argued that the inclusion of a right in the Bill of Rights meant that by definition it was "fundamental" enough to apply to the states. Black maintained that total incorporation was far less intrusive on the states than the subjective process of selective incorporation.

A Double Standard. Until the Bill of Rights was incorporated to apply to the states, the United States had two drastically different systems of criminal justice. Subject to the limitations in the Bill of Rights, federal prosecutors were required to use search warrants, the exclusionary rule, and

incorporation

process by which the Supreme Court has applied the Bill of Rights to the states through the Fourteenth Amendment

substantive due process

doctrine that the content of a law must be fair, not just its procedures

selective incorporation

the process of extending certain "fundamental" rights in the Bill of Rights to the states

total incorporation

the process of applying all the provisions in the Bill of Rights to the states

"A constitution is not intended to embody a particular economic theory."

—Justice Oliver Wendell Holmes

Justice Holmes was a pragmatist in his legal reasoning.

laissez faire

an economic policy opposing government regulation of business (from the French for "to let alone")

trial by jury. However, state prosecutors were not. One reason that the Supreme Court eventually extended most criminal procedure rights to the states was to avoid giving state law enforcement officials incentive to violate the U.S. Constitution.

Unincorporated Rights. The Supreme Court has not incorporated all provisions in the Bill of Rights. Those rights in the first eight amendments that have not been applied to the states are: the right to keep and bear arms (Second Amendment); the restriction on quartering troops (Third Amendment); the right to a grand jury indictment (Fifth Amendment); trial by jury in civil cases (Seventh Amendment); and the ban on excessive bail and fines (Eighth Amendment). The Ninth and Tenth Amendments also do not apply to the states, because they do not directly protect individual rights.

Substantive Due Process. As discussed in the chapter on the Ninth Amendment, the Supreme Court has protected unenumerated rights through the Due Process Clause of the Fourteenth Amendment. These rights not specifically listed in the Constitution have often been controversial. Under substantive due process, the Supreme Court decides which rights are "fundamental" and cannot be deprived by the states. These rights are generally categorized as "liberty" interests or "property" interests, because the Fourteenth Amendment states that no person shall be deprived of "life, liberty, or property" without due process of law. The Supreme Court favored property interests from the 1880s to the 1930s, but since then has principally protected liberty interests.

Property Interests. The most famous case upholding a property interest under substantive due process was *Lochner v. New York* (1905). Many states tried to regulate working conditions during the late nineteenth century to counteract the social problems of rapid industrialization. The Supreme Court ruled in *Lochner* that a New York law restricting bakers to sixty-hour work weeks was unconstitutional because it violated their "liberty of contract." Bakers should be allowed to work however long they wished, said the Court–although the law was being opposed by bakeries, not bakers. The Court's decision reflected an economic policy of *laissez faire,* or opposing government regulation of business. But Justice Oliver Wendell Holmes declared in dissent that "the Fourteenth Amendment does not enact Mr. Herbert Spencer's *Social Statics,*" a popular book advocating social Darwinism.

The *Lochner* case became symbolic of the Supreme Court imposing its own values on legislative decisions through substantive due process. This criticism of the Court increased when it routinely overturned New Deal legislation. Finally, in *United States v. Carolene Products Company* (1938), the Supreme Court began to back away from the *laissez-faire* policy. Instead, the Court declared that it would henceforth presume most economic regulations to be constitutional, but closely monitor infringements on individual liberties it regarded as fundamental.

Liberty Interests. During the 1920s, the Supreme Court used substantive due process to overturn state laws that prohibited the teaching of foreign languages and banned private schools. Other rights upheld under substantive due process have been the right to travel, the right to privacy, and the right to refuse medical treatment. Two of the most controversial issues that the Court has addressed under substantive due process are abortion and the right to assisted suicide.

> **"Substantive due process is a contradiction in terms—sort of like 'green pastel redness.'"**
>
> —John Hart Ely

Three Generations of Imbeciles Are Enough

One "liberty" interest that the Supreme Court did not protect under the Fourteenth Amendment was the right to be free from involuntary sterilization. Influenced by eugenics, a movement that promoted selective breeding to improve the human species, twenty-four states passed laws during the 1920s that allowed "imbeciles" to be sterilized against their will. But as one historian later noted, "people were sterilized not because they were feebleminded, but because they were 'poor white trash.'" In *Buck v. Bell* (1927), the Supreme Court heard a challenge to Virginia's Eugenical Sterilization Act on behalf of Carrie Buck, whose mother had been committed to an institution for the "feebleminded." Although Buck demonstrated normal intelligence in school, she was herself committed as "feebleminded" after she was raped and gave birth to an illegitimate child. Justice Oliver Wendell Holmes, writing on behalf of the Court's 8–1 majority, allowed Buck's forcible sterilization to go forward—comparing it to a compulsory vaccination. "Three generations of imbeciles are enough," said Holmes—a quote that would later be used by Nazi defense lawyers at the Nuremberg trials.

Abortion. In *Roe v. Wade* (1973), the Supreme Court held that the right to privacy included a woman's right to have an abortion. The Court ruled that the concept of personal liberty in the Fourteenth Amendment was "broad enough to encompass a woman's decision whether or not to terminate her pregnancy." The Court also held that a fetus was not a person under the Fourteenth Amendment, although the Court had previously ruled that a corporation was. The amendment itself refers to "all persons born," and the threshold for legal rights has traditionally been birth.

Justice Harry Blackmun's majority opinion in *Roe* was filled with medical terminology, befitting a former counsel for the Mayo Clinic. Following obstetrics of the time, Blackmun divided a pregnancy into three stages, or trimesters, during which a woman's interest in her privacy and the state's interest in the "potentiality of human life" were weighed. In the first trimester, a woman's privacy was paramount, and states could not forbid

> **"The issue is: Who should make the decision about abortion— the government, strangers, or women?"**
>
> —Sarah Weddington

abortions. During the second trimester, states could regulate abortions to safeguard the health of the woman, but not outlaw them. In the third trimester, states could forbid abortions as the fetus became viable and able to live outside the woman's body—unless the life or health of the woman were in jeopardy.

On January 22 every year, supporters and opponents of Roe v. Wade commemorate its anniversary at the Supreme Court.

With advances in medical technology, *Roe's* trimester framework became outdated. In *Planned Parenthood of Southeastern Pennsylvania v. Casey* (1992), the Supreme Court upheld a woman's right to an abortion but abandoned the trimester formula. Instead, states were allowed to regulate abortions if they did not place an "undue burden" on a woman's constitutional right to an abortion. According to the Court, an undue burden was a "substantial obstacle in the path of a woman seeking an abortion of a nonviable fetus."

In *Stenberg v. Carhart* (2000), the Supreme Court faced a challenge to a controversial procedure known as partial-birth abortion. This method, considered safest for women undergoing late-term abortions, involves removing the fetus from the uterus feet first and then collapsing the skull before complete extraction. In the *Stenberg* case, the Court struck down a Nebraska law outlawing partial-birth abortions as an "undue burden," because it was so broadly written that it could apply to all abortion methods and did not include an exception for safeguarding the life and health of the woman.

Norma McCorvey: The Real Jane Roe

When Norma McCorvey got pregnant for the third time in 1969, abortions were illegal in Texas. An uneducated bartender and carnival worker, McCorvey had led a tumultuous life: juvenile reform school, an abusive husband, drug and alcohol abuse, and two previous children given up for adoption. She could not face giving up a third child and sought an abortion instead. McCorvey later lied and said she had been raped—although that made no difference under

Texas law or in her court case.

McCorvey went to two young lawyers, Linda Coffee and Sarah Weddington, who were looking for a plaintiff to challenge the Texas abortion law. When she signed an affidavit for the lawsuit, Norma McCorvey became Jane Roe to remain anonymous. As the case wound its way through the legal system, McCorvey gave birth to her third child. She felt angry at her lawyers because she thought they had led her to believe she might actually get

an abortion. "I was nothing to Sarah and Linda, nothing more than just a name on a piece of paper," she wrote. Ironically, "Jane Roe" never had an abortion—although her lawyer, Sarah Weddington, had an illegal abortion in Mexico. In 1995, Norma McCorvey was baptized as a Christian and later renounced her pro-choice stand. She founded Roe No More Ministry in 1997 to campaign against abortions.

Assisted Suicide. The Supreme Court ruled that the Fourteenth Amendment protected a right to refuse medical treatment in *Cruzan v. Director, Missouri Department of Health* (1990). However, the Court also held that a state could require strong evidence that an incompetent person—such as accident victim Nancy Cruzan, who was in a persistent vegetative state—wanted to die in such circumstances before it ended medical treatment. In 1997, the Court ruled that a general right to commit suicide is not protected by substantive due process, thereby upholding state laws prohibiting physician-assisted suicide.

...nor deny to any person within its jurisdiction the equal protection of the laws.

Known as the Equal Protection Clause, this provision in the Fourteenth Amendment contains the first use in the Constitution of the word "equal" regarding the rights of individuals. The Equal Protection Clause prohibits unreasonable discrimination. If a law treats people differently, the state must demonstrate a good reason for that difference. Usually, the courts will defer to the legislature if it can show a "rational basis" for the law, a very easy test. But the Supreme Court has ruled that the government must meet a much higher test, and prove a "compelling interest" in the law, if it involves a "fundamental" right, such as free speech or voting, or a "suspect" class such as race.

The Supreme Court has ruled that the Due Process Clause of the Fifth Amendment forbids unreasonable discrimination by the federal government in the same way that the Equal Protection Clause of the Fourteenth Amendment restricts the states. The Court also held in the *Civil Rights Cases* (1883) that the Fourteenth Amendment only limits discrimination by the government, not private individuals or groups. In the *Slaughterhouse Cases* (1873), the Court initially ruled that the Equal Protection Clause was intended only to protect African Americans, but later decisions included other groups as well.

Racial Discrimination. Current Supreme Court rulings hold that one of the most pernicious forms of discrimination is that based on race, which is regarded as a "suspect class." But such was not always the case. For many years the Court upheld racially segregated public facilities, and it allowed Japanese American citizens to be interned during World War II.

Separate But Equal. The Supreme Court ruled in *Plessy v. Ferguson* (1896) that racial segregation in public facilities, if they were allegedly equal in quality, did not violate the Equal Protection Clause. Under this doctrine of "separate but equal," the Court upheld a Louisiana law that required separate railroad cars for whites and blacks. In his lawsuit, Homer Plessy

"The notion that the Constitution... prohibits the states from simply banning this visibly brutal means of eliminating our half-born posterity is quite simply absurd."
—Justice Antonin Scalia, on partial-birth abortion

"Our Constitution is colorblind, and neither knows nor tolerates classes among citizens."
—Justice John Marshall Harlan

Jim Crow laws

a system of segregation imposed by laws named after a minstrel show character

"God bless you all. I am a innocent man."

—Ed Johnson, lynching victim

maintained that segregation, enforced by the **Jim Crow laws** of the South, imposed a "badge of inferiority" on African Americans. But the Supreme Court's 8–1 majority disagreed. "If this be so," said the Court, "it is not by reason of anything found in the act, but solely because the colored race chooses to put that construction upon it." The lone dissenter in *Plessy*, Justice John Marshall Harlan, said in a famous dissent that the Constitution should be "colorblind" and not allow segregation.

Despite the *Plessy* ruling, segregated facilities for blacks were hardly ever equal to those for whites, especially in education. The National Association for the Advancement of Colored People (NAACP) devised a strategy to challenge segregation in education by suing to enforce the "separate but equal" ruling in *Plessy*. The NAACP reasoned that states would find it too expensive to maintain separate but truly equal public schools. In several NAACP cases during the 1930s and 1940s, the Supreme Court ordered that states admit black students to all-white graduate schools when black facilities were unequal or nonexistent.

Strange Fruit

Blues artist Billie Holiday sang of the "strange fruit" that hung from trees in the South. From 1882 to 1944, approximately forty-seven hundred persons were lynched across the United States. Of these, about seventy-three percent were African American. In many southern states, more than ninety percent of the lynching victims were black. The prevalence of lynching—despite the Fourteenth Amendment—helped lead to the founding of the National Association for the Advancement of Colored People (NAACP) in 1909.

That same year, in *United States v. Shipp*, the Supreme Court held a Tennessee sheriff and his deputies in criminal contempt for allowing the lynching of a black man whose case was being reviewed by the Court. Justice Thurgood Marshall later said that the *Shipp* case "was perhaps the first instance in which the Court demonstrated that the Fourteenth Amendment and the Equal Protection Clause have any substantive meaning to people of the African American race."

Internment of Japanese Americans. World War II brought discrimination against another racial group to the forefront. After Japan attacked Pearl Harbor in 1941, U.S. military officials forced Japanese Americans on the West Coast to obey curfews and leave their homes. President Franklin Roosevelt issued Executive Order 9066 authorizing the internment of 120,000 Japanese Americans in concentration camps. Two-thirds of them were natural-born U.S. citizens.

Fred Korematsu and Gordon Hirabayashi challenged this treatment of Japanese Americans, arguing that it violated the Equal Protection Clause.

However, the Supreme Court upheld the military orders in *Korematsu v. United States* (1944), saying they were not based on racial animosity but on the fact that Japan was an enemy. Yet as Justice Robert Jackson pointed out in his dissent, Americans of German and Italian ancestry were not treated similarly. In 1983, Fred Korematsu's criminal conviction was overturned because his attorney Peter Irons discovered that the U.S. solicitor general had lied to the Supreme Court in 1944. The solicitor general knowingly misinformed the Court that the U.S. military had evidence of disloyalty by Japanese Americans, but there was none. In 1988, Congress apologized to and compensated survivors of the internment camps.

"Ancestry is not a crime."

—Gordon Hirabayashi

The Mochida family awaits relocation from their California home to an internment camp in 1942.

Separate Is Unequal. After World War II ended, the NAACP challenged segregation in elementary and secondary schools in *Brown v. Board of Education of Topeka, Kansas* (1954). The Supreme Court ruled in Brown that "separate educational facilities are inherently unequal," unanimously overturning the *Plessy* decision. The Court held that, contrary to *Plessy,* segregation did create in black children "a feeling of inferiority as to their status in the community that may affect their hearts and minds in a way unlikely ever to be undone." In a study by psychologist Kenneth Clark, which the Court cited in its opinion, black children had chosen white dolls as being superior to black dolls. The Supreme Court ruled in a separate decision one year later that school districts should begin desegregation "with all deliberate speed."

Critics of the *Brown* decision argued that it relied too heavily on psychological data, not law, and that education was traditionally a power reserved exclusively to the states. Southern states organized massive resistance to the decision; 101 members of Congress signed a "Southern Manifesto" in 1956 opposing the Supreme Court's authority to desegregate the schools. In 1957, President Dwight Eisenhower ordered the 101st Airborne Division to protect nine black students who integrated Central High School in Little Rock, Arkansas. Some school districts, including Little Rock, closed entirely until federal courts reopened them. In 1969, after

affirmative action
program in which employers take positive steps to offer training and jobs to groups that have suffered discrimination in the past

fifteen years of delay, the Supreme Court finally ruled that schools must be desegregated "at once."

Besides education, the Supreme Court also struck down segregation in transportation, prisons, and public parks. In addition, the Court declared a Virginia law that banned interracial marriages to be unconstitutional. Yet it took a massive civil rights movement, in which thousands of citizens risked their lives, for the Supreme Court's desegregation decisions to be enforced.

Affirmative Action. Congress passed the Civil Rights Act of 1964 to prohibit discrimination in employment based on race, religion, or sex. However, the law did not address the effects of past discrimination, which could impede a person's success in the job market. Consequently, the federal government enacted a program of **affirmative action,** in which those who receive government funding must take positive steps to offer

I Don't Remember Feeling Frightened *Ruby Bridges*

In 1960, six-year-old Ruby Bridges became one of four black girls to integrate the first grade in New Orleans public schools. She spent most of the year in a class all by herself, escorted to school by federal marshals. Here she describes her first day.

I remember climbing into the back seat of the marshals' car with my mother, but I don't remember feeling frightened. William Frantz Public School was only five blocks away, so one of the marshals in the front seat told my mother right away what we should do when we got there.

"Let us get out of the car first," the marshal said. "Then you'll get out, and the four of us will surround you and your daughter. Just walk straight ahead, and don't look back."...

There were barricades and people shouting and policemen everywhere.... As we walked through the crowd, I didn't see

Federal marshals accompanied Ruby Bridges to and from school.

any faces. I guess that's because I wasn't very tall and I was surrounded by the marshals. People yelled and threw things. I could see the school building, and it looked bigger and nicer than my old school. When we climbed the high steps to the

front door, there were policemen in uniforms at the top. The policemen at the door and the crowd behind us made me think this was an important place.

It must be college, I thought to myself.

training and employment to groups that have suffered discrimination in the past—such as racial minorities and women. However, in *Richmond v. Croson* (1989), the Supreme Court said that such affirmative action programs at the state and local level must prove a "compelling interest" for discriminating against white men.

In education, the Supreme Court upheld a limited version of affirmative action in *Regents of the University of California v. Bakke* (1978). Although the Court ruled that strict racial quotas violated the Equal Protection Clause, it allowed universities to use race as one of several factors in admissions decisions. Wrote Justice Harry Blackmun: "In order to get beyond racism, we must first take account of race." But during the 1990s, several federal appellate courts ruled that race could not be considered at all during admissions decisions for state universities. As of 2001, however, the Supreme Court had not reconsidered its *Bakke* decision.

> **"It's all very well to talk about school integration—if you remember you may also be talking about social disintegration."**
>
> —President Dwight Eisenhower

At the Center of the American Mythology *Wynton Marsalis*

Jazz trumpeter and composer Wynton Marsalis believes that race is the key issue that will define the success of the American experiment.

For this country, [race is] like the thing in mythology that you have to do for the kingdom to be well. And it's always something you don't want to do.

And it's always about confronting yourself, always tailor-made for you to fail in dealing with it. And the question of your heroism and of your courage in dealing with this trial is the measure of your success. Can you confront it with honesty? And do you have the energy to sustain an attack on it? And since jazz music is at

the center of the American mythology, it necessarily deals with race because race is our black eye, to make a little pun. It's something that the more we run from it, the more we run into it. And it's an age-old story, if it's not race, it's something else. But in this particular instance, in this nation, it is race.

Gender Discrimination. In addition to race, discrimination based on sex is also prohibited by the Equal Protection Clause. Section 1 of the Fourteenth Amendment refers to "persons," not men or women. However, it was not until 1971 that the Supreme Court held that a law discriminating against women violated the Fourteenth Amendment. Instead, the Court's early decisions reflected stereotypes that limited the roles of women. In *Bradwell v. Illinois* (1873), the first Supreme Court case to challenge discrimination against women, the Court upheld a state law forbidding women to become lawyers. According to Justice Joseph P. Bradley, the "law of the Creator" made being a wife and mother "the paramount destiny and mission of woman."

During the late 1800s and early 1900s, the Supreme Court upheld state protective legislation that created limited hours and working conditions for women on the grounds that they were the weaker sex. However, the Court

"I'm sick and tired of being sick and tired."
—Fannie Lou Hamer, civil rights worker

had struck down similar laws for men. During both world wars, women filled critical labor shortages. After World War II, the Court again issued rulings enforcing stereotypes of women's behavior. The Supreme Court held in *Goesaert v. Cleary* (1948) that concerns about women's morality justified a Michigan law limiting their ability to serve as bartenders. And in *Hoyt v. Florida* (1961) the Court upheld a law that automatically exempted women from jury service unless they volunteered, on the grounds that women needed to be at home with their families.

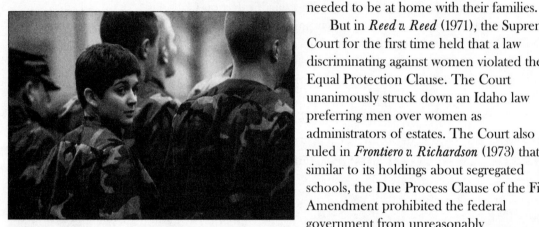

Women were first admitted to the Virginia Military Institute in 1997.

But in *Reed v. Reed* (1971), the Supreme Court for the first time held that a law discriminating against women violated the Equal Protection Clause. The Court unanimously struck down an Idaho law preferring men over women as administrators of estates. The Court also ruled in *Frontiero v. Richardson* (1973) that, similar to its holdings about segregated schools, the Due Process Clause of the Fifth Amendment prohibited the federal government from unreasonably discriminating against women. In that case, the Court overturned a military policy that automatically gave benefits to the families of male soldiers but not those of female soldiers.

Since 1973, the Supreme Court has issued a series of mixed rulings about sex discrimination, both against women and men. In 1976, the Court struck down a state law that allowed women but not men to buy beer at eighteen. But in *Rostker v. Goldberg* (1981), the Supreme Court upheld the exclusion of women from draft registration requirements because Congress banned women from serving in combat positions. Another controversial issue has been single-sex education in state schools. The Court declared that an all-female nursing school violated the Equal Protection Clause in *Mississippi University for Women v. Hogan* (1982). And in *United States v. Virginia* (1996), the Court ruled that women must be allowed to attend the all-male Virginia Military Institute.

In general, the Supreme Court has ruled that gender discrimination is more permissible under the Equal Protection Clause than racial discrimination. Sex is not a suspect class, as is race; therefore, the Court uses a less demanding test than "compelling interest" for classifications based on gender. However, in 1971 the Supreme Court began increasingly to strike down state laws that discriminated against women, even though it used a lesser constitutional standard to do so.

Many Americans supported the proposed Equal Rights Amendment to prohibit sex discrimination. First introduced in Congress in 1923, the amendment stated: "Equality of rights under the law shall not be denied or abridged by the United States nor by any state on account of sex." The amendment passed Congress in 1972, but failed to be ratified by its 1982 expiration deadline.

Other Types of Discrimination. Besides race and gender, the Supreme Court has ruled that the Equal Protection Clause forbids unreasonable discrimination in other areas as well. Included in these are alienage or citizenship status, sexual orientation, and voting rights.

Aliens. The Supreme Court held in *Yick Wo v. Hopkins* (1886) that aliens, those persons living in the United States who are not American citizens, were protected by the Fourteenth Amendment. That amendment specifically applies to all "persons" who were "subject to the jurisdiction" of the United States. Thus, the amendment prohibits states from restricting most benefits for legal immigrants—except those that are tied to citizenship, such as voting and serving on juries. However, Congress has total power over immigration, so it can outlaw benefits for immigrants. States may not deny certain benefits even to illegal aliens. The Supreme Court ruled in *Plyler v. Doe* (1982) that a Texas law forbidding illegal immigrants to attend public school violated the Equal Protection Clause.

Sexual Orientation. The Supreme Court has held that certain discrimination against homosexuals violates the Equal Protection Clause, even though they are not a "suspect class." In *Romer v. Evans* (1996), the Court struck down an amendment to the Colorado state constitution that forbade state and local governments to pass laws protecting lesbians and gay men from discrimination in housing, employment, and other areas. But even under the minimal "rational basis" test, the Supreme Court ruled that the amendment was a form of unreasonable discrimination. In his opinion for the Court, Justice Anthony Kennedy quoted Justice Harlan's dissent in the *Plessy* decision, affirming that the Constitution "neither knows nor tolerates classes among citizens." The Court held in *Romer* that no state could make any group "a stranger to its laws."

Voting Rights and Reapportionment. The Constitution does not include a general right to vote, although certain amendments give particular groups suffrage. However, the Supreme Court has ruled in a variety of cases that the Equal Protection Clause protects voting rights and equal access to the ballot. In *Bush v. Gore* (2000), the Supreme Court held that the lack of uniform recount procedures in Florida during the 2000 presidential election violated the Equal Protection Clause. But the Court warned that this ruling applied only to the unique circumstances of that contest, not to election procedures in general—which typically vary according to local practices.

reapportionment

reallocation of legislative seats based on changes in population

Another Equal Protection issue is **reapportionment,** in which state and federal legislative seats are reallocated based on changes in population. Many state constitutions require reapportionment, as does the U.S. Constitution for the House of Representatives (discussed in more detail under Article I, Section 2). But when population shifted from rural to urban areas after 1900, state legislators were reluctant to reapportion themselves out of jobs. Consequently, rural areas were vastly overrepresented in state legislatures.

The Supreme Court had traditionally avoided such "political questions" that it said should be solved by the legislative branch of government, not the judiciary. But in *Baker v. Carr* (1962), the Court held that federal courts could decide reapportionment cases based on the Equal Protection Clause. In *Gray v. Sanders* (1963), Justice William Douglas wrote for the Court: "The conception of political equality…can mean only one thing—one person, one vote." Moreover, the Court ruled in *Reynolds v. Sims* (1964) that both houses of a state legislature, unlike the U. S. Congress, must by apportioned according to population. During the 1990s, the Supreme Court ruled in a series of cases that, absent a "compelling interest," race cannot be the primary factor when redrawing the boundaries of legislative districts after reapportionment.

"Legislators represent people, not trees or acres."

—Chief Justice Earl Warren

SECTION 2. Representatives shall be apportioned among the several States according to their respective numbers, counting the whole number of persons in each State, excluding Indians not taxed….
This portion of the Fourteenth Amendment specifically counteracts the provision in Article I, Section 2, of the Constitution stating that slaves shall count as three-fifths of a person for representation purposes. Although the Thirteenth Amendment abolished slavery, it did not directly change the representation formula in Article I.

…But when the right to vote at any election for the choice of electors for President and Vice President of the United States, Representatives in Congress, the Executive and Judicial officers of a State, or the members of the Legislature thereof, is denied to any of the *male* inhabitants of such State, *being twenty-one years of age,* and citizens of the United States,…
The Fourteenth Amendment introduced the word "male" to the Constitution for the first time. The amendment explicitly links the right to vote to being male, and some advocates of women's suffrage opposed it for that reason. Despite this language, some women sued in federal court, claiming that voting was one of the privileges and immunities granted to them as citizens under the Fourteenth Amendment. But in *Minor v.*

Happersett (1875), the Supreme Court ruled that voting was not included as an automatic right of citizenship–for women or anyone else. Specific constitutional amendments were necessary to extend suffrage to black men, women, and eighteen-year-olds.

…or in any way abridged, except for participation in rebellion, or other crime, the basis of representation therein shall be reduced in the proportion which the number of such *male* citizens shall bear to the whole number of *male* citizens *twenty-one years of age* in such State. The purpose of this provision was to punish states for denying African American men the right to vote, although it did not forbid such practices. Section 2 also empowers states to deny the vote to veterans and supporters of the Confederacy, who were regarded as traitors. Today, it allows felons to be deprived of the right to vote.

SECTION 3. No person shall be a Senator or Representative in Congress, or elector of President and Vice President, or hold any office, civil or military, under the United States, or under any State, who, having previously taken an oath, as a member of Congress, or as an officer of the United States, or as a member of any State legislature, or as an executive or judicial officer of any State, to support the Constitution of the United States, shall have engaged in insurrection or rebellion against the same, or given aid or comfort to the enemies thereof. But Congress may by a vote of two-thirds of each House, remove such disability.
Section 3 prevented those who had held a federal office or certain state offices and then supported the Confederacy–thus committing treason–from becoming federal or state officials after the Civil War. At first, this limitation even applied to postmasters. But Congress narrowed the restriction in 1872, and then removed it entirely in 1898.

SECTION 4. The validity of the public debt of the United States, authorized by law, including debts incurred for payment of pensions and bounties for services in suppressing insurrection or rebellion, shall not be questioned. But neither the United States nor any State shall assume or pay any debt or obligation incurred in aid of insurrection or rebellion against the United States, or any claim for the loss or emancipation of any slave; but all such debts, obligations and claims shall be held illegal and void.
Section 4 acknowledges the validity of Union debts incurred during the Civil War, but makes clear that the neither the U.S. government nor state governments will assume any Confederate debts. This section also

> "While the Union survived the Civil War, the Constitution did not. In its place arose a new, more promising basis for justice and equality, the Fourteenth Amendment."
>
> —Justice Thurgood Marshall

specifically forbids any reimbursement to slaveholders for the emancipation of slaves.

SECTION 5. The Congress shall have the power to enforce, by appropriate legislation, the provisions of this article.

The Fourteenth Amendment expanded federal power by giving Congress the authority to pass enabling legislation to enforce its provisions. However, in early cases the Supreme Court limited the scope of Section 5. In the *Civil Rights Cases* (1883), the Court ruled that Congress could not prohibit private discrimination in the Civil Rights Act of 1875, thus instituting the state action requirement. Therefore, Congress relied on its Article I power to regulate interstate commerce when it passed the Civil Rights Act of 1964 to ban discrimination in privately owned motels and restaurants. But in a series of cases the Supreme Court did uphold the Voting Rights Act of 1965, which prohibited discrimination in election procedures, to be a valid exercise of congressional power under Section 5.

More recently, the Court has once again moved to limit the reach of Section 5. In *Adarand Constructors v. Pena* (1995), the Supreme Court ruled that Congress did not have more powers under Section 5 than the states to enact affirmative action programs. And in *City of Boerne v. Flores* (1997), the Court struck down the Religious Freedom Restoration Act (RFRA), holding that Congress could only act to remedy violations of rights, not redefine Supreme Court interpretations of what those rights were.

AMENDMENT XV

SECTION 1. The right of citizens of the United States to vote shall not be denied or abridged by the United States or by any State on account of race, color, or previous condition of servitude.

SECTION 2. The Congress shall have the power to enforce this article by appropriate legislation.

THE FIFTEENTH AMENDMENT: SUFFRAGE FOR BLACK MEN

The Fourteenth Amendment did not explicitly grant the vote to African American men, although it decreased congressional representation for states that denied them the vote. Congress debated proposals for an amendment forbidding discrimination in voting based on race, and some Americans argued that women's suffrage should also be included. But the amendment passed by Congress in 1869 and ratified in 1870 did not mention gender. As a result, it benefited only men until 1920, when the Nineteenth Amendment was ratified. And, for almost one hundred years after its ratification, the Fifteenth Amendment offered very little protection to African American men, either.

SECTION 1. The right of citizens of the United States to vote shall not be denied or abridged by the United States or by any State on account of race, color, or previous condition of servitude.

States sought many ways to subvert the Fifteenth Amendment for persons of color. They passed discriminatory laws regarding voting that did not mention race, yet had the effect of racial discrimination. One tactic was grandfather clauses, which allowed voters registered before the Fifteenth Amendment—or their descendants—to skip literacy tests. The Supreme Court struck down such grandfather clauses in 1915. Whites also tried to exclude blacks from political party conventions and primaries, claiming that they were private associations not regulated by the Fifteenth Amendment. But in *Terry v. Adams* (1953) the Court held that the Fifteenth Amendment applied to any election where a public official was chosen.

Born a slave in New York, Sojourner Truth became a national advocate of suffrage for both African Americans and women.

The Supreme Court has also extended Fifteenth Amendment protection to races other than African Americans. In *Rice v. Cayetano* (2000), the Court struck down a Hawaii law limiting voters for a state office to those whose ancestors lived in Hawaii before 1778, when Europeans first encountered the islands. Even though the state office administered funds designated for such Hawaiians, the Court ruled that the Hawaii law violated the Fifteenth Amendment. Although the law did not specifically mention race, the Supreme Court held that it clearly limited the ballot to voters of a certain race or ancestry.

"I have a dream that my four children will one day live in a nation where they will not be judged by the color of their skin but by the content of their character."

—Dr. Martin Luther King, Jr.

SECTION 2. The Congress shall have the power to enforce this article by appropriate legislation.

Congress enacted the Enforcement Act in 1870 to carry out the provisions of the Fifteenth Amendment, but to little effect. With the end of Reconstruction in 1876, and the Jim Crow laws enacted thereafter to discriminate against African Americans, southern states largely succeeded in keeping blacks away from the polls.

In the 1950s and 1960s, a massive civil rights movement sought to register African Americans to vote and change segregation laws. Leaders of the movement also wanted to pressure U.S. officials to support new laws strengthening voting rights. One of the key events in this movement was a voting rights march in Selma, Alabama, in March 1965. Before the march, only one percent of the African Americans of voting age in Selma were registered. Alabama state troopers on horseback attacked the marchers, and a week later President Lyndon Johnson submitted his voting rights bill to Congress.

Enacted five months later, the Voting Rights Act of 1965 prohibited literacy tests, allowed federal officials to supervise voter registration, and outlawed the dilution of minority voter strength in drawing the boundaries

Marchers crossed the Edmund Pettus Bridge in Selma, Alabama, to protest the denial of voting rights to blacks in March 1965.

of electoral districts. Its "preclearance" provision also required certain states to get approval from the federal government before enacting changes in their election laws. The Supreme Court upheld the Voting Rights Act in *South Carolina v. Katzenbach* (1966), even though the law allowed significant federal intrusion into the traditionally state-controlled domain of voting.

Dr. Martin Luther King: Free at Last!

After receiving his doctorate in theology at Boston University, the Rev. Martin Luther King, Jr., became a pastor in Montgomery, Alabama. When Rosa Parks refused to give up her seat on a city bus to a white man in 1955, Dr. King quickly emerged as a national leader of the civil rights movement. His eloquent speeches and nonviolent protests, focusing on the right of African Americans to vote, often earned him jail time in cities across the South. Dr. King's most famous address, delivered in 1963 before more than two hundred thousand people in the nation's capital, expressed his dream that one day all Americans would be able to say, "Free at last! Free at last! Thank God Almighty, we are free at last!" He won the Nobel Peace Prize in 1964.

Dr. King was assassinated on April 4, 1968, sparking riots nationwide.

AMENDMENT XVI

The Congress shall have power to lay and collect taxes on incomes, from whatever source derived, without apportionment among the several States, and without regard to any census or enumeration.

THE SIXTEENTH AMENDMENT: INCOME TAXES

During the early 1900s, as part of the Progressive Era, several amendments were added to the Constitution. The Sixteenth Amendment overturned a Supreme Court case in order to allow taxes on incomes. This increased federal revenue and allowed the national government to play a larger role in American life. It also gave many Americans a favorite target of criticism.

The Congress shall have power to lay and collect taxes on incomes, from whatever source derived, without apportionment among the several States, and without regard to any census or enumeration.
The Sixteenth Amendment made it clear that income taxes were constitutional when levied on individuals, without being apportioned among the states. During the Civil War, Congress had instituted an income tax, and the Supreme Court upheld it. But in *Pollack v. Farmers Loan & Trust Co.* (1895), the Court ruled that the income tax was a **direct tax,** which meant that under Article I it could not be levied as a uniform rate but instead had to be apportioned among the states. Such a complicated formula would be difficult to administer, so Congress passed the Sixteenth Amendment in 1909 and it was ratified in 1913.

direct tax
most commonly, a tax based on the value of land, as opposed to one based on privileges or uses

The Internal Rectal Service *Rep. James Trafficant*

Known for his colorful speeches on the floor of the House, former Rep. James Trafficant (D-Ohio) voiced the frustrations of many Americans about taxes in March 2001, using his signature cry from the television series Star Trek.

From the womb to the tomb, Madam Speaker, the Internal Rectal Service is one big enema. Think about it: they tax our income, they tax our savings, they tax our sex, they tax our property-sales profits, they

even tax our income when we die. Is it any wonder America is taxed off? We happen to be suffering from a disease called Taxes Mortis Americanus. Beam me up!

AMENDMENT XVII

The Senate of the United States shall be composed of two Senators from each State, elected by the people thereof, for six years; and each Senator shall have one vote. The electors in each State shall have the qualifications requisite for electors of the most numerous branch of the State legislatures.

When vacancies happen in the representation of any State in the Senate, the executive authority of such State shall issue writs of election to fill such vacancies: *Provided,* That the legislature of any State may empower the executive thereof to make temporary appointments until the people fill the vacancies by election as the legislature may direct.

This amendment shall not be so construed as to affect the election or term of any Senator chosen before it becomes valid as part of the Constitution.

THE SEVENTEENTH AMENDMENT: DIRECT ELECTION OF SENATORS

Another reform of the Progressive Era was allowing the people to select U.S. senators, rather than having state legislatures choose them, as originally provided in Article I. Advocates of the Seventeenth Amendment hoped to avoid the corrupt practice in which political machines, backed by corporate wealth, hand-picked senatorial candidates. Because of such practices, the Senate was often referred to as a "millionaire's club."

The Senate of the United States shall be composed of two Senators from each State, elected by the people thereof, for six years; and each Senator shall have one vote. The electors in each State shall have the qualifications requisite for electors of the most numerous branch of the State legislatures.

The Seventeenth Amendment changes Section 3 of Article I to allow direct election of senators by the people. It also allows states to determine what the qualifications of voters for senator shall be–subject of course to any further constitutional amendments. Therefore, women in some states, such as Wyoming, were allowed to vote for U.S. senator even before the Nineteenth Amendment gave women suffrage nationwide.

When vacancies happen in the representation of any State in the Senate, the executive authority of such State shall issue writs of election to fill such vacancies: *Provided,* **That the legislature of any State may empower the executive thereof to make temporary appointments until the people fill the vacancies by election as the legislature may direct.**

The governor of a state may make a temporary appointment for senator if the office becomes vacant. Article I does not contain similar provisions for the House of Representatives. As a result of the Cold War and the September 11, 2001 terrorist attacks, some scholars have proposed a constitutional amendment that would allow governors to make emergency appointments of House members if Congress was attacked and representatives were killed or disabled.

This amendment shall not be so construed as to affect the election or term of any Senator chosen before it becomes valid as part of the Constitution.

One obstacle to enacting the Seventeenth Amendment was Article V's requirement that before an amendment can be submitted to the states for ratification, it must be approved by a two-thirds vote of both houses of Congress (or a special convention called by two-thirds of the states). Not surprisingly, the incumbent U.S. senators did not want to vote themselves out of a job. However, by 1911 a majority of states had already enacted some provisions requiring their state legislatures to consider the results of voter primaries when selecting senators. Consequently, the Seventeenth Amendment was proposed in 1912 and ratified in 1913, although the House of Representatives had first passed it in the 1890s.

AMENDMENT XVIII

SECTION 1. *After one year from the ratification of this article the manufacture, sale, or transportation of intoxicating liquors within, the importation thereof into, or the exportation thereof from the United States and all territory subject to the jurisdiction thereof for beverage purposes is hereby prohibited.*

SECTION 2. *The Congress and the several States shall have concurrent power to enforce this article by appropriate legislation.*

SECTION 3. *This article shall be inoperative unless it shall have been ratified as an amendment to the Constitution by the legislatures of the several States, as provided in the Constitution, within seven years from the date of the submission hereof to the States by the Congress.*

THE EIGHTEENTH AMENDMENT: PROHIBITION

The temperance movement, which sought to restrict or ban the consumption of alcoholic beverages, had a long history in the United States. The first temperance organization was formed in 1808, and many states had outlawed alcohol before the Eighteenth Amendment nationalized its prohibition. But with the onset of the Progressive Era, Americans seemed more confident in the ability of constitutional amendments to reform human behavior. When the Eighteenth Amendment was ratified in 1919, many Americans believed that crime, poverty, and broken homes would be outlawed along with alcohol.

SECTION 1. *After one year from the ratification of this article the manufacture, sale, or transportation of intoxicating liquors within, the importation thereof into, or the exportation thereof from the United States and all territory subject to the jurisdiction thereof for beverage purposes is hereby prohibited.*

Women played a major role in the passage of laws prohibiting the sale of alcohol, even though they could not vote. Organizations such as the Women's Christian Temperance Union (WCTU) rallied on behalf of the women and children who were impoverished by drunken husbands, because they had no other means of support. The Prohibition movement also flourished among white fundamentalist Protestants, whose religion forbade the use of alcohol. But Catholic immigrants from Ireland and Italy opposed Prohibition, because alcohol was both part of their religion and part of their culture. As a result, Prohibition created conflict between the urban areas of the North, where immigrants concentrated, and the rural regions of the South and West. First introduced in Congress in 1876, a Prohibition amendment finally achieved the necessary two-thirds majority in both houses in 1917.

> "The saloon is the sum of all villainies. It is worse than war or pestilence. It is the parent of all crimes and the mother of all sins."
>
> —Billy Sunday

SECTION 2. *The Congress and the several States shall have concurrent power to enforce this article by appropriate legislation.*
After the Eighteenth Amendment was ratified in 1919, Congress passed the Volstead Act to enforce Prohibition. The law banned the consumption of beer and wine as well as distilled liquors. An exception was made for alcohol used in medicine and sacramental wine. Very quickly, an illegal bootlegging industry sprang up, with "rum runners" smuggling in liquor from the Caribbean and speakeasies, or illegal saloons, serving bathtub gin. Organized crime and police corruption flourished, especially in major cities like Chicago. Such widespread violations of the law caused many Americans to believe that the Volstead Act was unenforceable. Eventually, the Eighteenth Amendment was repealed by the Twenty-first Amendment in 1933.

SECTION 3. *This article shall be inoperative unless it shall have been ratified as an amendment to the Constitution by the legislatures of the several States, as provided in the Constitution, within seven years from the date of the submission hereof to the States by the Congress.*
Congressional opponents of Prohibition put a time limit on ratification of the Eighteenth Amendment, the first time such a restriction had ever been used. They believed that, with a small minority of states holding out, the amendment would fail ratification. But the "wets," as opponents of Prohibition were called, proved to be wrong, and the "drys" won ratification in a little over a year.

Cases of confiscated liquor were commonplace during Prohibition years.

AMENDMENT XIX

The right of citizens of the United States to vote shall not be denied or abridged by the United States or by any State on account of sex.

Congress shall have power to enforce this article by appropriate legislation.

THE NINETEENTH AMENDMENT: WOMEN'S SUFFRAGE

"If particular care and attention is not paid to the ladies we are determined to foment a rebellion, and will not hold ourselves bound by any laws in which we have no voice or representation."
—Abigail Adams

In 1776, Abigail Adams warned her husband John to "remember the ladies" in the new system of laws that America would adopt. But although women played a critical role in America's political life, they would not achieve the vote nationwide until almost 150 years later. In 1919, Congress finally approved the Nineteenth Amendment granting women suffrage throughout America. It was ratified in 1920, with Tennessee providing the necessary approval by one vote—after a mother lobbied her son in the state legislature on the amendment's behalf.

The right of citizens of the United States to vote shall not be denied or abridged by the United States or by any State on account of sex.

Congress shall have power to enforce this article by appropriate legislation.
The road to the Nineteenth Amendment was a long one. Women actively participated in the struggle for independence from England and in the fight to end slavery. But after the Civil War, their own quest for the vote took a backseat to suffrage for black men. Women fought for a Sixteenth Amendment to give themselves the vote after the Fifteenth Amendment was ratified in 1870, but it would be fifty years and three amendments later until at last they gained the ballot nationwide.

Revolutionary Roots. From the nation's beginning, women saw themselves as participants in America's experiment with liberty. During the 1770s, women across America were swept up in revolutionary fervor. In towns from Massachusetts to South Carolina, they issued declarations and resolves forswearing the use of tea, that hated symbol of England's taxation without representation. In 1774, ten months after the Boston Tea Party, fifty-one women in Edenton, North Carolina, issued their own nonimportation agreement to boycott British goods. London newspapers satirized their efforts as the "Edenton Ladies' Tea Party."

After independence, women were allowed to vote in at least one state in the new republic. New Jersey's constitution of 1776 allowed "all inhabitants" who met certain property requirements to vote, which for thirty years included both women and free blacks. But in 1807, New Jersey passed a law restricting the vote to free white males.

Seneca Falls. Women's lack of suffrage did not prevent them from being politically active. They were instrumental in the abolitionist movement, sending thousands of antislavery petitions to Congress. Indeed, it was after Elizabeth Cady Stanton and Lucretia Mott were denied admission to a London antislavery conference that they organized the first women's rights convention. It was held in Seneca Falls, New York, in 1848. Attended by abolitionist luminaries such as Frederick Douglass, the conference issued a "Declaration of Sentiments," modeled after the Declaration of Independence, which asserted that "all men and women are created equal."

An English cartoonist satirized the "patriotic ladies" at Edenton, North Carolina, as bawdy, drunk, and neglectful of their children.

Civil War Amendments. Women fought hard for the Thirteenth Amendment to abolish slavery, but some were dismayed when the Fourteenth Amendment introduced the word "male" as a qualification for voting for the first time in the Constitution. The Fifteenth Amendment's grant of suffrage for black men, without including women, caused a major split in the women's movement. Leading abolitionists favored the immediate adoption of the Fifteenth Amendment, arguing that women would be enfranchised later. These advocates included Frederick Douglass and famed orator Lucy Stone, who founded the American Woman Suffrage Association. Elizabeth Cady Stanton opposed ratification of the

Fifteenth Amendment without a companion amendment for women, and she formed the National Woman Suffrage Association.

Women's groups also filed test lawsuits across the country claiming that the Fourteenth Amendment's Privileges or Immunities Clause granted women, along with other citizens, the right to vote. However, the Supreme Court ruled in *Minor v. Happersett* (1875) that the Fourteenth Amendment did not protect the right to vote, leaving the determination of voters' qualifications up to the states.

Lucy Stone was nationally known as an eloquent orator for women's rights.

"Failure is impossible."

—Susan B. Anthony

We, the Whole People Susan B. Anthony

In 1872 Susan B. Anthony was arrested for attempting to vote in the presidential election. Known as the "Napoleon of women's rights," Anthony traveled thousands of miles speaking on behalf of the constitutional rights of women.

It was we, the people; not we, the white male citizens; nor yet we, the male citizens; but we, the whole people, who formed the Union. And we formed it, not to give the blessings of liberty, but to secure them; not to the half of ourselves and the half of our posterity, but to the whole people—women as well as men. And it is a downright mockery to talk to women of their enjoyment of the blessings of liberty while they are denied the use of the only means of securing them provided by this democratic-republican government—the ballot....

To them this government has no just powers derived from the consent of the governed. To them this government is not a democracy. It is not a republic. It is an odious aristocracy; a hateful oligarchy of sex...which ordains all men sovereigns, all women subjects, carries dissension, discord and rebellion into every home of the nation.

The Progressive Era. Women continued to play key roles in politics, serving on the front lines of the Progressive movement, which sought to reform government and society in the early 1900s. Even though they could not vote, women led the charge for the Eighteenth Amendment, banning the consumption of alcohol. And, although progress was slow for a constitutional amendment granting women suffrage, more and more states began to give women the right to vote in various forms. In 1890, the two wings of the women's suffrage movement reunited, and Wyoming became the first state to grant women the vote. Thereafter, thirty states had extended some form of suffrage to women by 1919, and Jeannette Rankin became the first woman to be elected to Congress in 1916.

Still, President Woodrow Wilson was a slow convert to women's suffrage. Wilson's campaign during World War I to "make the world safe for democracy" faced challenges at home by women, labor unions, and

African Americans. Suffragists pointed out that German women had the vote while American women did not. They chained themselves to the White House fence and were sent to prison. Wilson finally changed his mind when enough states had already granted women the vote that a national suffrage amendment seemed inevitable. In 1920, thanks to the Nineteenth Amendment, Warren G. Harding won the first presidential election in which women voted nationwide.

These picketers demonstrated outside the White House in 1917 to convince President Woodrow Wilson to support women's suffrage.

A Demand for Justice at Home Rose Winslow

A Polish immigrant, Rose Winslow (or Ruza Wenclawska) was among the suffragists jailed for picketing the White House in 1917. Claiming to be political prisoners, they waged a hunger strike and were force fed in prison during World War I.

If this thing is necessary we will naturally go through with it. Force is so stupid a weapon. I feel so happy doing my bit for decency—for our war, which is after all, real and fundamental....

We have been in solitary for five weeks.... I had a nervous time of it, gasping a long time afterward, and my stomach rejecting during the process.... The poor soul who fed me got liberally besprinkled during the process. I heard myself making the most hideous sounds.... One feels so forsaken when one lies prone and people shove a pipe down one's stomach....

This morning but for an astounding tiredness, I am all right. I am waiting to see what happens when the president realizes that brutal bullying isn't quite a statesmanlike method for settling a demand for justice at home....

All the officers here know we are making this hunger strike that women fighting for liberty may be considered political prisoners; we have told them. God knows we don't want other women ever to have to do this over again.

AMENDMENT XX

SECTION 1. The terms of the President and the Vice President shall end at noon on the 20th day of January, and the terms of Senators and Representatives at noon on the 3d day of January, of the years in which such terms would have ended if this article had not been ratified; and the terms of their successors shall then begin.

SECTION 2. The Congress shall assemble at least once in every year, and such meeting shall begin at noon on the 3d day of January, unless they shall by law appoint a different day.

SECTION 3. If, at the time fixed for the beginning of the term of the President, the President elect shall have died, the Vice President elect shall become President. If a President shall not have been chosen before the time fixed for the beginning of his term, or if the President elect shall have failed to qualify, then the Vice President elect shall act as President until a President shall have qualified; and the Congress may by law provide for the case wherein neither a President elect nor a Vice President elect shall have qualified, declaring who shall then act as President, or the manner in which one who is to act shall be selected, and such person shall act accordingly until a President or Vice President shall have qualified.

SECTION 4. The Congress may by law provide for the case of the death of any of the persons from whom the House of Representatives may choose a President whenever the right of choice shall have devolved upon them, and for the case of the death of any of the persons from whom the Senate may choose a Vice President whenever the right of choice shall have devolved upon them.

SECTION 5. Sections 1 and 2 shall take effect on the 15th day of October following the ratification of this article.

SECTION 6. This article shall be inoperative unless it shall have been ratified as an amendment to the Constitution by the legislatures of three-fourths of the several States within seven years from the date of its submission.

THE TWENTIETH AMENDMENT: LAME DUCKS

The Twentieth Amendment is best known for reducing the time in which members of Congress who had been voted out of office, or **lame ducks,** could continue to legislate. It accomplished this goal by moving the inauguration dates of the president and members of Congress from March to January. The Twentieth Amendment also specifies who shall act as president if the president-elect dies or has not been chosen by the date of inauguration. During the 2000 election, the latter provision—although not used—became increasingly more relevant.

lame ducks
incumbents who have not been reelected to office

SECTION 1. The terms of the President and the Vice President shall end at noon on the 20th day of January, and the terms of Senators and Representatives at noon on the 3d day of January, of the years in which such terms would have ended if this article had not been ratified; and the terms of their successors shall then begin.
After the Constitution was ratified, the Congress—still acting under the Articles of Confederation—had set March 4, 1789, as the date on which the new president and members of Congress would be inaugurated. But that created a four-month period between the November elections and the March inaugurations in which lame ducks could obstruct the work of Congress, without being accountable to voters. However, Congress could not change the inauguration dates by mere statute, because the Constitution guaranteed the president and members of Congress a fixed term that could not be shortened without a constitutional amendment. Therefore, Congress proposed the Twentieth Amendment to resolve this problem in 1932, and it was ratified in 1933. The amendment began the legislators' terms on January 3, so that the new Congress would have adequate time to choose the president—if so required—before the presidential inauguration on January 20.

SECTION 2. The Congress shall assemble at least once in every year, and such meeting shall begin at noon on the 3d day of January, unless they shall by law appoint a different day.

Section 2 changes the provision in Article I, Section 4, that Congress would begin its annual session on the first Monday in December. The four-month gap between the November election and the March inauguration was in the early days of the republic justified by poor transportation and communication. But on top of that delay, the newly elected Congress did not have its first official session until the following December–thirteen months after it had been elected. Section 2 ensured that the new Congress would begin work soon after its election.

SECTION 3. If, at the time fixed for the beginning of the term of the President, the President elect shall have died, the Vice President elect shall become President. If a President shall not have been chosen before the time fixed for the beginning of his term, or if the President–elect shall have failed to qualify, then the Vice President elect shall act as President until a President shall have qualified; and the Congress may by law provide for the case wherein neither a President elect nor a Vice President–elect shall have qualified, declaring who shall then act as President, or the manner in which one who is to act shall be selected, and such person shall act accordingly until a President or Vice President shall have qualified.

Section 3 addressed issues of presidential succession if the president-elect died or had not been chosen by the inauguration date. Coincidentally, only three weeks after the amendment's ratification, an assassin shot at president–elect Franklin Roosevelt in Miami, killing the mayor of Chicago. Section 3 also allows Congress to designate an acting president in the event that neither a president–elect nor a vice president–elect has qualified for office by the inauguration date. In the Presidential Succession Act of 1947, Congress specified that the order of succession after the vice president shall be the Speaker of the House of Representatives, the president pro tempore of the Senate, the Secretary of State, and then the remaining cabinet members according to the date their departments were created.

SECTION 4. The Congress may by law provide for the case of the death of any of the persons from whom the House of Representatives may choose a President whenever the right of choice shall have devolved upon them, and for the case of the death of any of the persons from whom the Senate may choose a Vice President whenever the right of choice shall have devolved upon them.

According to the Twelfth Amendment, the House of Representatives chooses among the top three candidates for president if no candidate has a majority in the electoral college. The Senate chooses among the top two candidates for vice president, if no candidate for that office has a majority in the electoral college. Section 4 allows Congress to specify what to do if any of those candidates dies between the meeting of the electoral college in December and the counting of the electoral votes in Congress on January 6.

SECTION 5. Sections 1 and 2 shall take effect on the 15th day of October following the ratification of this article.

Section 5 made sure that the amendment would not take effect too soon after an election had taken place. That way, members of Congress would have sufficient notice when their old terms would end and their new terms begin.

SECTION 6. This article shall be inoperative unless it shall have been ratified as an amendment to the Constitution by the legislatures of three-fourths of the several States within seven years from the date of its submission.

As in previous amendments, Section 6 sets a time limit by which the amendment must be ratified. It also establishes the method of ratification.

Amendment XXI

Section 1. The eighteenth article of amendment to the Constitution of the United States is hereby repealed.

Section 2. The transportation or importation into any State, Territory, or Possession of the United States for delivery or use therein of intoxicating liquors, in violation of the laws thereof, is hereby prohibited.

Section 3. This article shall be inoperative unless it shall have been ratified as an amendment to the Constitution by conventions in the several States, as provided in the Constitution, within seven years from the date of the submission hereof to the States by the Congress.

The Twenty-first Amendment: Repealing Prohibition

Only thirteen years after Prohibition took effect, the Eighteenth Amendment was repealed by the Twenty-first Amendment. This was the first time a constitutional amendment had ever been repealed. Widespread corruption and lawbreaking caused many Americans to believe that the "noble experiment" of Prohibition had failed. In addition, breweries and distilleries promised more jobs for the unemployed during the depths of the Great Depression. Some Americans argue that today's war on drugs is similar to the Prohibition movement, and with equal success.

SECTION 1. The eighteenth article of amendment to the Constitution of the United States is hereby repealed.

The Twenty-first Amendment was passed by Congress in February of 1933 and ratified by the states in December of the same year. A reapportionment of Congress due to population shifts from the rural South and West to the urban North caused legislators to be less sympathetic to Prohibition in 1933. The prospect of new jobs also increased the Twenty-first Amendment's support in Congress, and President Franklin Roosevelt advocated the repeal of Prohibition as well.

SECTION 2. The transportation or importation into any State, Territory, or Possession of the United States for delivery or use therein of intoxicating liquors, in violation of the laws thereof, is hereby prohibited.

This provision in the Twenty-first Amendment is one of two occasions where the Constitution directly forbids conduct by private individuals. The other is the Thirteenth Amendment's ban on slavery and involuntary servitude. The Supreme Court has ruled that Section 2, although it doesn't specifically say so, gives the states extensive authority to regulate alcoholic beverages. Normally, states would be prohibited by the Commerce Clause from restricting the transport of alcoholic beverages in interstate commerce. However, the Court has also held that states may only regulate alcohol in order to control consumption, not for economic protectionism. And in *South Dakota v. Dole* (1987), the Court ruled that the Twenty-first Amendment did not prohibit Congress from denying federal highway funds to states that did not enact a national minimum drinking age.

> "The Constitution may not be ruined by repeated hit-and-run attacks of the sort that Prohibition and its repeal entailed, but it may not emerge intact either."
>
> —Laurence Tribe

A Criminalizing Assembly Line *Salim Muwakkil*

Chicago journalist Salim Muwakkil argues that the war on drugs, like Prohibition, is a failed attempt to control human behavior at enormous cost to society.

Chicago was once defined by the violence wrought by a war on alcohol that we called Prohibition. In those days, drive-by shootings were the work of tommy-gun-toting

gangsters pushing that "demon rum" and other abominations of the era. That violent war ended in 1933 when Americans finally acknowledged the self-destructive futility of trying to prohibit alcohol use....

The "war on drugs" policy was officially launched in 1982 by the Reagan administration and since that time, drug arrests have soared and prison populations have exploded....

Law enforcement's inordinate focus on fighting a drug war has skewed law enforcement's crime-fighting priorities, channeling billions in resources to policies with few social rewards. By imprisoning record numbers of low-level drug dealers and users, society has created a criminalizing assembly line and deepened the saturation of prison culture into various inner-city communities.

SECTION 3. This article shall be inoperative unless it shall have been ratified as an amendment to the Constitution by conventions in the several States, as provided in the Constitution, within seven years from the date of the submission hereof to the States by the Congress.

The Twenty-first Amendment was ratified by state conventions, the first time that method of ratification under Article V had ever been used. All other amendments were ratified by state legislatures. Congressional opponents of Prohibition realized that rural interests still controlled most state legislatures, so they advocated ratification by state conventions specially elected for that purpose. Approximately seventy-three percent of the twenty-one million citizens who voted in those elections supported the Twenty-first Amendment.

The souped-up hot rods that had transported illegal booze soon found a home in the new sport of stock car racing after Prohibition ended.

AMENDMENT XXII

SECTION 1. No person shall be elected to the office of the President more than twice, and no person who has held the office of President, or acted as President, for more than two years of a term to which some other person was elected President shall be elected to the office of President more than once. But this Article shall not apply to any person holding the office of President when this Article was proposed by Congress, and shall not prevent any person who may be holding the office of President, or acting as President, during the term within which this Article becomes operative from holding the office of President or acting as President during the remainder of such term.

SECTION 2. This article shall be inoperative unless it shall have been ratified as an amendment to the Constitution by the legislatures of three-fourths of the several States within seven years from the date of its submission to the States by the Congress.

THE TWENTY-SECOND AMENDMENT: PRESIDENTIAL TERM LIMITS

George Washington established the tradition that a president would only seek two terms in office. But Franklin Delano Roosevelt broke that precedent. During the crises of the Great Depression and World War II, FDR was elected to his third term in 1940 and his fourth term in 1944. He died in April 1945, soon after his fourth inauguration. A new Republican Congress quickly sought to set term limits for future presidents in 1947, and the Twenty-second Amendment was ratified in 1951.

> "It's a good thing we've got a 22nd Amendment or I would run again."
> —Bill Clinton

SECTION 1. No person shall be elected to the office of the President more than twice, and no person who has held the office of President, or acted as President, for more than two years of a term to which some other person was elected President shall be elected to the office of President more than once. But this Article shall not apply to any person holding the office of President when this Article was proposed by Congress, and shall not prevent any person who may be holding

the office of President, or acting as President, during the term within which this Article becomes operative from holding the office of President or acting as President during the remainder of such term.

Section 1 forbids any person be elected president more than twice—and, if serving more than two years of another president's term, to be elected more than once. Therefore, ten years is the maximum term any president can serve. The amendment specifically did not apply to President Harry Truman, who had served almost all of FDR's fourth term. Truman was reelected in 1948, but chose not to run for a second full term in 1952. By denying even the prospect of a third term, the Twenty-second Amendment formally created a lame-duck president who tends to lose influence in office during the end of a second term.

SECTION 2. This article shall be inoperative unless it shall have been ratified as an amendment to the Constitution by the legislatures of three-fourths of the several States within seven years from the date of its submission to the States by the Congress.

Section 2 establishes the time limit for ratification and its method. Although the Twenty-second Amendment is usually regarded as a Republican measure to limit a popular Democratic president, many state legislatures controlled by Democrats nonetheless ratified the amendment.

In 1934, at his birthday party, President Franklin Roosevelt spoofed critics who charged that he behaved like an emperor—even before his fourth term.

AMENDMENT XXIII

SECTION 1. The District constituting the seat of Government of the United States shall appoint in such manner as Congress may direct:

A number of electors of President and Vice President equal to the whole number of Senators and Representatives in Congress to which the District would be entitled if it were a State, but in no event more than the least populous State; they shall be in addition to those appointed by the States, but they shall be considered, for the purposes of the election of President and Vice President, to be electors appointed by a State; and they shall meet in the District and perform such duties as provided by the twelfth article of amendment.

SECTION 2. The Congress shall have power to enforce this article by appropriate legislation.

THE TWENTY-THIRD AMENDMENT: ELECTORAL VOTES FOR THE DISTRICT OF COLUMBIA

Article I provides for the creation of a federal district to be the nation's capital, but it does not deal with suffrage for the District of Columbia's residents. Some scholars argue that the District of Columbia, like any other federal territory, was to be eligible for statehood once it reached sufficient population. Others believe that the District, which was once part of Maryland, must always remain under congressional control to preserve national interests. In 1960, Congress proposed the Twenty-third Amendment to give D.C. residents the vote in presidential elections, and it was ratified in 1961. However, D.C. residents remain the only U.S. citizens who pay federal income taxes and have no voting representation in Congress.

SECTION 1. The District constituting the seat of Government of the United States shall appoint in such manner as Congress may direct:

A number of electors of President and Vice President equal to the whole number of Senators and Representatives in Congress to which

the District would be entitled if it were a State, but in no event more than the least populous State; they shall be in addition to those appointed by the States, but they shall be considered, for the purposes of the election of President and Vice President, to be electors appointed by a State; and they shall meet in the District and perform such duties as provided by the twelfth article of amendment.

An earlier version of the Twenty-third Amendment would have given the District of Columbia representation in the House of Representatives as well as the electoral college. The amendment would also have banned the poll tax. But in negotiations between the House and the Senate, these additional provisions were removed. As of 1960, the District of Columbia had about eight hundred thousand citizens—more than thirteen other states. African Americans constituted a large majority of these citizens, which raised racial justice issues during the onset of the civil rights movement. The District's population has decreased significantly since that time—to six hundred thousand as of the 2000 census, and only Wyoming had a smaller population. In addition, whites composed a greater proportion of the District's population in 2000.

Congress passed a constitutional amendment in 1978 that would have given the District full voting representation in the House and the Senate, but it failed to be ratified. Under the Twenty-third Amendment, the District of Columbia receives three electoral votes (the same electoral votes as the least populous state) for president—regardless of its own population. This brings the total number of electoral votes to 538; a candidate must then have 270 electoral votes to become president.

SECTION 2. The Congress shall have power to enforce this article by appropriate legislation.

As with some other amendments, Congress has enforcement powers under the Twenty-third Amendment. In addition, Congress retains ultimate control under Article I for legislation affecting the District of Columbia, so District residents have only a limited form of self-government known as home rule.

AMENDMENT XXIV

SECTION 1. The right of citizens of the United States to vote in any primary or other election for President or Vice President, for electors for President or Vice President, or for Senator or Representative in Congress, shall not be denied or abridged by the United States or any State by reason of failure to pay any poll tax or other tax.

SECTION 2. The Congress shall have power to enforce this article by appropriate legislation.

THE TWENTY-FOURTH AMENDMENT: BANNING THE POLL TAX

The Twenty-fourth Amendment prohibits the use of **poll taxes** in federal elections, either in primaries or general elections. Such taxes, also known as head taxes, were often used in a discriminatory manner to prevent access to the ballot, especially for poor whites and racial minorities. Although only a few states still used the poll tax in the early 1960s, Congress thought the problem was best solved by a constitutional amendment, since states traditionally controlled elections. The amendment was passed by Congress in 1962 and ratified in 1964.

poll taxes

head taxes that can be used in a discriminatory way to prevent participation in voting

SECTION 1. The right of citizens of the United States to vote in any primary or other election for President or Vice President, for electors for President or Vice President, or for Senator or Representative in Congress, shall not be denied or abridged by the United States or any State by reason of failure to pay any poll tax or other tax.

SECTION 2. The Congress shall have power to enforce this article by appropriate legislation.

Property qualifications for voting began in the early days of American government, but with the expansion of the franchise in the Jacksonian era they were gradually eliminated. However, after Reconstruction many southern states began using a poll or head tax as a requirement for voting. Although the amount of the tax was small, it was often implemented in a way to discourage political participation by poor whites and African Americans. The Twenty-fourth Amendment only affects the use of poll taxes in federal elections. However, in *Harper v. Virginia State Board of Elections* (1966), the Supreme Court ruled that the use of poll taxes in state and local elections violated the Equal Protection Clause of the Fourteenth Amendment.

AMENDMENT XXV

SECTION 1. In case of the removal of the President from office or of his death or resignation, the Vice President shall become President.

SECTION 2. Whenever there is a vacancy in the office of the Vice President, the President shall nominate a Vice President who shall take office upon confirmation by a majority vote of both Houses of Congress.

SECTION 3. Whenever the President transmits to the President pro tempore of the Senate and the Speaker of the House of Representatives his written declaration that he is unable to discharge the powers and duties of his office, and until he transmits to them a written declaration to the contrary, such powers and duties shall be discharged by the Vice President as Acting President.

SECTION 4. Whenever the Vice President and a majority of either the principal officers of the executive departments or of such other body as Congress may by law provide, transmit to the President pro tempore of the Senate and the Speaker of the House of Representatives their written declaration that the President is unable to discharge the powers and duties of his office, the Vice President shall immediately assume the powers and duties of the office as Acting President.

Thereafter, when the President transmits to the President pro tempore of the Senate and the Speaker of the House of Representatives his written declaration that no inability exists, he shall resume the powers and duties of his office unless the Vice President and a majority of either the principal officers of the executive department or of such other body as Congress may by law provide, transmit within four days to the President pro tempore of the Senate and the Speaker of the House of Representatives their written declaration that the President is unable to discharge the powers and duties of his office. Thereupon Congress shall decide the issue, assembling within forty-eight hours for that purpose if not in session. If the Congress, within twenty-one days after receipt of the latter written declaration, or, if Congress is not in session, within twenty-one days after Congress is required to assemble, determines by two-thirds vote of both Houses that the

President is unable to discharge the powers and duties of his office, the Vice President shall continue to discharge the same as Acting President; otherwise, the President shall resume the powers and duties of his office.

THE TWENTY-FIFTH AMENDMENT: PRESIDENTIAL SUCCESSION AND DISABILITY

After the assassination of President John F. Kennedy, Lyndon Johnson took the oath of office aboard Air Force One *with Mrs. Kennedy at his side, still wearing her blood-soaked suit from the Dallas motorcade.*

The assassination of President John F. Kennedy in 1963 brought to the forefront many long-standing questions about presidential succession. When the president died, did the vice president automatically become president, or only serve as acting president? What happened when the vice presidency was vacant? Who determined when the president was disabled and incapable of carrying out official duties? The Twenty-fifth Amendment, passed by Congress in 1965 and ratified in 1967, at long last answered these questions.

SECTION 1. In case of the removal of the President from office or of his death or resignation, the Vice President shall become President.

Section 1 clearly establishes the custom begun in 1841 with John Tyler, who became the first vice president to assume the presidency. Tyler maintained that in such circumstances the vice president became president, not just served as acting president. Before the Twenty-fifth Amendment was ratified, the president had died in office eight times, and the vice president assumed the job thereafter.

SECTION 2. Whenever there is a vacancy in the office of the Vice President, the President shall nominate a Vice President who shall take office upon confirmation by a majority vote of both Houses of Congress.

The vice presidency had been vacant sixteen times before the Twenty-fifth Amendment was ratified. Although the president had never died without a vice president in place, Congress was concerned when Lyndon Johnson–who had a previous heart attack–took office in 1963 without a vice president. Section 2 was implemented for the first time when Spiro Agnew resigned the vice presidency in October 1973 and was convicted of tax evasion. President Richard Nixon, in the midst of the Watergate scandal, nominated Gerald Ford to be vice president, and Ford was confirmed by Congress in December 1973. In August 1974, Nixon resigned the presidency and Ford became president. He nominated Nelson Rockefeller to fill the vacant vice presidency. For the first time in American history, neither the president nor the vice president had been selected by the voters.

> **"Our long national nightmare is over. Our Constitution works."**
>
> —President Gerald R. Ford

SECTION 3. Whenever the President transmits to the President pro tempore of the Senate and the Speaker of the House of Representatives his written declaration that he is unable to discharge the powers and duties of his office, and until he transmits to them a written declaration to the contrary, such powers and duties shall be discharged by the Vice President as Acting President.

Under Section 3, the president may voluntarily turn over the reins of power to the vice president when suffering from a temporary disability. The Twenty-fifth Amendment was not invoked when President Ronald Reagan was shot in 1981. Nor did Reagan formally invoke Section 3 when undergoing surgery in 1985, although he sent letters to congressional leaders informing them that Vice President George Bush would assume presidential duties while Reagan was under anesthesia.

Neither Vice President Nelson Rockefeller nor President Gerald Ford had been elected to their offices by the American people.

SECTION 4. Whenever the Vice President and a majority of either the principal officers of the executive departments or of such other body as Congress may by law provide, transmit to the President pro tempore of the Senate and the Speaker of the House of Representatives their written declaration that the President is unable to discharge the powers and duties of his office, the Vice President shall immediately assume the powers and duties of the office as Acting President....

Several times in American history the president has been disabled for a prolonged period of time. After James Garfield was shot in 1881, he lingered for more than two months. Woodrow Wilson was disabled from a stroke during the last eighteen months of his second term. And Dwight Eisenhower suffered a heart attack and stroke during his administration. Section 4 allows the vice president and a majority of the cabinet officers to declare that the president is disabled, so that the vice president can assume the president's official duties until the disability ends.

...Thereafter, when the President transmits to the President pro tempore of the Senate and the Speaker of the House of Representatives his written declaration that no inability exists, he shall resume the powers and duties of his office unless the Vice President and a majority of either the principal officers of the executive department or of such other body as Congress may by law provide, transmit within four days to the President pro tempore of the Senate and the Speaker of the House of Representatives their written declaration that the President is unable to discharge the powers and duties of his office. Thereupon Congress shall decide the issue, assembling within forty-eight hours for that purpose if not in session. If the Congress, within twenty-one days after receipt of the latter written declaration, or, if Congress is not in session, within twenty-one days after Congress is required to assemble, determines by two-thirds vote of both Houses that the President is unable to discharge the powers and duties of his office, the Vice President shall continue to discharge the same as Acting President; otherwise, the President shall resume the powers and duties of his office.

Section 4 also allows the president to contest a decision of disability made by the vice president and a majority of the cabinet. Under such circumstances, Congress will decide the issue by a two-thirds vote–if the vice president and a majority of the cabinet continue to claim that the president is disabled.

I Am in Control Here *Al Haig*

When President Ronald Reagan was shot on March 30, 1981, Secretary of State Al Haig answered questions by White House reporters. Haig mistakenly believed he was next in the line of succession after the vice president, but the Speaker of the House of Representatives and the president pro tempore of the Senate were ahead of him.

PRESS REPRESENTATIVE: Who is making the decisions for the government right now? Who is making the decisions?

HAIG: Constitutionally, gentlemen, you have the President, the Vice President, and the Secretary of State, in that order, and should the President decide he wants to transfer the helm to the Vice President, he will do so. As of now, I am in control here, in the White House, pending the return of the Vice President and in close touch with him. If something came up, I would check with him, of course.

Amendment XXVI

SECTION 1. The right of citizens of the United States, who are eighteen years of age or older, to vote shall not be denied or abridged by the United States or by any State on account of age.

SECTION 2. The Congress shall have power to enforce this article by appropriate legislation.

The Twenty-sixth Amendment: Suffrage for Young People

With the escalation of the Vietnam War came increased pressure to lower the voting age from twenty-one to eighteen. Young people argued that if they were old enough to die for their country, they were also old enough to vote for the leaders who sent them to war. Consequently, Congress proposed the Twenty-sixth Amendment on March 23, 1971, and it was ratified by three-fourths of the states on July 1, 1971–the fastest ever.

SECTION 1. The right of citizens of the United States, who are eighteen years of age or older, to vote shall not be denied or abridged by the United States or by any State on account of age.

SECTION 2. The Congress shall have power to enforce this article by appropriate legislation.
Section 2 of the Fourteenth Amendment had implied that twenty-one was the minimum age for voting. However, some states allowed individuals younger than twenty-one to vote during and after World War II. Congress passed a Voting Rights Act in 1970 that set eighteen as the minimum age for voting in national and state elections, arguing that it had broad power to protect voting rights under Section 5 of the Fourteenth Amendment. In *Oregon v. Mitchell* (1970), the Supreme Court ruled that the law was valid only for national elections, not for the states. As a result, states faced a monumental task of maintaining separate voting registrations for national and state elections. To solve the problem, Congress quickly passed the proposed Twenty-sixth Amendment, and the states ratified it in a record 107 days.

Amendment XXVII

No law, varying the compensation for the services of the Senators and Representatives, shall take effect, until an election of Representatives shall have intervened.

The Twenty-seventh Amendment: Limiting Congressional Pay Raises

When James Madison submitted his proposals for a Bill of Rights in 1789, he included a provision that prevented members of Congress from voting themselves a pay raise before the voters had a chance to kick them out of office for doing so. This amendment was approved as one of the twelve amendments submitted to the states on September 25, 1789. Only ten of these were ratified in 1791, and they became known as the Bill of Rights because they mainly protected individual rights. However, Congress had not established an official time limit for ratification of the 1789 amendments. During the 1980s, more and more states ratified the amendment limiting congressional pay raises, and it became the Twenty-seventh Amendment in 1992–the longest ratification in U.S. history.

No law, varying the compensation for the services of the Senators and Representatives, shall take effect, until an election of Representatives shall have intervened.
In 1982, during his sophomore year, Gregory Watson wrote a paper for a class at the University of Texas. He argued that since the congressional pay raise amendment proposed in 1789 contained no time limit, it still could be ratified by the states. Watson discovered that after six states had ratified the amendment by 1791, Ohio had ratified it in 1873 and Wyoming in 1978. Watson's instructor gave him a "C" on the paper, maintaining that the amendment was a dead letter. And, based on Supreme Court doctrine, the instructor was right. The Court had ruled that, even though Article V included no time limits in the amendment process, ratification by the states should be "sufficiently contemporaneous…to reflect the will of the people in all sections at relatively the same period."

But after Watson conducted a ten-year national campaign, more than three-fourths of the state legislatures had ratified the amendment in 1992.

> **"It's short-term political pandering without regard to long-term consequences to the Constitution."**
>
> —Rep. Neal Smith

The archivist of the United States, who by statute had the responsibility for certifying the amendment as ratified, did so in May 1992. Both houses of Congress passed resolutions agreeing with that decision, although some questioned whether four other amendments proposed without time limits might still be valid. Those included the 1789 amendment on the reapportionment of Congress, the 1810 amendment on titles of nobility, the 1861 Corwin Amendment to allow slavery in the states, and the 1924 amendment banning child labor.

A Better Way *Gregory D. Watson*

In 1982, while still in college, Gregory Watson began a campaign to resurrect ratification of an amendment limiting congressional pay raises that had been submitted to the states in 1789 as part of the Bill of Rights. After his success in 1992, Watson proposed a new method of amending the Constitution.

Long before I launched the movement to ratify what is today the Twenty-seventh Amendment..., I knew that the manner in which the Constitution is changed was, and remains, in need of dramatic updating....

I have a better way. First, require the proposal of a constitutional amendment by a two-thirds vote of the *entire* membership elected and serving in each house of Congress. Second, eliminate the state legislatures. Ratification should be accomplished via a national referendum in an election year, when voters are going to the polls anyway.

A proposed amendment would have to receive the approval of a simple majority of all votes cast in not less than two-thirds of the geographic districts that comprise the U.S. House of Representatives....

My proposals would streamline the process and eliminate many of the needless eccentricities of the current procedure, while not making it "easier" to amend the Constitution.

TO DECIDE FOR OURSELVES
WHAT FREEDOM IS

What amendments might come next in the U.S. Constitution? In 1992, constitutional scholars were startled by the resurrection of one of James Madison's original amendments. In 2002, all fifty states had passed resolutions saying they would ratify an amendment prohibiting flag burning if it passed the Congress. Will such a flag burning amendment become the first constitutional limitation to the First Amendment?

Americans have disagreed throughout their history about the real meaning of freedom. To many Americans, freedom means freedom *from* government authority. Such negative rights include freedom of religion, freedom of speech, and freedom of the press. To other Americans, freedom includes the freedom *to* achieve the fullness of human potential—through positive rights such as the right to education, the right to health care, and the right to meaningful employment. Thus far, the U.S. Constitution has opted in favor of negative rights over positive rights.

But historian Eric Foner points out that Americans are constantly redefining what freedom means. As Foner wrote in his book, *The Story of American Freedom:*

> Americans have sometimes believed they enjoy the greatest freedom of all—freedom from history. No people can escape being bound, to some extent, by their past. But if history teaches anything, it is that the definitions of freedom and of the community entitled to enjoy it are never fixed or final. We may not have it in our power, as Thomas Paine proclaimed in 1776, "to begin the world over again." But we can decide for ourselves what freedom is.

To decide for ourselves what freedom is. That is the greatest gift that our Constitution gives us—a way to decide, along with our fellow citizens, what words we will live by.

"I think there are only three things that America will be known for 2,000 years from now when they study this civilization: the Constitution, jazz music, and baseball."

—Gerald Early,
author

ENDNOTES

PAGE
9   Constitution as conversation: See Tribe and Dorf, *On Reading the Constitution*, 31.
9   Learned Hand: "The Spirit of Liberty," speech in New York, May 21, 1944.
9   Garrett Epps: David Ignatius, "Not Their Finest Hour," *Washington Post*, Nov. 12, 2000, B7.
10   Oliver Wendell Holmes: *Abrams v. United States*, 250 U.S. 616, 630 (1919).
10   Steve Chapman: Hentoff, *Free Speech for Me*, vii.
12   Lucy Stone: Partnow, *The Quotable Woman*, 167.
12   Thurgood Marshall: Remarks to San Francisco Patent and Trademark Law Association, May 6, 1987.
12   Akhil Reed Amar: Amar and Hirsch, *For the People*, 24–25.
12   Ruth Bader Ginsburg: Monk, *The Bill of Rights*, 8.
13   Charlton Heston: Diaz, *Making a Killing*, 192.
13   Gouverneur Morris: Morris, *The Framing of the Federal Constitution*, 66.
13   Shelby Foote: Ward, *The Civil War*, 273.
14   George Washington: Letter to John Jay, Aug. 1, 1786, in Peters, *A More Perfect Union*, 1.
14   *Jacobson:* 197 U.S. 11, 22 (1905).
14   James Madison: Koch, *Notes*, 352.
15   Patrick Henry: Bailyn, *Debate*, Part One, 596–97.
15   *McCulloch:* 17 U.S. 316, 403–5 (1819).
15   Clarence Thomas: *U.S. Term Limits v. Thornton*, 514 U.S. 779, 846 (1995).
16   William Gladstone: Platt, *Respectfully Quoted*, 66.
16   Thurgood Marshall: Remarks to San Francisco Patent and Trademark Law Association, May 6, 1987.
16–17   "with all its faults": Bailyn, *Debate*, Part One, 3–4.
17   Boston critic: Bailyn, *Debate*, Part One, 8.
17   "a rising . . . sun": Koch, *Notes*, 659.
17   "miracle at Philadelphia": Bowen, *Miracle at Philadelphia*.
17   George Washington: Letter to the Marquis de Lafayette, Feb. 7, 1788, in Bailyn, *Debate*, Part Two, 178-79.
17   Warren G. Harding: Neil A. Grauer, "Founding Fathers' Unlikely Sire," *Washington Post*, July 3, 1997, B.5.
17   "founding father knows best": Mark Tushnet, "The U.S. Constitution and the Intent of the Framers," *Tikkun*, Vol. 1, No. 2 (1986), 35.
17   George Washington: Letter to Bushrod Washington, Nov. 10, 1787, in Bailyn, *The Debate on the Constitution*, Part One, 306.
24   Richard Neustadt: Neustadt, *Presidential Power*, 29.
26   Mark Twain: Flexner and Soukhanov, *Speaking Freely*, 322.
26   George Washington: Hutson, *To Make All Laws*, 5.
26   James MacGregor Burns: Eigen and Siegel, *Macmillan Dictionary*, 79.
27   Jeannette Rankin: Partnow, *Quotable Woman*, 294.
27   New Jersey Constitution: Agel, *Words That Make America Great*, 109.
28   Benjamin Franklin: Keyssar, *The Right to Vote*, 3.
29   Henry Hyde: Wolfensberger, *Congress and the People*, 217.
29   George Will: Will, *Restoration*, 3, 211.
30   William Lloyd Garrison: Fehrenbacher, *The Slaveholding Republic*, 39.
30   Don Fehrenbacher: Ibid., 47.
31   sampling case: *Wisconsin v. City of New York*, 517 U.S. 1 (1996).
31   Census Act case: *Dept. of Commerce v. U.S. House of Representatives*, 525 U.S. 316 (1999).
32   Montana lawsuit: *Department of Commerce v. Montana*, 503 U.S. 442 (1992).
32   John Fund: John Fund, "The Ghost of Elbridge Gerry," *Wall Street Journal*, Apr. 23, 2001, A22.
33   Newt Gingrich: Gingrich, *Lessons Learned the Hard Way*, 3.
34   Tip O'Neill: O'Neill, *All Politics Is Local*, xv–xvi.
35   Barbara Jordan: Gill, *African American Women in Congress*, 40.
37   "His Rotundity": McCullough, *John Adams*, 408.
37   "a government of laws": McCullough, *John Adams*, 222.

PAGE

40 Norman Ornstein: Norman Ornstein, "Make Sure Congress Can Survive the Worst-Case Scenario," *Washington Post,* Oct. 23, 2001, A23.

41 Woodrow Wilson: Wilson, *Congressional Government,* 69.

42 expulsion case: *In re Chapman,* 166 U.S. 661 (1897).

42 Edward R. Murrow: Jensen, *Stories That Changed America,* 142.

44 Will Rogers: Platt, *Respectfully Quoted,* 56.

46 Tammany Hall politician: Fisher, *The Constitution Between Friends,* v.

49 Robert H. Jackson: *United States v. Women's Sportswear Manufacturing Association,* 336 U.S. 460 (1949).

50 Chief Joseph: Kaplan, *Bartlett's,* 541.

50 Cherokee Nation: Monk, *Ordinary Americans,* 51–52.

52 Ted Nugent: Ted Nugent, "Want to Hear My Songs? Pay Up," *Wall Street Journal,* Mar. 13, 2001, A26.

54 Korean War case: *Youngstown Sheet & Tube Company v. Sawyer,* 343 U.S. 579 (1952).

54 draft case: *Arver et al. v. United States,* 245 U.S. 366 (1918).

54 military bases: *Greer v. Spock,* 424 U.S. 828 (1976).

54 yarmulke case: *Goldman v. Weinberger,* 475 U.S. 503 (1986).

57 "We must never forget": *McCulloch v. Maryland,* 17 U.S. 316, 407 (1819).

57 Felix Frankfurter: Schwartz, *History of the Supreme Court,* 38.

57 Benjamin Franklin: Brands, *The First American,* 702.

58 Olaudah Equiano: Monk, *Ordinary Americans,* 9.

58 *Ex Parte Milligan:* 71 U.S. 120, 121 (1866).

59 habeas corpus case: *Felker v. Turpin,* 518 U.S. 651 (1996).

59 income tax case: *Pollack v. Farmer's Loan & Trust Co.,* 157 U.S. 429 (1895).

60 John Hart Ely: Ely, *Democracy and Distrust,* 183.

60 James Madison: *Federalist* 48.

60 bankruptcy case: *Ogden v. Saunders,* 25 U.S. 213 (1827).

61 Barber B. Conable, Jr.: Ed Magnuson, "Free at Last," *Time,* Oct. 22, 1984, 39.

61 Thomas Jefferson: Maroon, *The United States Capitol,* 22.

61 Abraham Lincoln: U. S. Capitol Historical Society, *We the People,* 10.

65 Roger Sherman: Koch, *Notes of Debates,* 46.

65 Thomas Jefferson: Letter to John Adams, Nov. 13, 1787, in Kammen, *Origins of the American Constitution,* 84.

65 inherent power case: *U.S. v. Curtiss-Wright Export Corp.,* 299 U.S. 304 (1936).

65 Korean War case: *Youngstown Sheet & Tube Company v. Sawyer,* 343 U.S. 579 (1952).

66 Woodrow Wilson: Eigen and Siegel, *Macmillan Dictionary,* 565.

66 immunity case: *Nixon v. Fitzgerald,* 457 U.S. 731, 750 (1982).

66 Arthur Schlesinger, Jr.: Schlesinger, *The Imperial Presidency,* viii.

66 Gerald Ford: Ibid., 425.

66 Harry Truman: Neustadt, *Presidential Power,* 10.

66 Alexander Hamilton: Koch, *Notes of Debates,* 589.

66 Gouverneur Morris: Ibid., 310.

67 John Adams: McCullough, *John Adams,* 639.

67 Roger Sherman: Koch, *Notes of Debates,* 596.

67–68 "a man of moderate talents": Witcover, *Crapshoot,* xiii.

68 Adlai Stevenson: Jay, *Oxford Dictionary,* 347.

68 George Mason: Koch, *Notes of Debates,* 308.

69 "national bonus plan": Arthur M. Schlesinger, Jr., "Fixing the Electoral College," *Washington Post,* Dec. 19, 2000, A39.

70 Charles Fried: Charles Fried, "How to Make the President Talk to the Local Pol," *New York Times,* Nov. 11, 2000, A19.

72 Doris Kearns Goodwin: *NBC Today Show,* Nov. 10, 2000.

72 loyalty pledge case: *Ray v. Blair,* 343 U.S. 214 (1952).

73 George Washington: Rhodehamel, *George Washington: Writings,* 969.

73 "the office should seek the man": Goodwin, *Every Four Years,* 5.

73 Mark Hanna: Ibid.

PAGE

73 Kathleen Sullivan: Kathleen M. Sullivan, "One Nation, One Standard Way to Ballot," *New York Times,* Nov. 15, 2000, A29.

74 John Lewis: John Lewis, "Now We Know That Not All Votes Count," *New York Times,* Dec. 2, 2000, A19.

75 Arthur Miller: Arthur Miller, "American Playhouse: Politics and the Art of Acting," *Harper's Magazine,* June 2001, 34–36.

76 national bank case: *McCulloch v. Maryland,* 17 U.S. 316 (1819).

76–77 George Washington: Letter to Henry Knox, April 1, 1789, in Rhodehamel, *George Washington: Writings,* 726.

78 George Bush: Texas State Republican Convention, June 20, 1992, in Ely, *War and Responsibility,* 3.

78 Abraham Lincoln: Rehnquist, *All the Laws But One,* vii.

78 John Hart Ely: Ely, *War and Responsibility,* ix.

78 John F. Kennedy: Neustadt, *Presidential Power,* 180.

79 Francis Biddle: Rehnquist, *All the Laws But One,* 191.

79 executive branch statistics: U.S. Office of Personnel Management, Central Personnel Data File (CPDF), 2000.

80 Taiwan case: *Goldwater v. Carter,* 444 U.S. 654 (1988).

81 Charles E. Schumer: Charles E. Schumer, "Judging by Ideology," *New York Times,* June 26, 2001, A19.

82 "First in war": Bailyn, *The Debate on the Constitution,* Vol. I, 991.

83 Richard Neustadt: Neustadt, *Presidential Power,* x.

83 George Will: George Will, "Devil's Island! Guillotines!" *Newsweek,* Dec. 10, 2001, 84.

84 "If the emergency arises": *In re Debs,* 158 U.S. 564, 578–79 (1895).

85 Benjamin Franklin: Koch, *Notes of Debates,* 332.

85 impeachment case: *Nixon v. United States,* 506 U.S. 224 (1993).

85 Eleanor Roosevelt: Clift and Brazaitis, *Madam President,* 9.

85 Eleanor Clift: Ibid., 30.

86 William H. Rehnquist: Rehnquist, *Grand Inquests,* 97.

87 Bill Clinton: Grand jury testimony, August 17, 1998.

87 Paula Jones case: *Clinton v. Jones,* 520 U.S. 681 (1997).

87 Barney Frank: Smith, *Talk to Me,* 285–87.

88 Bill Clinton: Bunch, *The American Presidency,* 110.

88 John Adams: Letter to Abigail Adams, Nov. 2, 1800, in McCullough, *John Adams,* 551.

91 "to say what the law is": 5 U.S. 137, 177 (1803).

91 Andrew Jackson: Platt, *Respectfully Quoted,* 180.

91 "the federal judiciary is supreme": 358 U.S. 1, 18 (1958).

91 "ultimate interpreter": 369 U.S. 186, 211 (1962); 418 U.S. 683, 703–5 (1974).

91 Cass Sunstein: Sunstein, *The Partial Constitution,* vi.

91 Charles Evans Hughes: Kammen, *Machine,* 194.

92 Gordon Wood: Scalia, *A Matter of Interpretation,* 49.

93 Robert H. Jackson: Concurring, in *Brown v. Allen,* 344 U.S. 443, 540 (1953).

93 Abe Fortas: Tribe, *God Save This Honorable Court,* 66.

93 apprenticeships: O'Brien, *Storm Center,* 34.

93 Roman Hruska: Tribe, *God Save This Honorable Court,* 82.

94 "potato hole": Friendly, *The Constitution: That Delicate Balance,* 11.

94 "nine black beetles": Lieberman, *Practical Companion,* 493.

95 Thomas Jefferson: Letter to Thomas Ritchie, Dec. 25, 1820, in Peterson, *Thomas Jefferson: Writings,* 1446.

95 "play in the joints": Oliver Wendell Holmes, "The Theory of Legal Interpretation," *Harvard Law Review,* Vol. 12 (1899), 417.

95 "We must never forget": 17 U.S. 316, 407 (1819).

96 "I am not a strict constructionist": Scalia, *A Matter of Interpretation,* 23.

96 "The ascendant school": Scalia, *A Matter of Interpretation,* 38, 41.

96 Oliver Wendell Holmes: Letter to Harold Laski, March 4, 1920, in Howe, *Holmes-Laski Letters,* Vol. 1, 248–49.

97 Clarence Thomas: Francis Boyer Lecture, American Enterprise Institute for Public Policy Research, Feb. 13, 2001; http://www.aei.org/boyer/thomas.htm

97 Laurence H. Tribe: Tribe, *God Save This Honorable Court,* 46–48.

100 jurisdiction case: *Ex Parte McCardle,* 74 U.S. 506 (1869).

100 habeas corpus case: *Felker v. Turpin,* 518 U.S. 1051 (1996).

PAGE

101 Akhil Reed Amar: Amar and Hirsch, *For the People,* 55.

101 Thomas Jefferson: Amar and Hirsch, *For the People,* 58.

101 Sandra Day O'Connor: O'Connor, "Portia's Progress," 66 *N.Y.U. Law Review* 1546 (1991).

102 treason case: *Haupt v. United States,* 330 U.S. 631 (1947).

103 Wen Ho Lee: Lee, *My Country Versus Me,* 209–10, 251–52.

105 Sonny Bono: Sullivan, *Same-Sex Marriage,* 222–23.

106 Robert Bork: Robert Bork, "Stop Courts From Imposing Gay Marriage," *Wall Street Journal,* Aug. 7, 2001, A14.

106 "a national economic union": *Supreme Court of New Hampshire v. Piper,* 470 U.S. 274, 280 (1985).

107 personal liberty case: *Prigg v. Pennsylvania,* 41 U.S. 539 (1842).

107 runaways: Franklin and Schweninger, *Runaway Slaves,* 282.

108 Charles E. Stevens: Monk, *Ordinary Americans,* 82–83.

108 state capital case: *Coyle v. Smith,* 221 U.S. 559 (1911).

110 Guarantee Clause case: *Pacific States Telephone & Telegraph Co. v. Oregon,* 223 U.S. 118 (1912).

110 John Hart Ely: Ely, *Democracy and Distrust,* 118, 123.

110 Benjamin Franklin: Brands, *The First American,* 232–33.

113 "A bill of rights": Letter to James Madison, Dec. 20, 1787, in Peterson, *Thomas Jefferson: Writings,* 916.

114 George Washington: Letter to Patrick Henry, Sept. 24, 1787, in Kammen, *Origins,* 56.

115 Daniel Lazare: Lazare, *The Frozen Republic,* 5.

117 Thomas Jefferson: Letter to Samuel Kercheval, July 12, 1816, in Peterson, *Thomas Jefferson: Writings,* 1401.

119 "You give me a credit": Monk, *The Bill of Rights,* 21.

120 Jonas Phillips: http://press-pubs.uchicago.edu/founders/print_documents/a6_3s11.html; spelling and punctuation have been modernized.

123 John Hancock: Bailyn, *Debate,* Part One, 942.

123 Richard Henry Lee: Wood, *Creation,* 469.

123 Daniel Carroll: Smith, *John Marshall,* 111.

124 Hugo Black: Wagman, *The First Amendment Book,* 85.

124 Richard Henry Lee: Bailyn, *Debate,* Part One, 465.

124 Alexander Hamilton: *Federalist* 83.

124 Constitution took effect: *Owings v. Speed,* 18 U.S. 420 (1820).

124 George Mason: Koch, *Notes of Debates,* 566.

124 "Our new Constitution": Letter to Jean-Baptiste Leroy, Nov. 13, 1789, in Kaplan, *Bartlett's,* 310.

125 George Washington: Letter to Marquis de Lafayette, Sept. 18, 1787, in Kammen, *Origins,* 55.

125 "if you can keep it": Farrand, *Records,* 3:85.

125 Mercy Otis Warren: Bailyn, *Debate,* Part Two, 295–96, 303.

126 Alexis de Tocqueville: Tocqueville, *Democracy in America,* 165.

129 George Washington: Letter to Hebrew Congregation of Newport, Rhode Island, in Rhodehamel, *George Washington: Writings,* 767.

129 Virginia Statute for Religious Freedom: Peterson, *Thomas Jefferson: Writings,* 347.

129 Mary Dyer: Noonan, *The Lustre of Our Country,* 41.

129 Danbury Baptist Association: *Church & State,* January 2002, 13.

129 "a wall of separation": Peterson, *Thomas Jefferson: Writings,* 510.

130 "It does me no injury": Peterson, *Thomas Jefferson: Writings,* 285.

130 John Williams: Isaac, *The Transformation of Virginia,* 162–63; spelling and punctuation have been modernized.

130 *Everson:* 330 U.S. 1, 15 (1947).

131 *Mergens:* 496 U.S. 226, 250 (1990).

132 *Engel:* 370 U.S. 421, 422, 425 (1962).

132 *Jaffree:* 472 U.S. 38, 60 (1985).

132 Fred Gedicks: Freedom Forum, *First Amendment Calendar,* Sept. 29, 2001.

134 *Reynolds:* 98 U.S. 145, 164 (1879).

134 *Cantwell:* 310 U.S. 296, 303–4 (1940).

135 Harlan Fiske Stone: Peters, *Judging Jehovah's Witnesses,* v.

135 "fixed star": 319 U.S. 624, 642 (1943).

135 "the very purpose": 319 U.S. 624, 638 (1943).

136 *Ballard:* 322 U.S. 78, 86 (1944).

PAGE

136 unemployment benefits cases: *Sherbert v. Verner,* 374 U.S. 398 (1963); *Hobbie v. Florida* 480 U.S. 136 (1987).

136 RFRA case: *City of Boerne, Texas v. Flores,* 521 U.S. 507 (1997).

137 Garrett Epps: Epps, *To an Unknown God,* 256–57.

137 Wynton Marsalis: Ward, *Jazz,* 116.

138 Matthew Lyon: Monk, *The Bill of Rights,* 61.

138 Espionage Act: Monk, *The Bill of Rights,* 62.

138 James Madison: "Memorial and Remonstrance Against Religious Assessments," in Rakove, *James Madison: Writings,* 31.

138 Elizabeth Gurley Flynn: Monk, *Ordinary Americans,* 140–42.

140 "government may not prohibit": 491 U.S. 397, 414 (1989).

140 Jim Kolbe: "That's Some Star-Spangled Debating," *Washington Post,* July 4, 1999, B5.

140 "It was a chance": *Profiles of Freedom* (Alexandria, Va.: Close Up Publishing, 1997).

140 "An exploiter's vision": Gregory "Joey" Johnson, "An Exploiter's Vision of Freedom," *Perspectives: Readings on Contemporary American Government* (Alexandria, Va.: Close Up Publishing, 1993), 31.

140 "My point was not": *Profiles of Freedom* (Alexandria, Va.: Close Up Publishing, 1997).

141 "money is speech": 424 U.S. 1, 262 (1976).

141 Paul Gigot: Paul A. Gigot, "The Left Discovers the First Amendment," *Wall Street Journal,* March 9, 2001, A14.

141 Mitch McConnell: Mitch McConnell, "In Defense of Soft Money," *New York Times,* Apr. 1, 2001, Sect. 4, 17.

142 Michael Moore: Moore, *Downsize This!,* 4.

142 Doris Haddock: Haddock, *Granny D,* 276, 278.

143 *Miller:* 413 U.S. 15, 24 (1973).

143 Warren Burger: 413 U.S. 15, 32 (1973).

143 Potter Stewart: *Jacobellis v. Ohio,* 378 U.S. 184, 197 (1963).

144 "a damn Fascist": Peters, *Judging Jehovah's Witnesses,* 215.

144 "fighting words": 315 U.S. 568, 573 (1942).

144 Alan Dershowitz: Dershowitz, *Shouting Fire,* 36.

145 *Tinker:* 393 U.S. 503, 506 (1969).

145 Colin Powell: http://www.quotationspage.com

145 Randall Kennedy: Kennedy, *Nigger,* 3, 173–76.

146 Oliver Wendell Holmes: *Schenck v. United States,* 249 U.S. 47, 52 (1919).

146 Robyn Blummer: Freedom Forum, *First Amendment Calendar,* Sept. 20, 1999.

147 Thomas Jefferson: Letter to Edward Carrington, Jan. 16, 1787, in Peterson, *Thomas Jefferson: Writings,* 880.

147 Nat Hentoff: Hentoff, *Free Speech for Me–But Not for Thee,* 17.

147 Hugo Black: *New York Times v. United States,* 403 U.S. 713, 717 (1971).

147 Daniel Ellsberg: Daniel Ellsberg, "Lying About Vietnam," *New York Times,* June 29, 2001, A23.

148 Katharine Graham: Graham, *Personal History,* 450.

148 "with knowledge that it was false": 376 U.S. 254, 280 (1964).

148 Anthony Lewis: Lewis, *Make No Law,* 35–36, 42.

148 Oprah Winfrey: Peggy Noonan, "Expect the Unexpected: Why the Third Amendment May Once Again Be Needed," MightyWords.com, 2000.

149 broadcast media case: *Red Lion Broadcasting v. FCC,* 395 U.S. 367 (1969).

149 cable company case: *Turner Broadcasting System v. FCC,* 520 U.S. 180 (1997).

149 Anna Quindlen: Anna Quindlen, "A Conspiracy of Notebooks," *Newsweek,* Feb. 18, 2002, 80.

150 Frank Hague: Monk, *Bill of Rights,* 84.

150 loyalty oaths for teachers: *Keyishian v. Board of Regents,* 385 U.S. 589 (1967).

150 parade case: *Hurley v. Irish-American Gay, Lesbian, and Bisexual Group of Boston,* 515 U.S. 557 (1995).

151 "the body of the people": Cogan, *The Complete Bill of Rights,* 181–82.

151 Akhil Reed Amar: Amar and Hirsch, *For the People,* 171–72.

152 Sanford Levinson: Sanford Levinson, "The Embarrassing Second Amendment." *Yale Law Journal,* Vol. 99, No. 3 (December 1989), 637–59.

152 Ted Nugent: Nugent, *God, Guns, & Rock'n'Roll,* 81–82.

152 Charlton Heston: Charlton Heston, "The Second Amendment: First-Line Defense of Americans' Liberties and Their Lives," MightyWords.com, 2000.

PAGE

153 federal appellate court ruling: *United States v. Emerson,* 270 F.3d 203 (5th Cir. 2001).

153 Supreme Court ruling that Second Amendment does not apply to states: *Presser v. Illinois,* 116 U.S. 252 (1886).

153 Morton Grove case: *Quilici v. Morton Grove,* 695 F.2d 261 (1982).

153 Wendy Kaminer: Wendy Kaminer, "Second Thoughts on the Second Amendment," in Dizard, *Guns in America,* 498.

153 Daniel Lazare: Daniel Lazare, "Your Constitution Is Killing You," *Harper's Magazine,* Oct. 1999, 65.

153 Pete Hamill: Pete Hamill, "Twenty-seven Words: The Bloody Problem of the Second Amendment," MightyWords.com, 2000.

156 Joseph Story: Monk, *Bill of Rights,* 103.

156 William Douglas: 367 U.S. 497, 522 (1961).

156 Peggy Noonan: Peggy Noonan, "Expect the Unexpected: Why the Third Amendment May Once Again Be Needed," MightyWords.com, 2000.

157 Louis Brandeis: *Olmstead v. United States,* 277 U.S. 438, 478 (1928).

158 John Adams: McCullough, *John Adams,* 62.

158 James Otis: Monk, *Bill of Rights,* 106.

158 "people, not places": 389 U.S. 347, 351 (1967).

160 Caroline Kennedy and Ellen Alderman: Caroline Kennedy and Ellen Alderman, "Expectations of Privacy: The Fourth Amendment in the 21st Century," MightyWords.com, 2000.

160 William Safire: William Safire, "Threat of National ID," *New York Times,* Dec. 24, 2001, A15.

162 Tom Clark: 367 U.S. 643, 657 (1961).

162 Benjamin Cardozo: *People v. Defore,* 242 N.Y. 13, 21 (1926).

162 Tom Clark: *Mapp v. Ohio,* 367 U.S. 643, 659 (1961).

162 admission by Mapp's arresting officer: Friendly, *The Constitution: That Delicate Balance,* 132.

163 Alan Dershowitz: Dershowitz, *Reasonable Doubts,* 50–51.

165 "indict a ham sandwich": Alderman and Kennedy, *In Our Defense,* 154.

166 double jeopardy in capital sentencing: *Bullington v. Missouri,* 451 U.S. 430 (1981).

168 Kenneth Lay: "Perspectives," *Newsweek,* Feb. 25, 2002, 17.

168 Earl Warren: 384 U.S. 436, 457 (1966).

168 *"Miranda* announced a constitutional rule": 530 U.S. 428, 444 (2000).

169 Louis Brandeis: *Olmstead v. United States,* 277 U.S. 438, 485 (1928).

169 Akhil Reed Amar: Akhil Reed Amar, "Taking the Fifth Too Often," *New York Times,* Feb. 18, 2002, A15.

169 Ernesto Miranda: Riley, *Miranda,* 46.

170 Felix Frankfurter: *Malinski v. New York,* 324 U.S. 401, 414 (1945).

171 Arthur Goldberg: *Kennedy v. Mendoza-Martinez,* 372 U.S. 144, 160 (1963).

173 Alan Dershowitz: Dershowitz, *Shouting Fire,* 33.

174 "a safeguard against any attempt": *In re Oliver,* 333 U.S. 257, 270 (1948).

174 "a Roman holiday": 384 U.S. 333, 356 (1966).

174 public trial for benefit of defendant: *Gannett Co. v. De Pasquale* (1979).

174 gag order case: *Nebraska Press Association v. Stuart* (1976).

175 federal jury trials statistics: William Glaberson, "Juries, Their Powers Under Siege, Find Their Role Is Being Eroded," *New York Times,* March 2, 2001, A1.

176 "representative cross-section": *Taylor v. Louisiana,* 419 U.S. 522, 528 (1975).

176 Betsy Streisand: Betsy Streisand, *U. S. News & World Report,* Oct. 9, 1995, 47–51.

176 George Will: George Will, "Circus of the Century," *Washington Post,* Oct. 4, 1995, A25.

177 Anise Aschenbach: Dershowitz, *Reasonable Doubts,* 129 (photo caption).

178 Sandra Day O'Connor: 497 U.S. 836, 849 (1990).

178 Antonin Scalia: *Coy v. Iowa,* 487 U.S. 1012, 1018 (1988).

179 "though he be not guilty": 287 U.S. 45, 59 (1932).

179 right to counsel for misdemeanors: *Argersinger v. Hamlin,* 407 U.S. 25 (1972).

179 "If the exercise of constitutional rights": 378 U.S. 478, 490 (1964).

180 "Of all the prisons": Lewis, *Gideon's Trumpet,* 67.

180 "I suppose I am": Lewis, *Gideon's Trumpet,* 66.

180 "It has become almost axiomatic": Lewis, *Gideon's Trumpet,* 227–28.

182 Mark Twain: Adler, *The Jury,* 249.

PAGE

182 Akhil Reed Amar: Amar and Hirsch, *For the People,* 54.
183 case restricting jury awards: *Gasperini v. Center for Humanities,* 517 U.S. 1102 (1996).
183 Whoopi Goldberg: Whoopi Goldberg, "We, the People–I, the Jury–You, the Man," MightyWords.com, 2000.
185 punitive damages case: *Browning-Ferris v. Kelco Disposal,* 492 U.S. 257 (1989).
185 Coretta Scott King: Coretta Scott King, "Challenge of the Eighth Amendment: Humane Treatment of All Offenders," MightyWords.com, 2000.
185 "evolving standards of decency": 356 U.S. 86, 101 (1958).
185 "the punishment of death": 428 U.S. 153, 169 (1976).
185 Potter Stewart: 428 U.S. 153, 183 (1976).
185 William Brennan: 428 U.S. 153, 229 (1976).
186 capital punishment of juveniles: *Stanford v. Kentucky,* 492 U.S. 361 (1989).
187 Harry Blackmun: U.S. 1141, 1145 (1994).
187 William Brennan: *Glass v. Louisiana,* 471 U.S. 1080, 1094 (1985).
188 George Will: George Will, "Innocent on Death Row," *Washington Post,* Apr. 6, 2000, A23.
187 Kirk Bloodsworth: Scheck, *Actual Innocence,* 222.
187 Walter Berns: Walter Berns, "Where Are the Death Penalty Critics Today?" *Wall Street Journal,* June 11, 2001, A22.
189 George Carlin: Carlin, *Napalm & Silly Putty,* 215.
191 William O. Douglas: 381 U.S. 479, 484 (1965).
191 "This right of privacy": 410 U.S. 113, 153 (1973).
191 Michael Hardwick: Irons, *The Courage of Their Convictions,* 403.
192 "a fundamental right": 478 U.S. 186, 191 (1986).
192 "Unlike the Court": 478 U.S. 186, 200 (1986).
192 Robert Bork: Barnett, *The Rights Retained by the People,* 1.
192 Randy Barnett: Barnett, *The Rights Retained by the People,* 4.
193 John Hart Ely: Ely, *Democracy and Distrust,* 34.
194 "will probably continue to arise": *McCulloch v. Maryland,* 17 U.S. 316, 405 (1819).
196 J. Harvie Wilkinson, III: Charles Lane, "Scope of Federal Authority at Issue in Supreme Court," *Washington Post,* Oct. 1, 2000, A3.
196 "an indestructible Union": 74 U.S. 700, 725 (1869).
197 Southern Manifesto: Monk, *The Bill of Rights,* 205.
197 John F. Kennedy: Carson, *The Eyes on the Prize Civil Rights Reader,* 160.
198 William Simmons: Hampton and Fayer, *Voices of Freedom,* 120–21.
200 private causes of action cases: *Florida Prepaid v. College Savings Bank,* 527 U.S. 666 (1999); *Kimel v. Florida Board of Regents,* 528 U.S. 62 (2000); and *Alden v. Maine,* 527 U.S. 706 (1999).
202 "a man of moderate talents": Witcover, *Crapshoot,* xiii.
205 Frederick Douglass: Speech on July 5, 1852, in Foner, *Lift Every Voice,* 258.
206 Thomas Jefferson: Letter to John Holmes, Apr. 22, 1820, in Peterson, *Thomas Jefferson: Writings,* 1434.
206 slaves in British North America: Thomas, *The Slave Trade,* 804–5.
207 Harriet Tubman: Taylor, *Harriet Tubman,* 37.
207 "beings of an inferior order": 60 U.S. 393, 407 (1857).
208 "a house divided": Agel, *Words That Made America Great,* 192.
208 James McPherson: McPherson, *Abraham Lincoln,* 34.
208 "In giving freedom to the slave": McPherson, *Abraham Lincoln,* 110.
209 Petition by Massachusetts Slaves: Monk, *Ordinary Americans,* 31–32.
209 Frederick Douglass: Tushnet, *Taking the Constitution Away from the Courts,* 12.
210 Randall Robinson: Robinson, *The Debt,* 216.
210 Barbara J. Fields: Barbara Fields, "Who Freed the Slaves?" in Ward, *The Civil War,* 178, 181.
210 real estate discrimination case: *Jones v. Alfred H. Mayer Co.,* 392 U.S. 409 (1968).
210 peonage case: *Bailey v. Alabama,* 219 U.S. 219 (1911).
211 IRS reparations claims: Glenn Kessler, "IRS Paid $30 Million in Credits for Slavery," *Washington Post,* Apr. 13, 2002, A1.
211 Henry Louis Gates, Jr.: Henry Louis Gates, Jr., "The Future of Slavery's Past," *New York Times,* July 29, 2001, Sect. 4, 15.

PAGE

211 Linda Chavez: Linda Chavez, "Reparations Will Make Lawyers Richer," *Chicago Tribune,* Nov. 9, 2000, 31.

214 Hugo Black: *Adamson v. California,* 332 U.S. 46, 89 (1947).

215 "equal rights of conscience": Veit, *Creating the Bill of Rights,* 13.

215 "the most valuable amendment": Veit, *Creating the Bill of Rights,* 188.

215 "a scheme of ordered liberty": 302 U.S. 319, 325 (1937).

216 "the Fourteenth Amendment does not enact": 198 U.S. 45, 75 (1905).

216 "A Constitution is not intended": *Lochner v. New York,* 198 U.S. 45, 75 (1905).

217 John Hart Ely: Ely, *Democracy and Distrust,* 18.

217 "people were sterilized": Craig Timberg, "Virginia House Voices Regret for Eugenics," *Washington Post,* Feb. 3, 2001, A1.

217 "broad enough to encompass": 410 U.S. 113, 153 (1973).

217 Sara Weddington: Weddington, *A Question of Choice,* 237.

218 "substantial obstacle": 505 U.S. 833, 877 (1992).

218 federal discrimination case: *Bolling v. Sharpe,* 347 U.S. 497 (1954).

218 "I was nothing": McCorvey, *I Am Roe,* 127.

219 physician-assisted suicide cases: *Washington v. Glucksberg,* 521 U.S. 702 (1997); *Vacco v. Quill,* 521 U.S. 793 (1997).

219 Antonin Scalia: *Stenberg v. Carhart,* 530 U.S. 914, 953 (2000).

219 "Our Constitution is colorblind": *Plessy v. Ferguson,* 163 U.S. 537, 559 (1896).

220 "If this be so": 163 U.S. 537, 551 (1896).

220 Ed Johnson: Curriden and Phillips, *Contempt of Court,* xiii.

220 Thurgood Marshall: Curriden and Phillips, *Contempt of Court,* xvii.

221 no evidence of disloyalty: Irons, *A People's History of the Supreme Court,* 362.

221 "separate educational facilities": 347 U.S. 483, 495 (1954).

221 "a feeling of inferiority": 347 U.S. 483, 494 (1954).

221 Gordon Hirabayashi: Irons, *A People's History of the Supreme Court,* 364.

221 "all deliberate speed": *Brown v. Board of Education, Part II,* 349 U.S. 294, 301 (1955).

222 "at once": *Alexander v. Holmes County Board of Education,* 396 U.S. 19, 20 (1969).

222 interracial marriages case: *Loving v. Virginia,* 388 U.S. 1 (1967).

222 Ruby Bridges: Bridges, *Through My Eyes,* 15–16.

223 "In order to get beyond racism": 438 U.S. 265, 407 (1978).

223 Dwight Eisenhower: Peltason and Davis, *Understanding the Constitution,* 383.

223 Wynton Marsalis: Ward, *Jazz,* 118.

223 "law of the Creator": 83 U.S. 130, 141 (1873).

224 Fannie Lou Hamer: Monk, *The Bill of Rights,* 228.

224 beer case: *Craig v. Boren,* 429 U.S. 190 (1976).

225 "a stranger to its laws": 527 U.S. 620, 635 (1996).

226 "one person, one vote": 372 U.S. 368, 381 (1963).

226 Earl Warren: *Reynolds v. Sims,* 377 U.S. 533, 562 (1964).

228 Thurgood Marshall: Remarks at the Annual Seminar of the San Francisco Patent and Trademark Law Association, May 6, 1987.

229 grandfather clause case: *Guinn v. United States,* 238 U.S. 347 (1915).

230 "I have a dream": Dr. Martin Luther King, Jr., "I Have a Dream," Aug. 28, 1963.

231 Sheyann Webb: Monk, *Ordinary Americans,* 233.

233 James Trafficant: *Washington Post,* May 5, 2001, C1, C10.

237 Billy Sunday: Lucas, *The Eighteenth and Twenty-first Amendments,* 38.

238 "If particular care": Letter to John Adams, March 31, 1776, in McCullough, *John Adams,* 104.

238 "remember the ladies": Ibid.

240 "Failure is impossible": Partnow, *Quotable Woman,* 176.

240 "We, the Whole People": Ravitch, *The Democracy Reader,* 167–68.

241 Rose Winslow: Monk, *Ordinary Americans,* 157–58.

247 State regulation of alcohol case: *Bacchus Imports, Ltd. v. Dias,* 468 U.S. 263 (1984).

247 Laurence Tribe: Laurence Tribe, "How to Violate the Constitution Without Really Trying: Lessons from the Repeal of Prohibition to the Balanced Budget Amendment," in Eskridge and Levinson, *Constitutional Stupidities,* 100.

PAGE

247 Salim Muwakkil: Salim Muwakkil, "The Body Count Continues: Who's Winning America's War on Drugs?" *Chicago Tribune,* July 9, 2001, 13.

249 Bill Clinton: John Fund, "Catch-22: Three Cheers for Two Terms," *Wall Street Journal,* Feb. 27, 2001; http://www.opinionjournal.com/diary/?id=85000644

252 Anthony Williams: Craig Timberg, "Williams, in State of District Speech, Urges Voting Rights for City," *Washington Post,* March 6, 2002, B4.

257 Gerald Ford: Eigen and Siegel, *Macmillan Dictionary,* 89.

259 Al Haig: Richard V. Allen, "The Day Reagan Was Shot," *Atlantic Monthly,* April 2001, 66.

261 "sufficiently contemporaneous": *Dillon v. Gloss,* 256 U.S. 368, 375 (1921).

262 Neal Smith: Bernstein, *Amending America,* 247.

262 Gregory D. Watson: Gregory D. Watson, "I Have a Better Way," *Insights on Law & Society,* Vol. 1, No. 1 (Fall 2000), 16.

263 Gerald Early: Ward and Burns, *Baseball,* 463.

263 Eric Foner: Foner, *The Story of American Freedom,* 332.

SELECTED BIBLIOGRAPHY

Adler, Stephen J. *The Jury: Trial and Error in the American Courtroom.* New York: Times Books, 1994.

Agel, Jerome, ed. *Words That Make America Great.* New York: Random House, 1997.

Alderman, Ellen, and Caroline Kennedy. *In Our Defense: The Bill of Rights in Action.* New York: William Morrow, 1991.

Amar, Akhil Reed. *The Bill of Rights: Creation and Reconstruction.* New Haven: Yale University Press, 1998.

Amar, Akhil Reed, and Alan Hirsch. *For the People: What the Constitution Really Says About Your Rights.* New York: Free Press, 1998.

Anthony, Carl Sferrazza. *First Ladies: The Saga of the Presidents' Wives and Their Power, 1789–1961.* New York: William Morrow, 1990.

Bailyn, Bernard, ed. *The Debate on the Constitution.* New York: Library of America, 1993.

Banner, Stuart. *The Death Penalty: An American History.* Cambridge: Harvard University Press, 2002.

Barnett, Randy E., ed. *The Rights Retained by the People: The History and Meaning of the Ninth Amendment.* Fairfax, Va.: George Mason University Press, 1989.

Bernstein, Richard B., with Jerome Agel. *Amending America: If We Love the Constitution So Much, Why Do We Keep Trying to Change It?* New York: Times Books, 1993.

Bork, Robert H. *The Tempting of America: The Political Seduction of the Law.* New York: Free Press, 1990.

Bowen, Catherine Drinker. *Miracle at Philadelphia.* Boston: Little, Brown and Company, 1966, 1986.

Brands, H. W. *The First American: The Life and Times of Benjamin Franklin.* New York: Doubleday, 2000.

Bridges, Ruby. *Through My Eyes.* New York: Scholastic Press, 1999.

Bunch, Lonnie G. III, et al. *The American Presidency: A Glorious Burden.* Washington, D.C.: Smithsonian Institution Press, 2000.

Carlin, George. *Napalm & Silly Putty.* New York: Hyperion, 2001.

Carson, Clayborne, David J. Garrow, Gerald Gill, et al. *The Eyes on the Prize Civil Rights Reader.* New York: Penguin, 1991.

Clift, Eleanor, and Tom Brazaitis. *Madam President: Shattering the Last Glass Ceiling.* New York: Scribner, 2000.

Cogan, Neil H., ed. *The Complete Bill of Rights: The Drafts, Debates, Sources, and Origins.* New York: Oxford University Press, 1997.

_____. *Contexts of the Constitution: A Documentary Collection on Principles of American Constitutional Law.* New York: Foundation Press, 1999.

Curriden, Mark, and Leroy Phillips, Jr. *Contempt of Court: The Turn-of-the-Century Lynching That Launched a Hundred Years of Federalism.* New York: Faber and Faber, 1999.

DePauw, Linda Grant. *Founding Mothers: Women of America in the Revolutionary Era.* Boston: Houghton Mifflin, 1975.

Dershowitz, Alan M. *Reasonable Doubts: The O. J. Simpson Case and the Criminal Justice System.* New York: Simon & Schuster, 1996.

_____. *Shouting Fire: Civil Liberties in a Turbulent Age.* Boston: Little, Brown and Company, 2002.

Diaz, Tom. *Making a Killing: The Business of Guns in America.* New York: The New Press, 1999.

Dionne, E. J., and William Kristol, eds. *Bush v. Gore: The Court Cases and the Commentary.* Washington, D.C.: Brookings Institution Press, 2001.

Dizard, Jan E., Robert Merrill Muth, and Stephen P. Andrews, Jr., eds. *Guns in America: A Reader.* New York: New York University Press, 1999.

Dray, Philip. *At the Hands of Persons Unknown: The Lynching of Black America.* New York: Random House, 2002.

Eigen, Lewis D., and Jonathan P. Siegel, eds. *The Macmillan Dictionary of Political Quotations.* New York: Macmillan Publishing Company, 1993.

Ely, John Hart. *Democracy and Distrust: A Theory of Judicial Review.* Cambridge, Mass.: Harvard University Press, 1980.

————————. *War and Responsibility: Constitutional Lessons of Vietnam and Its Aftermath.* Princeton, N.J.: Princeton University Press, 1993.

Epps, Garrett. *To an Unknown God: Religious Freedom on Trial.* New York: St. Martin's Press, 2001.

Eskridge, William N., Jr., and Sanford Levinson, eds. *Constitutional Stupidities, Constitutional Tragedies.* New York: New York University Press, 1998.

Farrand, Max, ed. *Records of the Federal Convention of 1787.* New Haven: Yale University Press, 1966.

Fehrenbacher, Don E. *The Dred Scott Case: Its Significance in American Law and Politics.* New York: Oxford University Press, 1978.

————————. *The Slaveholding Republic: An Account of the United States Government's Relations to Slavery.* New York: Oxford University Press, 2001.

Fisher, Louis. *The Constitution Between Friends: Congress, the President, and the Law.* New York: St. Martin's Press, 1978.

Flexner, Stuart Berg, and Anne H. Soukhanov. *Speaking Freely: A Guided Tour of American English from Plymouth Rock to Silicon Valley.* New York: Oxford University Press, 1997.

Foner, Eric. *The Story of American Freedom.* New York: W. W. Norton, 1998.

Foner, Philip S., and Robert James Branham, eds. *Lift Every Voice: African American Oratory, 1787–1900.* Tuscaloosa, Ala.: University of Alabama Press, 1998.

Franklin, John Hope, and Loren Schweninger. *Runaway Slaves: Rebels on the Plantation.* New York: Oxford University Press, 1999.

Friendly, Fred, and Martha J. H. Elliott. *The Constitution: That Delicate Balance.* New York: Random House, 1984.

Garrow, David J. *Liberty & Sexuality: The Right to Privacy and the Making of Roe v. Wade.* New York: Macmillan Publishing Company, 1994.

Gill, LaVerne McCain. *African American Women in Congress: Forming and Transforming History.* New Brunswick, N.J.: Rutgers University Press, 1997.

Gingrich, Newt. *Lessons Learned the Hard Way: A Personal Report.* New York: HarperCollins, 1998.

Glennon, Michael J. *When No Majority Rules: The Electoral College and Presidential Succession.* Washington, D.C.: Congressional Quarterly, 1992.

Goldstein, Joseph. *The Intelligible Constitution: The Supreme Court's Obligation to Maintain the Constitution as Something We the People Can Understand.* New York: Oxford University Press, 1992.

Goldstein, Robert Justin. *Flag Burning & Free Speech: The Case of Texas v. Johnson.* Lawrence, Kans.: University Press of Kansas, 2000.

Goodman, James. *Stories of Scottsboro: The Rape Case That Shocked 1930's America and Revived the Struggle for Equality.* New York: Pantheon Books, 1994.

Goodwin, Doris Kearns. *Every Four Years: Presidential Campaign Coverage 1896–2000.* Arlington, Va.: Newseum, 2000.

Graham, Katharine. *Personal History.* New York: Vintage Books, 1998, 1997.

Haddock, Doris, with Dennis Burke. *Granny D: Walking Across America in My Ninetieth Year.* New York: Villard Books, 2001.

Halbrook, Stephen P. *That Every Man Be Armed: The Evolution of a Constitutional Right.* Albuquerque, N.M.: University of New Mexico Press, 1984.

Hall, Kermit L., ed. *The Oxford Companion to the Supreme Court of the United States*. New York: Oxford University Press, 1992.

Hamilton, Alexander, James Madison, and John Jay. *The Federalist Papers*. New York: New American Library, 1961.

Hampton, Henry, and Steve Fayer, with Sarah Flynn, eds. *Voices of Freedom: An Oral History of the Civil Rights Movement from the 1950s Through the 1980s*. New York: Bantam Books, 1990.

Hentoff, Nat. *Free Speech for Me—But Not for Thee: How the American Left and Right Relentlessly Censor Each Other*. New York: HarperCollins, 1992.

Howe, Mark DeWolfe, ed. *Holmes-Laski Letters*. Cambridge: Harvard University Press, 1953.

Hutson, James H. *To Make All Laws: The Congress of the United States 1789–1989*. Washington, D.C.: Library of Congress, 1989.

Irons, Peter. *The Courage of Their Convictions: Sixteen Americans Who Fought Their Way to the Supreme Court*. New York: Free Press, 1988.

——————. *A People's History of the Supreme Court*. New York: Viking Penguin, 1999.

Isaac, Rhys. *The Transformation of Virginia, 1740–1790*. New York: W. W. Norton, 1982.

Jaffa, Harry V. et al. *Original Intent and the Framers of the Constitution: A Disputed Question*. Washington, D.C.: Regnery Publishing, 1994.

Jay, Antony, ed. *Oxford Dictionary of Political Quotations*. New York: Oxford University Press, 2001.

Jensen, Carl. *Stories That Changed America: Muckrakers of the 20th Century*. New York: Seven Stories Press, 2000.

Jensen, Merrill. *The Articles of Confederation*. Madison, Wisc.: University of Wisconsin Press, 1940, 1970.

Johnson, Charles, and Patricia Smith. *Africans in America: America's Journey Through Slavery*. New York: Harcourt Brace and Company, 1998.

Kammen, Michael, ed. *The Origins of the American Constitution: A Documentary History*. New York: Penguin Books, 1986.

——————. *A Machine That Would Go of Itself: The Constitution in American Culture*. New York: Vintage, 1987.

Kaplan, Justin, ed. *Bartlett's Familiar Quotations*, 16th ed. Boston: Little, Brown and Company, 1992.

Keen, Lisa, and Suzanne B. Goldberg. *Strangers to the Law: Gay People on Trial*. Ann Arbor: University of Michigan Press, 1998.

Kelly, Alfred H., Winfred A. Harbison, and Herman Belz. *The American Constitution: Its Origins & Development*, 6th ed. New York: W. W. Norton, 1983.

Kennedy, Randall. *Nigger: The Strange Career of a Troublesome Word*. New York: Pantheon Books, 2002.

Keyssar, Alexander. *The Right to Vote: The Contested History of Democracy in the United States*. New York: Basic Books, 2000.

Killian, Johnny H., and George A. Costello. *The U.S. Constitution, with Annotations of Cases Decided by the Supreme Court of the United States to June 29, 1992*. Washington, D.C.: Government Printing Office, 1996. Available online at http://www.findlaw.com/casecode/constitution/

Kluger, Richard. *Simple Justice: The History of Brown v. Board of Education and Black America's Struggle for Equality*. New York: Alfred A. Knopf, 1975.

Koch, Adrienne, ed. *Notes of Debates in the Federal Convention of 1787 Reported by James Madison*. New York: W. W. Norton, 1987.

Kurland, Philip, and Ralph Lerner, eds. *The Founders' Constitution*. Chicago: University of Chicago Press, 1986. Available online at http://press-pubs.uchicago.edu/founders/

Kyvig, David E. *Explicit & Authentic Acts: Amending the U.S. Constitution 1776–1995*. Lawrence, Kans.: University Press of Kansas, 1996.

Lazare, Daniel. *The Frozen Republic: How the Constitution Is Paralyzing Democracy.* New York: Harcourt Brace and Company, 1996.

Lee, Wen Ho, with Helen Zia. *My Country Versus Me: The First-Hand Account by the Los Alamos Scientist Who Was Falsely Accused of Being a Spy.* New York: Hyperion, 2001.

Lewis, Anthony. *Gideon's Trumpet.* New York: Vintage, 1964.

——————. *Make No Law: The Sullivan Case and the First Amendment.* New York: Random House, 1991.

Lieberman, Jethro K. *A Practical Companion to the Constitution.* Berkeley, Ca.: University of California Press, 1999.

Longley, Lawrence D., and Neal R. Peirce. *The Electoral College Primer 2000.* New Haven: Yale University Press, 1999.

Lucas, Eileen. *The Eighteenth and Twenty-first Amendments.* Springfield, N.J.: Enslow Publishers, Inc., 1998.

Lyons, Oren, and John Mohawk, eds. *Exiled in the Land of the Free: Democracy, Indian Nations, and the U.S. Constitution.* Santa Fe: Clear Light Publishers, 1992.

Maroon, Fred J. *The United States Capitol.* New York: Stewart, Tabori & Chang, 1993.

McCorvey, Norma, with Andy Meisler. *I Am Roe: My Life, Roe v. Wade, and Freedom of Choice.* New York: HarperCollins, 1994.

McCorvey, Norma, with Gary Thomas. *Won by Love: Norma McCorvey, Jane Roe of Roe v. Wade, Speaks Out for the Unborn as She Shares Her New Conviction for Life.* Nashville: Thomas Nelson Publishers, 1997.

McCullough, David. *John Adams.* New York: Simon & Schuster, 2001.

McPherson, James M. *Abraham Lincoln and the Second American Revolution.* New York: Oxford University Press, 1991.

McPherson, James M., ed. *"To the Best of My Ability": The American Presidents.* London: Dorling Kindersley, 2000.

Michel, Lou, and Dan Herbeck. *American Terrorist: Timothy McVeigh & the Oklahoma City Bombing.* New York: HarperCollins, 2001.

Monk, Linda R. *The Bill of Rights: A User's Guide,* 3rd ed. Alexandria, Va.: Close Up Publishing, 2000.

——————. *Ordinary Americans: U.S. History Through the Eyes of Everyday People.* Alexandria, Va.: Close Up Publishing, 1994.

Moore, Michael. *Downsize This!* New York: HarperPerennial, 1997.

Morris, Richard B. *The Framing of the Federal Constitution.* Washington, D.C.: U.S. Department of the Interior, 1986.

Murray, William J. *My Life Without God.* Nashville: Thomas Nelson Publishers, 1982.

Nelson, William E. *Marbury v. Madison: The Origins and Legacy of Judicial Review.* Lawrence, Kans.: University Press of Kansas, 2000.

Neustadt, Richard E. *Presidential Power and the Modern Presidents.* New York: Free Press, 1990.

Noonan, John T., Jr. *The Lustre of Our Country: The American Experience of Religious Freedom.* Berkeley: University of California Press, 1998.

Norris, Clarence, and Sybil D. Washington. *The Last of the Scottsboro Boys.* New York: G. P. Putnam's Sons, 1979.

Norton, Mary Beth. *Liberty's Daughters: The Revolutionary Experience of American Women, 1750–1800.* Ithaca, N.Y.: Cornell University Press, 1996.

Nugent, Ted. *God, Guns, & Rock'n'Roll.* Washington, D.C.: Regnery Publishing, 2000.

O'Brien, David M. *Storm Center: The Supreme Court in American Politics,* 5th ed. New York: W. W. Norton, 2000.

O'Neill, Thomas P., and Gary Hymel. *All Politics Is Local and Other Rules of the Game.* New York: Times Books, 1994.

Partnow, Elaine T., ed. *The Quotable Woman: The First 5,000 Years.* New York: Checkmark Books, 2001.

Peltason, J. W., and Sue Davis. *Corwin & Peltason's Understanding the Constitution,* 15th ed. New York: Harcourt College Publishers, 2000.

Perry, Barbara A. *The Priestly Tribe: The Supreme Court's Image in the Public Mind.* Westport, Conn.: Praeger Publishers, 1999.

Peters, Shawn Francis. *Judging Jehovah's Witnesses: Religious Persecution and the Dawn of the Rights Revolution.* Lawrence, Kans.: University Press of Kansas, 2000.

Peters, William. *A More Perfect Union: The Making of the United States Constitution.* New York: Crown Publishers, 1987.

Peterson, Merrill D., ed. *Thomas Jefferson: Writings.* New York: Library of America, 1984.

Platt, Suzy, ed. *Respectfully Quoted: A Dictionary of Quotations Requested from the Congressional Research Service.* Washington, D.C.: Library of Congress, 1989.

Posner, Richard A. *An Affair of State: The Investigation, Impeachment, and Trial of President Clinton.* Cambridge, Mass.: Harvard University Press, 1999.

_____. *Breaking the Deadlock: The 2000 Election, the Constitution, and the Courts.* Princeton, N.J.: Princeton University Press, 2001.

Rakove, Jack N. *Original Meanings: Politics and Ideas in the Making of the Constitution.* New York: Alfred A. Knopf, 1996.

Rakove, Jack N., ed. *James Madison: Writings.* New York: Library of America, 1999.

Ravich, Diane, and Abigail Thernstrom, eds. *The Democracy Reader.* New York: HarperCollins, 1992.

Rehnquist, William H. *Grand Inquests: The Historic Impeachments of Justice Samuel Chase and President Andrew Johnson.* New York: William Morrow, 1992.

_____. *All the Laws But One: Civil Liberties in Wartime.* New York: Alfred A. Knopf, 1998.

_____. *The Supreme Court,* new ed. New York: Alfred A. Knopf, 2001.

Rhodehamel, John, ed. *George Washington: Writings.* New York: Library of America, 1997.

Riley, Gail Blasser. *Miranda v. Arizona: Rights of the Accused.* Hillside, N.J.: Enslow Publishers, 1994.

Robinson, Randall. *The Debt: What America Owes to Blacks.* New York: Dutton, 2000.

Rutland, Robert Allen. *The Birth of the Bill of Rights, 1776–1791,* rev. ed. Boston: Northeastern University Press, 1983.

Scalia, Antonin. *A Matter of Interpretation: Federal Courts and the Law.* Princeton, N.J.: Princeton University Press, 1997.

Scheck, Barry, Peter Neufeld, and Jim Dwyer. *Actual Innocence: Five Days to Execution, and Other Dispatches from the Wrongly Convicted.* New York: Doubleday: 2000.

Schlesinger, Arthur M., Jr. *The Imperial Presidency.* Boston: Houghton Mifflin, 1973, 1989.

Schwartz, Bernard. *A History of the Supreme Court.* New York: Oxford University Press, 1993.

Smith, Anna Deavere. *Talk to Me: Listening Between the Lines.* New York: Random House, 2000.

Smith, Jean Edward. *John Marshall: Definer of a Nation.* New York: Henry Holt, 1996.

Stampp, Kenneth M. *America in 1857: A Nation on the Brink.* New York: Oxford University Press, 1990.

Storing, Herbert J. *What the Anti-Federalists Were For.* Chicago: University of Chicago Press, 1981.

Strum, Philippa. *When the Nazis Came to Skokie: Freedom for Speech We Hate.* Lawrence, Kans.: University Press of Kansas, 1999.

Sullivan, Andrew, ed. *Same-Sex Marriage: Pro and Con: A Reader.* New York: Vintage Books, 1997.

Sunstein, Cass R. *The Partial Constitution.* Cambridge, Mass.: Harvard University Press, 1993.

Taylor, M. W. *Harriet Tubman: Antislavery Activist.* New York: Chelsea House Publishers, 1991.

Thomas, Hugh. *The Slave Trade: The Story of the Atlantic Slave Trade, 1440–1870.* New York: Simon & Schuster, 1997.

Tocqueville, Alexis de. *Democracy in America.* Trans. George Lawrence. New York: Harper & Row, 1966, 1988.

Tribe, Laurence. *God Save This Honorable Court.* New York: Random House, 1985.

_____. *American Constitutional Law,* 3rd ed. New York: Foundation Press, 2000.

Tribe, Laurence, and Michael C. Dorf. *On Reading the Constitution.* Cambridge, Mass.: Harvard University Press, 1991.

Tushnet, Mark. *Taking the Constitution Away from the Courts.* Princeton, N.J.: Princeton University Press, 1999.

U.S. Capitol Historical Society. *We the People: The Story of the United States Capitol.* Washington, D.C.: 1991.

Veit, Helen E. et al., eds. *Creating the Bill of Rights: The Documentary Record from the First Federal Congress.* Baltimore: Johns Hopkins University Press, 1991.

Wagman, Robert J. *The First Amendment Book.* New York: Pharos Books, 1991.

Ward, Geoffrey C. *The Civil War: An Illustrated History.* New York: Alfred A. Knopf, 1990.

_____. *Jazz: A History of America's Music.* New York: Alfred A. Knopf, 2000.

Ward, Geoffrey C., and Ken Burns. *Baseball: An Illustrated History.* New York: Alfred A. Knopf, 1994.

Weddington, Sarah. *A Question of Choice.* New York: G. P. Putnams's Sons, 1992.

White, G. Edward. *Oliver Wendell Holmes: Sage of the Supreme Court.* New York: Oxford University Press, 2000.

Will, George. *Restoration: Congress, Term Limits, and the Recovery of Deliberative Democracy.* New York: Free Press, 1992.

Wilson, Woodrow. *Congressional Government: A Study in American Politics.* Baltimore: Johns Hopkins University Press, 1981, 1885.

Witcover, Jules. *Crapshoot: Rolling the Dice on the Vice Presidency.* New York: Crown Publishers, 1992.

Wolfensberger, Donald R. *Congress and the People: Deliberative Democracy on Trial.* Washington, D.C.: Woodrow Wilson Center Press, 2000.

Wood, Gordon S. *The Creation of the American Republic 1776–1787.* Chapel Hill: University of North Carolina Press, 1969, 1998.

INDEX

Page numbers in **boldface** indicate extended discussion of topic. Those in *italics* indicate illustrations.

T = top of the page; B = bottom of the page

6T: Library of Congress, Prints and Photographs Division [LC-USZ62-995]
6B: Library of Congress, Prints and Photographs Division [LC-USZ62-119343]
7: Library of Congress, Prints and Photographs Division [LC-D416-9858]
11: Smithsonian American Art Museum, Washington, D.C./Art Resource, NY
13: National Archives and Records Administration, 306-PS-D-52-13183
16T: Library of Congress, Prints and Photographs Division [LC-USZ62-995]
16B: National Archives and Records Administration, NWDNS-148-CC-11 (3)
25: National Archives and Records Administration, NLR-PHOCO-A-71140
26: Library of Congress, Prints and Photographs Division [LC-USZ62-126500]
27: Library of Congress, Prints and Photographs Division [LC-USZ62-8422]
32: Library of Congress, Prints and Photographs Division
    [Portfolio 0, Folder 1]
33: Library of Congress, Prints and Photographs Division [LC-USZ62-121290]
34T: Library of Congress, Prints and Photographs Division [LC-USZ62-98908]
34B: Library of Congress, Prints and Photographs Division
    [LC-USZ62-106849]
36: Library of Congress, Prints and Photographs Division [LC-USZ62-98798]
41: Library of Congress, Prints and Photographs Division [LC-USZ62-9242]
45: Library of Congress, Prints and Photographs Division [LC-USZ62-1562]
46: Chicago Historical Society, ICHI-01813, Carey Orr
47: Library of Congress, Prints and Photographs Division [LC-USZC4-9018]
50: Library of Congress, Prints and Photographs Division [LC-USZ62-129681]
56: National Archives and Records Administration, 57-PS-233
58: Library of Congress, Prints and Photographs Division [LC-USZ62-41678]
61: Library of Congress, Prints and Photographs Division [LC-USZC4-3595]
66: Used with permission, Paul Conrad, © Tribune Media Services, Inc.,
    2001. All Rights Reserved.
67: Library of Congress, Prints and Photographs Division [LC-USZ62-91638]
68: Copyright 2000 by Herblock in *The Washington Post*
69: Larry Downing/Reuters/TimePix
72: Harry S. Truman Library
73: Courtesy Ronald Reagan Library
75: Rutherford B. Hayes Library
76: John Fitzgerald Kennedy Library
77: Courtesy Winterthur Museum
79: LBJ Library Photo by Jack Kightlinger
80T: Boondocks © 2001 Aaron McGruder. Distributed by Universal Press
    Syndicate. All rights reserved. Reprinted with permission.
80B: George Bush Presidential Library
83: National Archives and Records Administration, NWDNS-111-B-2325
84: The Richard Nixon Library & Birthplace
85: Library of Congress, Prints and Photographs Division [LC-USZ62-2045]
88: Library of Congress, Prints and Photographs Division [LC-USZ62-46804]
94T: Library of Congress, Prints and Photographs Division [LC-USZ62-96380]
94B: Collection of the Supreme Court of the United States
96: From *Herblock on All Fronts* (New American Library, 1980)
97: Collection of the Supreme Court Historical Society, photographed by
    Hugh Tallman, Smithsonian Institution
99: Collection of the Supreme Court Historical Society, photographed by
    Richard Strauss, Smithsonian Institution
100: Library of Congress, Prints and Photographs Division [LC-D416-29922]
101: Collection of the Supreme Court Historical Society, photographed by
    Richard Strauss, Smithsonian Institution
102: Library of Congress, Prints and Photographs Division [LC-USZ62-117772]
103: AP/Wide World Photos
105: AP/Wide World Photos
108: Library of Congress, Prints and Photographs Division [LC-USZ62-90750]

111: Library of Congress, Prints and Photographs Division [LC-USZ62-38902]
114: Courtesy Jimmy Carter Library
115: National Archives and Records Administration, NWDNS-102-LH-1056
119: Library of Congress, Prints and Photographs Division [LC-USZ62-3462]
123: Negative number 33959, Collection of the New-York Historical Society
126: National Archives and Records Administration, RP001O
128: Library of Congress, Prints and Photographs Division [LC-USZ62-77730]
129: Boston Public Library/Herald-Traveler
133: AP/Wide World Photos
134: AP/Wide World Photos
135: Library of Congress, Prints and Photographs Division
    [LC-USF33-T01001180-M3]
138: Library of Congress, Prints and Photographs Division [LC-USZ62-96665]
140: AP/Wide World Photos
142: AP/Wide World Photos
143: AP/Wide World Photos
148: AP/Wide World Photos
151: Library of Congress, Prints and Photographs Division [LC-USZ62-60085]
152: AP/Wide World Photos
155: Library of Congress, Prints and Photographs Division [LC-USZ62-35522]
158: Library of Congress, Prints and Photographs Division [LC-USZ62-102561]
159: AP/Wide World Photos
165: AP/Wide World Photos
168: AP/Wide World Photos
169: Arizona State Library Archives and Public Records, Archives Division,
    Phoenix #00-0517PHD043
176: AP/Wide World Photos
178: Library of Congress, Prints and Photographs Division [LC-USZ62-84031]
179: Florida State Archives
183: AP/Wide World Photos
187: AP/Wide World Photos
188: AP/Wide World Photos
192: AP/Wide World Photos
195: Library of Congress, Prints and Photographs Division [LC-USZ62-107588]
197: AP/Wide World Photos
203T: Library of Congress, Prints and Photographs Division
    [LC-USZ62-119056]
203B: Library of Congress, Prints and Photographs Division [LC-D416-9858]
207: National Archives and Records Administration, NWDNS-165-JT-230
208: Library of Congress, Prints and Photographs Division [LC-USA7-16837]
209: New York Public Library Portrait Collection, SC-CN-85-0428
216: Library of Congress, Prints and Photographs Division [LC-USZ62-92753]
218: AP/Wide World Photos
221: National Archives and Records Administration, NWDNS-210-G-C153
222: AP/Wide World Photos
224: AP/Wide World Photos
230: Library of Congress, Prints and Photographs Division [LC-USZ62-119343]
231: Library of Congress, Prints and Photographs Division [LC-USZ62-126846]
232: National Archives and Records Administration,
    NWDNS-306-SSM-4C (51) 13
237: Library of Congress, Prints and Photographs Division [LC-USZ62-96021]
239: Library of Congress, Prints and Photographs Division [LC-USZ62-12711]
240: Library of Congress, Prints and Photographs Division [LC-USZ62-29701]
241: Library of Congress, Prints and Photographs Division [LC-USZ62-31799]
248: Library of Congress, Prints and Photographs Division [LC-USZ62-96757]
250: Franklin Delano Roosevelt Library
256: LBJ Library (Cecil Stoughton)
257: Courtesy Gerald R. Ford Library